Before Memories Fade

Memoirs

SPIEGEL

Pearl Fichman

October 27, 2005

2

*Dedicated with love to my husband Yuda
and our sons Mark and Eytan.*

Contents

CONTENTS

Photo Album

Pearl Fichman

Pearl and Yuda Fichman in New York (1981)

Pearl Fichman (Spiegel) with her friend in Czernowitz (1939)

Paul Celan in Czernowitz from the background of the street snapshot

Pearl's class in Czernowitz high school

Pearl with her friends at the entrance to her house in Czernowitz

Pearl's father (stands) with a neighbor in Czernowitz (late 1930's)

Pearl's father in the Czernowitz ghetto

Preface

After over forty years, why the decision to bring up old, painful memories? After all, they have haunted my nights all along; nightmares brought up vividly some childhood fears, many later encounters, all mixed up and all in confusing patterns and usually, my awakening dispels them. Yet they keep returning.

Some pleasant memories return, too: some are sentimental as they evoke old friendships, loves, unusual and unexpected encounters - a kaleidoscope of memories.

My sons Mark and Eytan heard a number of stories in the course of their growing-up years, yet the events seemed disjointed. Talking to Eytan last summer, he exhorted me to write a real account of my life. He had heard bits and pieces, yet not the whole story. I mulled over that conversation and realized that it would be right to do it now - I have ample time and can still remember fairly well what went on when I grew up, how I matured under highly adverse conditions. After all, my memory may fail as time goes on. I decided to write before memories fade. The time and place of my youth were so different from the place and time of my children's and grandchildren's lives.

My grandchildren may catch a glimpse of the life of their grandparents and greatgrandparents, a life before cars, television, telephone, refrigerators, dishwashers, washing machines, air conditioners, frozen foods and disposable diapers. Imagine a world like that? It looks impossible from the vantage point of to-day, yet life had its joys and sorrows, just the same. Life was simpler, people worked harder, physically, expectations were lower.

Besides, how can one put in a nutshell the years that followed, years of such turbulence, of such upheaval, fear and danger and political convulsions, the years from 1939 to the end of the Second World War? It was open hunting season on the Jews in Europe and thorough German hunters achieved great successes - they almost annihilated the Jewish communities of Europe. The ones who remained have a duty to tell the events, as they experienced them, as a sad reminder and as a warning, for "history repeats itself".

The question in my mind and in the minds of those reading these pages would necessarily come up: How does one have the courage to continue living under such circumstances? Why does one not commit suicide? A great number of people took their own lives. Was their despair any greater? Did they display more courage or less?

Among my own circle, three women committed suicide: a former classmate of mine, the young woman upstairs, who jumped to her death from the fifth floor, was picked up, carried in by her father and set on my bed. I could never erase that picture from my mind. That fateful day was December 7, 1941, where half a world away from us, the Japanese attacked the U.S. navy at Pearl Harbor. The third was the wife of a doctor, a former neighbor on Mehlplatz. She was a few years older than myself. Yuda's family physician and her husband took their lives in the ghetto, in October 1941.

I could see that it seemed simple, bloodless and freeing one of further struggle, yet I never considered that solution. I had that magic thinking, that innate optimism, that in the long run, we'll come out on top, survive the catastrophe, live to tell the tale. The fact that an entire community went through the same suffering made it easier to endure. Everybody hoped that through some unusual event, the war would end. One hoped for Hitler's assassination, for a special bomb that would bring to an end German power, deus ex machina, a deliverance, somehow.

However, in retrospect, I realize that had anybody known that the war would stretch to such length, six years, one would not have struggled to keep alive.

Six years are an eternity in wartime, especially when you are among the ones the government is out to exterminate, to wipe off the face of the earth. Luckily for the ones who survived, the war was over in 1945, forty years ago, but the struggle did not end. The new endeavor was to rebuild a life out of the ashes. One had lost home, friends, family, a way of life. People came out full of scars, from wounds that had been inflicted along the way. All were poor, penniless, homeless. Some survivors became aggressive, some became resigned, some ruthless, others restless and others compassionate. Some felt they were wiser but not calloused, still quite vulnerable.

When my father found out, in 1944, that his entire family had been wiped out in Poland - brothers, sisters, nephews, nieces - he said to my Mother and myself: I don't think I will ever laugh again. He never did.

No two people who survived those awful years could tell the same story. Everybody went through a different course, each one's experiences were unique, different, all bitter. My husband Yuda lost his parents and did not know whether his only brother, Michael, was alive. Yuda himself went through the ghetto and labor camps, arrived in Israel and fought an entire year in the War of Independence (1948-1949). For him, the war that had started in 1939 ended in 1949.

The same was true for the different Jewish communities all over Europe. The isolation of those years was such, nobody knew what was going on in the next town or village. The utter splintering of the Jewish communities brought along the isolation, intended by the oppressors. All during the war, I never heard of Treblinka or Auschwitz, while in Poland or in Austria they never knew about Bershad or Obadovka or Michailovka, in Transnistria, where the Jews from Bucovina were deported and most of them did not survive.

It may be of interest to my grandsons Michael and Jonathan and their future brothers or sisters and to Eytan's future family to read an account of grandmother's and grandfather's lives and to know more about their family than they ordinarily would. Of course, for my daughter-in-law Ruth, this is a revelation of our past.

My fervent hope for my children and grandchildren and generations to come is never to have to endure anything comparable to the barbarity that occurred in the first half of our century. If anything, the world should have learned from the senselessness of the destruction. My fervent wish is for a peaceful, happy life. Lechaim - to life.

Two Questions

In the course of conversations, people will often ask a naturalized American citizen, like myself: "What country did you come from?" and upon hearing that I settled here after the Second World War, they will invariably ask: "How did you survive?" I find both queries difficult to answer, since a simple name of a country does not really tell what my background is and the second question defies a simple retort altogether. The closest I came to giving a fair answer as to how I survived, was: "I kept breathing."

Actually, the bulk of the following writing constitutes an answer to these inquiries - therefore this piece of writing deserves to come at the beginning of my reminiscences.

To tell that I was born in Romania is correct, historically, yet my surroundings, my first language, my first registered impressions, the first songs I sang, the first fairy tales told to me, the first jokes I heard and understood - all those were German, based on the life of a province, of a town, of a family that existed within the Austrian culture. Up to the age of six, when I started first grade, I did not understand a single word of Romanian. Growing up, the Romanian education went on side by side with the accustomed life of before - no cutting off of the former, just adding another facet to my life. I became bilingual by necessity, by circumstance.

As history intruded onto the scene, when I was 20, the Soviet Union took over the province where I lived and another layer was about to be added to the former. The war and Nazi occupation brought a sharp interruption of the Russian-Ukrainian scene and the Romanians came back for three years. As the Soviets returned in 1944, I lived under them another year and left Czernovitz for good, in 1945. After an interim of two years in Bucharest, I came to the United States for slightly over two years of studies and then settled for seven years in Israel. For the last thirty years, my home is in the United States, my language English. My native town has been Russian ever since 1944.

Now, considering layer upon layer of languages and cultures and regimes, how can I easily answer a seemingly simple question? As a rule, I say: "I was born in Romania." This often calls forth a remark about liking gratar, mamaliga, red wine, ţuica and gypsy music and dancing the hora. Well, I really do not stem from that background. We liked different foods: we ate wiener schnitzel and drank spritz - a mixture of wine and soda-, we listened to German classics, we enjoyed German literature, we loved the poetry of Schiller, Goethe, Heine; we sang songs by Schubert and Lehar, we danced to Strauss waltzes. "What kind of a fake Romanian are you?" would be a natural reaction. We followed the Austrian tradition because the area had been for generations part of the Austro-Hungarian Empire, those were the customs familiar to us. Little by little the Romanian customs started to appeal to the younger generation, yet old traditions are hard to erase, it takes generations for the new ones to set in.

"So what is the area now?" It is part of the Soviet Union now. In fact, Bukovina was located in the North-Eastern corner of Romania and is now the Western part of the Ukraine. Hard to explain to any person who does not exactly follow the vagaries of European history in the 20th century. Instead of trying to clarify this complicated matter orally, I rather take a detailed map of Europe and try, if possible, to clarify and show where all this took place.

The answer to the second question proves even more treacherous to elucidate. The fact of one's presence is in itself the answer: I survived, I am here. The hard part is to explain: how? I won't go into that again because the whole story is the answer to this question. For the first time, I have given a full, detailed reply, a complete account of my own survival as well as that of my parents and of a fraction of the Jewish community of my home town Czernovitz.

Next time, when asked, I will tell the questioner: Read this book.

Chapter 1

Childhood

Czernovitz, my hometown, was my universe, the place to be. It was a hilly, densely populated town. We lived in a centrally located square. I remember the house where I was born and where I lived up to the age of fifteen. I was surrounded by parents, older brothers and sisters, very friendly neighbors - the youngest child among them all.

It was an old three-story building, situated on Mehlplatz (Flour Square). It must have been at one time a square, where traders in flour would do their business on market days. By the time I grew up, the old Austrian name of the square had been renamed by the new Romanian administration Piaţa Dacia (Dacia Square). Dacia was the Latin name of the territories, North of the Danube, conquered by the Romans during the reign of emperor Trajan, about 100 A.D.

As is the case with many Eastern European towns, situated in areas always coveted by neighboring nations in Central Europe and the Balkans, Czernovitz had had a very colorful history. This part of Eastern Europe belonged in turn to the Romans, the Greeks, the Turks and the Austrians till 1918. After the defeat and dismemberment of the Austro-Hungarian empire, the province Bukovina became overnight part of Romania.

Thus, when I was born in 1920, our town, the capital of the province Bukovina, had had its name changed to Cernauţi and the official language changed from German to Romanian.

People were always talking about the times "before the war", meaning life as Austrian citizens, among German-speaking folk, before 1914; "during the invasion" - meaning the occupation by the tsarist Russian army, during the First World War; during the second invasion, the flight - meaning my parents' flight to Vienna, and after the war. That was the First World War (1914- 1918).

My earliest recollections were conversations about inflation, valueless "Kerenskys", which I found out was Russian money before the Communist Revolution; hunger during my family's flight through Hungary, Moravia and Bohemia and their arrival in Vienna.

Whenever grown-ups got together and talked about the years in Vienna or Budapest or Slovakia - I realized that the families I knew had gone through turmoil; most had survived enemy occupations, times of starvation and dislocation and we were already enjoying that elusive peace. I was already living in "peace-time".

Every now and then, a distant cousin would visit and when he would talk about having been a prisoner of war - I was told then that he had spent years as a war prisoner on the Italian front. (Interesting, this same cousin later became a lawyer, lost his citizenship in Romania in 1938, during a highly antisemitic administration. Since he could not exercise his profession, he emigrated to Chile, where he worked as a professor of Latin. He was killed, an old man by that time, during the Allende revolution. His wife and son had remained in Romania, waiting for him to establish himself in Chile and then join him. The war broke out in the meantime; his wife and son were killed by the Germans in 1941.)

Amid all the talk of upheaval that had preceded me, life started to open up before me. In our house and all around me people spoke German, read German books and the daily local German newspapers. Once a month we would get Scherl's magazine, published in Berlin, the equivalent of Life magazine, combined with articles similar to the New Yorker. The pictures of glamorous movie stars like Marlene Dietrich; luminaries of opera and stage like Max Reinhardt, Emil Jannings, Helene Weigel, Paula Wessely and Gustav Frölich and many, many more filled its pages; also the cartoons of Georg Grosz, an artist, who later fled to the U.S.A.

In my Father's store, a wholesale haberdashery, many customers would come to shop from the outlying villages surrounding town. Many of them were Ukrainians. Ukrainian village girls came to do housework in town. The peasant women, who sold chickens, fruits and vegetables on the market - they too were mostly Ukrainian. A small number of villages had a German population, originally from Swabia, a province of South-East Germany. They spoke a dialect called Schwäbish.

The most colorful group of people lived in the mountains, which separated the Carpatho-Ukraine from Bukovina. They were called Huțul (Hootsool) and were a tribe, apart from the Ukrainians. They were mountain people, a colorful lot, who were raising horses. Accomplished riders, they kept very much to themselves. The men had long, fierce-looking moustaches; they came to town on horseback, in order to sell horses and to purchase some goods in the stores. They spoke a Slav dialect, not real Ukrainian.

Yet, in my small universe, I knew my family, distant cousins — since my mother's family lived in the U.S.A. and my father's in Poland — and our neighbors — all Jews who spoke German or Yiddish or both.

And yet I lived in Romania. Since kindergarten was not compulsory, I did not go. Mother would have had to walk me back and forth as school was far. Until first grade, at the age of six and a half, I had no concept of anything Romanian, although I was born in Romania.

Czernovitz was the capital of the province Bukovina, the most North-Eastern section of Romania. Poland was about 50 miles to the North and the Soviet Union about 60 miles East. Yet our life was not touched by the fact that we were within arm's reach of Russia. The Soviet Union kept herself completely insulated from the rest of Europe. There were no diplomatic relations with her neighbors. Thus, to us, the Dniester River, the Eastern border between Romania and Russia was like the end of Europe. It was less accessible to people in the 1920s and the 30s than the moon is to-day.

Thus, to me and the people around me, Czernovitz was our home, the center of my world. It was a hilly town, in the style of most old European cities. The central square, Unity Square, had an imposing City Hall building, a monument in honor of a united Romania, represented by several soldiers, holding on to one flag - of Great Romania. Streets were radiating from that hub. The Residence of the Patriarch, head of the Greek-Orthodox church, was a massive, palatial structure, situated within a big, secluded park, surrounded by thick walls. There were many other public buildings like: the university, official buildings, schools, churches, synagogues, a temple, hospitals, barracks. All were massive stone structures, almost exactly like the ones in Vienna and Budapest - just scaled down.

In the 1920s life was simple and little dependent on machinery or mechanical contrivances. We had electricity, which provided us with lights in the home and lighted streets. Our town was rightfully proud of an electric streetcar, referred to as the tramway, which had cars going in one direction: North- South. You couldn't use it much if you did not happen to live exactly in the area where it ran. Nevertheless it played a pivotal role in running towards the railroad station and further, on its last stop, to the river Prut.

The Prut meant a great deal to us, especially to the young. It was our summer recreation. The sandy beaches along both banks were adequately built up with booths, where one changed clothes, kept the sandwiches and fruit for lunch. All this made it possible to spend summer days bathing, swimming, sunning, reading, playing ball, flirting, romancing, discussing - just enjoying life. This was often the essence of one's summer vacation.

Astride the Prut stood the bridge with no particular name. It connected Czernovitz with many outlying villages and small towns, known nowadays as "shtetls". Most people came to town to shop, or see a "famous doctor", or go to the movies or the theater. People from small towns came to doctors in Czernovitz, while the Czernovitzers, when very sick, travelled to Vienna. At the time, the professors at that Medical School were the most famous in the world. My Father had his tonsils removed by a professor in Vienna.

Many youngsters from the outlying areas went to high school or university in our town. They did not commute daily as transportation was not readily available. Thus, whoever studied in Czernovitz used to rent a furnished room in a private home. University students could choose to stay at a students' dorm. Interestingly, since Jews and non-Jews never mixed socially, there were several dormitories near the university, yet those were financed by the government and accommodation was reserved for Christians only. The sons and daughters of poor Jewish families, who could not afford private accommodation, stayed at a Jewish student hostel, supported by the Jewish community. No state aid was available to them.

The reality of life was such that at any time Christian discontent could spill into an attack on Jewish students. Thus, they faced real dangers because of antisemitic feelings, which were just below the surface and could erupt at any time. When trouble loomed for Jewish students because of a slight incident, the Romanian, Ukrainian and German students felt united in their hatred for the Jews. An incident need not result from a special disagreement. If a Jewish student looked at a Christian female student in a way as to arouse her boyfriend's jealousy, he might start an incident, start hitting the Jewish young man. Soon enough others would spread rumors and incidents would occur all over town.

When the students were in a foul mood, the Jewish population tried as much as possible to avoid any contacts with non-Jews. Our students would cut some of the classes for a time, until the atmosphere of danger would somehow subside. However, the uncertainty, the anguish of people, living in a society, where any small provocation or imagined slight could provoke an outburst of physical attacks at any time - that way of life on the brink was a permanent state of affairs.

Coming back to my early youth, I remember it as an Austrian way of life. Those traditions stayed on and were nurtured in the home as if Romania was only an incidental whim of history. Though the theater changed into the Romanian National Theater, which aimed to propagate Romanian literature and drama, yet all this made a difference only to the young, who learned the new language in school and became gradually knowledgeable of Romanian culture. The administrators, officers and teachers who had been sent from the "Old Kingdom" to make the regime work, they became a new intelligentsia and started to effect a gradual changeover from a German to a Romanian life style.

My mother, who loved the German language classics and the Austrian operettas, never went to a Romanian play in all the years, up to 1940, when our town was occupied by the Soviet Union. The older people just never learned the language.

A joke made the rounds:

Teenager: Did you see that hilarious Romanian comedy at the National Theater?

Adult: Of course not. Do you take me for a child?

As life in Czernovitz changed by necessity, yet the Austrian and German theatrical producers never forgot the appreciative audiences in our town. Thus, every year, the Viennese Burg Theater, the Operetta Theater and the Reinhardt Buhne came for a week's stay and the faithful theater lovers bought tickets in advance and awaited impatiently the performances. In time they introduced their growing children to the coming shows.

I'll never forget that by the age of five, my mother took me for the first time to a Strauss operetta: "Viennese Blood", and little by little, every year from then on, I could see more and more serious plays.

I remember my older brother Bernie (Bubi as he was called at home) trying to get into practically every show. He certainly did not buy tickets to all of them. Thus, on a signal, somebody took a slip to go out during the intermission and through some trick both went back in. This way he saw at least the second part of the performance. Year by year the expectations built up and we became lovers of the theater and of concerts. We had a Music Conservatory and a Philharmonic Orchestra, too.

Of course, we enjoyed the movies and saw the most noteworthy films, from the earliest on. I remember the "Jazz Singer" with Al Jolson and the early movies with Greta Garbo and Ramon Navarro. The silents just had a piano player hacking along constantly. We saw French and lots of German films. The operettas enchanted us. We youngsters, up to the age of 12 could go on a child's ticket. So we sat two or three times over, in order to memorize the songs with the lyrics. We loved the actors and actresses and knew all about them - who marries whom, who divorces whom.

Of course, our entire town felt great pride in the success of Joseph Schmidt, a world renowned tenor, who appeared in a number of German movies. Whether he portrayed a gondolier or an opera singer, his lyrical tones melted our hearts. He sang Mozart like an angel. As a youngster he sang in the choir of our Temple, he was my brother Eli's classmate. Later on, he would come home every year for the holidays in the fall and do part of the services in the Temple. To our eternal regret, he perished during the Holocaust.

The German film industry developed most rapidly in Europe. While the Austrians filmed musicals endlessly, the German directors like Fritz Lang and Max Reinhardt created notable mysteries, tragedies, classics and modern, some experimental, plays about the social upheavals around us, the labor tensions, strikes of the 20s and 30s. Actors like Emil Jannings, Albert Bassermann, Frieda Richard and Brigitte Helm are forever imprinted in my memory.

I remember my earliest playmate, a boy with the nickname Bunziu, probably Benno, son of a restaurateur. Around the square used to be a stop for carts, with a pair of Belgian draft horses each. There may have been 10 to 15 drivers coming out every morning and waiting there for business. They used to be called upon to move furniture or transport crates for businessmen. Of course, they would come into that restaurant for food, but more often for beer. They would sit around, smoke, talk, joke. When a customer came, he would call on the driver from this inn. Bunziu Ellenberg was the only child of the owners.

I would come down and we would play together. Sometimes his mother would call him in to eat and I would share his meal just as he sometimes ate in my house. One day I came home and told my Mother that I had eaten something wonderful in Bunziu's house.

What was it Mrs. Ellenberg treated you to?

Mamaliga with something - little ones - like this. . .

I did not know what it was, but it tasted like ambrosia. Mother asked and was told that I had mamaliga with mushrooms and sour cream. Thus started my love for mushrooms, which to this day is one of my favorite foods. Of course, in Europe, the peasants would pick them fresh after the rain and bring them the same day to market. Those really tasted special. What is mamaliga? Yellow corn mush, the national dish of Romania.

However, Mehlplatz with the horses around the square was also a very scary place for a little girl. I feared those big Belgian horses with their heavy, hairy legs and heavy hoofs. Their manes were long and thick and when a wagon passed by, the clanking of the hoofs on the cobblestones was hard and metallic, their nostrils would quiver and they would emit heavy breath, the manes would shake. Some of these horses were of chestnut color, sprinkled with white; they were powerful and would make me shiver with fright.

Whenever I went to my father's store, I would have to cross the square and pass between two carts, in front of a pair of horses. I never dared tell my parents how scared I was, but often, in a nightmare throughout my life, to this day, I've been trampled by such horses.

I was also afraid of drunkards and there were some coming out of my childhood friend's inn. They were loud, boisterous, would sing and stagger, but never did any harm to anybody and yet, I was scared. My father would smile when he heard of my fear and would say: "If you are afraid of them when they are sober, that I understand; but drunk? Just run away, he can hardly move." It was reasonable advice, yet it didn't help.

In these old houses there were mice. Everybody kept cats as an antidote. In our house, any time we went into the cellar, where we kept provisions for the winter: potatoes, carrots, beets I never dared to go down alone, for fear of mice. Mother understood that and spared me the ordeal; she never sent me down alone.

Of course I was afraid of storms, thunder and lightning. In the days before radios and weather reports, nobody knew what weather to expect. Once we went to the Prut; Bernie took Sali and me along. In the middle of the day a severe thunderstorm caught us unawares. People crowded onto a pavilion and some took refuge under the wooden structure, below the stairs. When Bernie saw that press of people, he called us to stand outside, in the rain, rather than in a place that might collapse. And it did. People were injured, one woman was killed and we escaped unscathed. We had a smart brother who was about 16 years old then.

The loveliest childhood memories include the holidays and preparations for them. Mother used to cook and bake all the traditional foods for each holiday. For Passover everything in the apartment was cleaned, rearranged, washed, polished - so that no "khametz" remained anywhere, no bread, no breadcrumbs. The preparations also meant buying lots of food: eggs by the hundred, goose fat that had to be rendered and the cracklings, called "greeven" reserved for the holiday, potatoes by the sackful, nuts, wine, and of course matza. Father ate a different matza called "shmoora". It was baked of less refined wheat flour, under special supervision, with him present at the baking. Even to-day orthodox rabbis eat "matza shmoora".

On the day before the Seder, all the dishes and glasses were put away and the pessach stuff put in place. All this to commemorate the exodus of our Israelite ancestors from bondage in Egypt and the rejoicing in freedom. In their hurry, they baked unleavened bread-matza. It was a time of good food, great expectations; it was also the joyous expectation of spring and warmth after our long, cruel winters. We would always get new shoes, socks, a new spring coat or a dress. We would put on the new clothes for the seder.

Father, who was a deeply religious Jew, without being fanatical, took his social responsibilities seriously. He belonged to the Jewish Community Board and was an unpaid member in charge of social aid. Since there were large numbers of poor Jews in town, his responsibility, by his own choice, was to see that nobody goes without Pessach kosher food - matza, meat, potatoes, eggs, sacramental wine. The same care was applied to see to it that Jews in hospitals, the insane asylum and prison were provided with kosher food for the holiday. By the time he had satisfied all these provisions, he came home to celebrate the seder. By that time Mother was almost asleep from the accumulated tiredness after all the work that had gone into preparing the holiday and the hour was late.

However, by the time he arrived, everything went into motion. He sat on a "hesse bed" - three chairs along which was spread a feather bed. Father put on a white "kittel" - a wide, white linen garment with wide sleeves and he began to read the Haggadah, the story of the Exodus.

I, as the youngest child, enjoyed the privilege of sitting next to him and I asked the four questions. One of the great attractions of the seder were the different wine glasses reserved for everybody year to year. The children had small blue or green or yellow glasses, with little handles. As one grew older, one advanced to a bigger ornamental glass, or a different color. Since every celebrant was supposed to drink four glasses, the parents made sure the children should not get tipsy.

There was laughter and merriment about the prophet Elijah. His glass stood filled all evening and at one time, during the seder, one opens the door for Elijah to appear. There were anecdotes about youngsters, who would play pranks on a family and would jump in, all wrapped in a white sheet, the moment the door was opened for the prophet.

There were also funny moment at the reading of the haggadah, the story of Pessach. Everyone had a text. Some of them were illustrated, some were really hilarious. They showed the father and the four sons asking the questions. One was supposed to be wise, one wicked, the third a simpleton and the forth was noncommittal, he didn't care to ask a question about the exodus from Egypt. We invariably thought that all four didn't look too smart in the illustrations.

In my haggadah, when it came to eat dinner, there was a piece of advice: Eat and drink and just be merry. We thought it was good advice - so why did we have to read so much after dinner? That did not make us merry, for we were all sleepy. Of course, we read to the end and sang Chadgadia and finished with the wish expressed by all the generations throughout our long history: Next year in Jerusalem. Of course, before we could reach Jerusalem, we had to reach the kitchen and wash all the dishes.

The message of joy on the liberation from slavery has achieved a very immediate meaning to me later in life, in the years since my own liberation from bondage in 1945. It has been 40 years since and yet, when I ponder about the course of my life, I should sing "Hallelujah" more often than just at the seder, for freedom must not be taken for granted. One feels how indispensable it is only when one has been deprived of it. Every seder since, I celebrate my own liberation from slavery. Hallelujah.

Other holidays that stand out in my memory as very enjoyable: Purim in the spring and Sukkoth in the fall. On Purim, to celebrate the defeat of Haman, who intended to kill all the Jews of Persia and also to praise the deeds of Queen Esther and her cousin Mordechai, who were instrumental in saving the Jews, we read "Megillat Esther", a scroll, a rolled up parchment in which the ancient story is told. Whenever the name Haman was read, children used to rattle a noisemaker called a "grager". My Father, who had a beautiful voice, would read the Megilla at home for Mother and the children; we would call in the neighbors and the gragers were going with great glee. After the reading of the megilla, being sure that the Jews had all been saved, we all sat down to a fine traditional meal of pot roast, potato pancakes, a strudel with honey, apples and nuts called "flooden" and the traditional Hamantaschen, a triangular yeast cake filled with poppy seeds and honey.

The other lovely holiday was Sukkoth, which starts four days after Yom Kippur. For eight days one is supposed to eat in a sukkah, a booth covered with greenery. It is a reminder of the wandering of the Jews through the wilderness, after the exodus from Egypt, when all shelter was make-shift. It is also a harvest festival. We would bring Father his food into the sukkah in the neighbor's house. Of course, we lived on the second floor and by the time I or my older sister Sali brought down the soup one long flight of stairs in our building, half a block to the next house and one flight up to the sukkah, half was spilled and the remainder was cold. However, all this was fun.

Only Father observed this tradition to the letter. Mother and we, the children just made the blessing over the etrog - a perfect lemon from Palestine - and the lulav - a palm branch, a sprig of willow and myrtle - every morning for eight days. Father went to the synagogue every day and made those prayers there. Sukkoth being a harvest festival, we blessed these symbolic fruits and grains of the land of Israel.

My greatest enjoyment, as a child, was the privacy that a sukkah offered me and my childhood friends Chavale and Lucie. Since none of us had ever had our own room, we were chatting for hours, unheard and unseen by the adult world. Here I found out about the differences between boys and girls and about sexual matters, of which I was completely unaware up to the age of six or seven. I was much too bashful to ask whether all this was true, but I trusted Lucie, who was a little older than myself and had older brothers and sisters who were more outspoken than my own family.

I was the youngest at home and my parents not able to pay too much attention to me. They were 36 and 39 when I was born and they had endured a lot together. A week before Sali was born, they had lost a four year old daughter, Lotti, dead from meningitis. The two years as refugees in Vienna were a time of deprivation, standing in line for food, overcrowding in a small apartment, the load of a family of five children, Mother herself and my Father's sister Sali.

My aunt had come for a visit to Czernovitz to see her brother and his family and, maybe, to help a little with the children. The war broke out and she stayed with my parents for about eight years, until she got married in 1921, from my Father's house.

My Mother's parents emigrated to the United States in 1920, after having lost their house and farm during the war (1914-1918). My grandfather had been an overseer of a big landed estate near Kolomija, Galicia. Thus, my Mother grew up in a village. The landowner kept teachers on the estate to educate his children as well as grandfather Stadler's sons and daughter. The sons were taught Hebrew, too. My Mother, the only daughter, was instructed only to read and write Hebrew, not the rigorous studies meant for sons. Girls were just supposed to be able to read the prayers. She received an education in German.

Mother's brothers Solomon, Louis, Meyer, Max and Morris had been already well established in New York before the war. They made my grandparents' passage possible through Romania. They stayed a few months in our house before their departure in 1920. I was a few months old then. My Mother never saw her parents again. Grandfather died in New York of Buerger's disease, a consequence of years of heavy smoking. He lived just eight months in the United States. My own Father's fate was similar. He died of cancer about eight months after his arrival in America. Both of them lived through hard years of wandering and homelessness during the world wars and survived but could not enjoy the ensuing peace, could not share life with children and grandchildren. They lived through the wars, yet peace was not theirs to savor.

The joy of experiencing the gentle care and love of grandparents was never mine. My Father had lost his mother at a very tender age and by the time I was born, his father had gone to rest, too. I often wrote to my grandmother Esther in New York, without ever getting any answer. Her letters were always written by a niece. She could not write, I presume.

By the time Sali, who was four years older than myself, started to learn to read and write Hebrew, I was given lessons, too, by the same old teacher, Mr. Lecker. I could read and write Yiddish by the age of four. It enabled me to send my first letters to grandmother.

As for myself, as a child, I was surrounded by people, all older than myself. The closest in age was Sali. I used to see older brothers and sisters going to school, reading and learning. It seemed the only activity to do: read and write.

Thus, at a very tender age, besides reading and writing Yiddish, I somehow taught myself to read German in the Gothic alphabet. Circumstances surely govern daily life. Since my family had lived in Vienna for two years (1916-1918) during the war, the older sisters and brothers Eli, Betty, Gertie, and Bernie went to elementary school there. On the family's return home, they brought along some of their school books: readers and a song book.

Two books with lovely illustrations and symbols intrigued me more than any others: the Wiener Lesebuch, which means Viennese Reader and a Liederbuch - Songbook. They fascinated me. I asked one or the other of the older siblings what one sign or another meant, for those were the letters, cursive and print. That way, by curiosity and imitation, all this brought about my reading and writing German, at the age of four or five.

However, the song book was used by the older sisters, for they sang many of those Schubert songs and folk tunes for their enjoyment. In those years, before radio, records and television, the only music one could enjoy was offered at concerts, at musical theaters or, at home, playing an instrument or singing. Movies, in black and white, were silent, with subtitles. A lonely pianist would accompany the action on the screen. I learned to sing a number of classical and operetta songs at that time.

By the time I started school, at the age of six-and-a-half I was a veteran reader, but I knew two distinct alphabets - the Hebrew and the Gothic, not the Latin, which I had to learn in order to read and write Romanian.

Funny, when I think back, I don't remember to have feared facing a completely alien environment, where people spoke a language that I had never really heard.

In school, all the children faced the same predicament, for they were Ukrainian children, many Jewish, some Polish but none Romanian. In fact, the first years in school seemed like a fairly easy time. Learning came easily to me. The teacher, for all four years in elementary school was the same loving, motherly Mrs. Weiner. She may have been impatient with some, but I sailed through with top grades. One of the difficulties of those years were the repeated bouts with tonsillitis. At the end of the fourth grade I had my tonsils removed.

The winters were extremely harsh so that the snow that fell in November would melt in March. When I was in second grade, in the winter of 1928, the bitter frosts persisted all through the winter months; the temperature dropped to -40 degrees Celsius or Fahrenheit. (At -40 the two measurements are the same)

The newspapers wrote about the Danube, being frozen solid and that people from Bulgaria skated across the river to Romania. It probably happens once in a century for a winter to be so severe. People used to say that the wolves were coming out from the woods into the villages.

As much as the apartments were heated with fire-wood, the moment we stopped stoking the fire, the apartment cooled off, at night. One covered up with featherblankets, over the shoulders, just the nose stuck out, for air.

On the windowpanes, the indoor humidity froze forming ice flowers, but, at the bottom of the window, nearer the frame, toward the sill, the ice got to a thickness of a finger or two. We had double windows and in between, on the sill, we placed a sort of longish pillow stuffed with sawdust, to prevent the frosty air from penetrating through any crack. In order to air the rooms and the kitchen, the windows had a top part, which could be opened. That was called "Oberlicht" (top-light).

I remember one Saturday afternoon, on my return from school, (school was on six days a week) Mother and Sali were in the apartment, all wrapped in blankets. Since Mother would not light a fire on the Sabbath, the person who came around to do it at lunchtime, didn't come back again to renew it later. The embers had burned out, only ashes remained and the room was cold. Mother would start heating the house again after the first star had appeared. When I came home, jolly and happy and with rosy cheeks, Mother asked anxiously: "How is it outside?" She heard the whistling of the wind all around. She thought that I would be frozen. I answered that it was so nice and breezy, that I crossed the road a few times back and forth, for it was windier that way.

I read recently the memoirs of the Bulgarian writer Elias Canetti and he describes the severe winter of 1928 and how they crossed the frozen Danube by sleigh into Romania.

As I am thinking of these childhood years, the atmosphere and the general tone in the family was restrained, contained, often matter of fact, never sentimental. There was warmth and care and love, and yet it was not communicated in words. I do not remember my parents ever telling me that they loved me, yet I felt that they did; I knew that they did. It was taken for granted that parents and children loved one another and it need not be articulated. I wish they did, I never heard it from them.

The only time my Father almost said it was by the time he was very sick, a few weeks before the end. I would go daily to Columbia University, where I was studying for my master's and would come back home to Brooklyn in the afternoon. As soon as I came home, I would come to say hello to my Father and talk to him. I always tried to tell him something cheerful, something to make him smile - if possible. That prompted him to say: "Lucky the man who will marry you." I got married a year and a half after his death. I miss him to this day.

The neighbors on Mehlplatz 3 were like an extended family. In the three story building lived eight families: the owners, the Welts, whose sons were the first people in town to own a motorcycle, a car, a radio. We were among the seven tenants. Our next door neighbors were the Gottliebs, who had four sons and a daughter. When I grew up, the older sons and the daughter were married; the youngest two sons were ten and eight years older than myself. The youngest son was the only Jewish kid that I had ever heard of who failed twice third grade in elementary school. His father referred to him as "Malaikopf", the equivalent of dumbbell.

Mrs. Gottlieb was a tall, slender, graceful, blond woman, kind and helpful, the resident healer in the house. I don't know whether she had ever stepped into a school, but she knew all the remedies against coughs, burns, fevers, upset stomachs - anything. I remember, once, Sali spilling a glass with hot tea and scalding her knees and legs. Pronto Mrs. Gottlieb mixed a salve of oil, honey and egg yolk, applied it and watched over her for the next few days Sali never had any scar left. In case of fever, she would apply leeches on the chest and back. It probably worked.

Her husband was the absolute opposite kind of person. He was short and heavy, had a ruddy complexion, a fierce temper. He hit his sons at the slightest provocation and was feared by them for his nasty outbursts. Whenever one of the sons would tremble before his father's return home, he would come into our house and wait for the storm to subside. Chaim, the youngest son, knew what to expect after getting his report card.

They were always afraid of the tax collector; they probably owed a pretty sum. They bribed him and he promised not to return for another month. As the month was over, he would return. Whenever we saw one come, we'd inform the neighbor. She would lock the door and wait in our apartment until the danger passed.

Their grandchildren were singing a little ditty in Ukrainian to this effect:

> I stole a horse in Sadagura, tra, la, la
> I sold it in Czernovitz, tra, la, la.

Incidentally, the family came originally from Sadagura, a small town across the river Prut. Some of them were horse traders. I guess every song has a kernel of truth.

Their son Simon trained to become a printer and later worked at a newspaper. He saw workers eating different foods and he dared try some of them.

The former Austrians had never seen eggplant, tomato, mustard, Turkish coffee. One day he brought home smoked sliced meat, made a sandwich and spread mustard on it. His father looked at it and asked him what it was. Simon offered his father a taste of it. Scandalized by a food of this color and consistency, he came into our house and said: "Come in, come in all of you, Simon is eating shit." We came in and dared to try and quieted his shock. During the war, in 1941 or 42, Simon perished in a German prisoner of war camp. His younger brother is alive, in Israel. A few years ago we visited him in Tel Aviv.

Our upstairs neighbors, the Körners, were the first to acquire a Victrola. Their youngest son Joseph, Eli's age, bought also one record. It had two songs sung by a famous soprano of the Vienna Opera - Selma Kurtz. One was an aria, the other: The Bird In the Forest, a bravura soprano song, with endless trills. Whenever he played the record, with windows open, of course, the entire house would listen, all the neighbors. The trill were stupendous and we told him how much we admired his eminent taste. Soon after, he bought another one, the Caucasian Suite by Ippolitov-Ivanov.

Next to them lived the Morgensterns with two very pretty daughters. The older, Blanca, used to work in a bank and whenever she came home, she had a young man accompanying her. They used to stand in front of the entrance door and talk endlessly. Finally, the young man would kiss her hand in a gallant fashion and leave. That leave-taking was often observed by my playmate Bunziu. He could not understand why they were standing and talking so much. What were they talking about?

One day he came to my house to play and started a conversation with Bernie, who was about ten years older than Bunziu and a few years Blanca's junior. He asked whether Bernie had noticed that Blanca was coming home, every time with a different beau. Then he remarked: "One day she is going to go out with you, too. Perhaps one day also with me."

Downstairs lived the family Klein. Their daughter Rella was a piano teacher, who taught Sali for a while. Their son Gustav went to Vienna to study medicine when I was about five years old. By the time he was supposed to come home for summer vacation and his parents were anxiously awaiting him, I was trying to figure out what medical question to ask him. After all, he was one sixth of a doctor. I came up with the question why tears are salty. He looked amused at me and retorted: "Because suffering is bitter."

Once, my Father was travelling to Vienna and the Kleins wanted him to visit Gustav and see how and where he lived. Thus, my Father came to his address, knocked on his door and Gustav answered. Yet, it took a few minutes before he admitted his visitor. He lived in a small room, sparsely furnished with a bed, a table, two chairs and a washstand. Upon Father's question why it took him so long to open the door, Gustav avowed that he was studying and since he had only one pair of pants, he had to put on his pants. He could not afford to wear them when he was alone, in his room, studying. Dr. Gustav Klein is an old doctor, in his eighties, still living in Czernovitz. The two sisters Morgenstern are living in Israel. I spoke to both of them on our visit in Israel in 1983. Two grandchildren of the Gottliebs are residing in Venezuela; one visited me in New York.

The awakening of a social conscience stemmed from those childhood years. First, my Father's concern for the poor and the sick and the imprisoned showed me that people don't just think only of themselves. Whether the performance of those "good deeds" or "mitzvoth" in Hebrew, were the sum total of what a devoted believer is supposed to do, so as to earn for himself a seat in paradise, or it was my Father's natural inclination to do good, I can not really judge at this time. He was a born social worker, without knowing the term. I never discussed with him the roots of his religious beliefs, but his own father was a "chasid", a Hebrew teacher by profession. He may have followed his direction without wavering. His kindness and compassion were so genuine, his desire to alleviate suffering so real. Among the organizations he belonged to was "Bikur Kholim". Its members were religious Jews; the aim was to visit sick people in the hospitals, people who had no family of their own. Without the study of sociology or psychology, they felt that patients who were destitute and had nobody to care for them and give them encouragement, would not recover as well as those who did.

No misunderstanding about it, my Father never accepted any remuneration for any of his services to people in the community, nor was any of it intended to influence their degree of religiosity. It was done within the Jewish community only. Christians, as I mentioned before, had their own social services provided by the state or by the city, they rarely extended to the Jewish population.

The world around me and the poverty of so many became very real, when on Thursdays or Fridays groups of beggars would come to the house, walk from door to door, for alms. Mother was cooking for the Sabbath from early Friday morning. She cooked a little extra and those who came were given a bowl of soup and a slice of bread. Two women used to come on Fridays and expected to be offered borscht or cabbage soup cooked with meat. The usual compliment earned by my Mother was: "For your borscht, I gladly give up chicken soup." I still remember the sound of her raspy voice and the zest with which she attacked the gift of food.

Of course, when I started school, I felt it my responsibility to do something for the poor, just like my parents. In our compulsory public schools were children of all strata. I picked myself the girls to help. Olga Slugotzka was a Ukrainian janitor's daughter. She was cross-eyed, had mousy-looking hair and was evidently poor. In warm weather she came to school barefoot. No hippy she, just poor.

School was on from 1 - 5 p.m. six times a week. Whenever I came home, there would be a snack, called Jause, of bread and butter and jam or cookies and milk. I invited Olga to come home with me so that she could share a treat with me. Mother didn't mind serving both of us. One day Bernie came in and saw her and said: "Out, out of the house. She is crawling with lice."

Another classmate in first grade seemed to be just as worthy of my attention. She was a Jewish girl, Anna Ruff, who was so shy, one could hardly hear her whispered answers to the teacher's questions. She was so cross-eyed, one could hardly see more than the white of one eye. As I felt badly about her reclusiveness, I approached her and asked her to come to my house after school. At home, Sali and Bernie told me that she looked scary. "Are there only such unusual children in your class?" they remarked. They really meant scarecrows. A few incidents of this kind dampened my personal attempts at satisfying a social responsibility.

Of course, there were also the usual children - apple-cheeked Bella Weinstein, whose birthday was on March 21, the first day of spring; fat little Rita Rosenkranz, who was always anxiously awaiting the ten minute break, to eat some sweets and one very pale, solemn-looking girl, for ever afraid of the teacher.

Talking about childhood and the seasons, the spring delighted us with the variety of flowers: lilies-of-the-valley, pansies, lilac in all hues, from white to deepest purple, white daffodils and tulips. We savored them all, the colors and the scents. Later in the season would follow hedge roses, irises, lilies, dahlias, carnations, roses and the harbingers of fall, asters.

Any time Mother went to market for food, she would also bring home flowers in season. Peasant women offered vegetables, fruit or poultry and they also brought flowers from their gardens. We always had some on the big dining room table; they gave the room a special fragrance.

The fruits paraded through the season in a natural sequence. We first enjoyed cherries - white, pink, red and the last in the season, sour cherries. Mother made preserves from pink and white cherries; Father sometimes made "Vishniak" from sour cherries. It became a kind of "Cherry Heering", more substantial than wine but less concentrated that liqueur. In the summer, fruits and berries were a string of delights. Tiny wild strawberries, picked in the woods - a treat with sweet cream. Gooseberries and raspberries were made into syrup of brilliant scarlet color and stored in bottles, for use all through the year. A summer treat used to be: cold soda water with syrup.

In early summer, we loved currants. They grew very low, the height of lilies- of-the-valley. On a thin stem would be six or up to ten little, red, bead- like fruits, very sour. As they puckered your mouth, they were like an addiction. Any time a bowlful was on the table, it was finished by the people around it. None were ever left. Yet, the big guns of the season were just around the corner: apricots, pears, apples, grapes, plums and quinces.

Since, at that time, you could buy in the grocery just staples, like flour, salt, sugar, rice, butter, herring, everything else had to be prepared at home and at the right time. Thus summer and the beginning of autumn were the seasons to make jams, marmalade, preserves, syrup and pickles.

The end of August, when fruits were ripe, in abundance and inexpensive, the real busy time started. All this before the fall holidays: Rosh Hashanah (New Year's) and Yom Kippur (Day of Atonement). Povidla, plum marmalade, was prepared in a big caldron. First, for a day or two, big quantities would be bought and the peasants from the market would bring them home. Then, everybody in the family pitched in washing them, removing the pits and, next day, in the early hours of the morning Mother would start boiling it, stirring in the sugar. As the liquid would evaporate, the povidla became thicker and it became hard to stir, with that enormous, wooden spatula. By evening it would be done. It cooled off through the night and next day it was time to fill the jars or big ceramic crocks. Mother also made quince marmalade and it was about the same procedure. (Quinces look like greenish-yellowish apples; are hard and sour and can't be eaten raw.) All these jams were intended for sandwiches or snacks for the entire year, until next season.

Preserves were prepared in smaller quantities and were made of apricots, strawberries, cherries, different berries and roses. Those were more delicate fruits, made to taste sweeter than jam and were mostly used for baking or as a treat, with cold water, in the summer. The preparation of rose confiture resulted in a double delight. Mother would buy one or two big bags full of hedge roses, freshly cut from the garden. She would shake the petals into a big basin and pick out just the petals, for there were leaves and impurities mixed in. Then boil them gently in water with sugar, for a short time; let it cool off. The entire house smelled of rose perfume. In the rose season, different neighbors prepared these preserves on different days-the entire house was perfumed.

All these preparations for the winter meant an inordinate amount of work for Mother. Although we helped some, yet that was negligible. Work began early in the morning, the fire in the kitchen stove kept going and so did the busy sorting, cooking, boiling, washing of dishes. To keep in mind, that was before air-conditioning. Mother used to say: "Morgenstund hat Gold im Mund." (Morning hours are golden ones).

Cucumbers were pickled in the fall and kept in a barrel or big jars. Of course, spices were boiled, garlic and greens added. That, too, emanated a special aroma in the autumn. Every once in a while, not yearly, Father would make wine, in a large glass jar. That was a hit or miss proposition. Sometimes the wine would be delightful, at other times a pure waste. It was done for sheer fun, with a 50/50 expectation.

The sour cherry wine, a small quantity - perhaps four or five bottles - would be enjoyed as a special pleasure. You had to deserve a glass; it was a conversation piece, an artistic creation. My friends knew about the "Vishniak" (Vishni, in Slav languages means sour cherries. Vishniak is an alcoholic drink made of sour cherries) and about the special people or occasions for its consumption.

Once I told a friend that this year the drink is excellent. He started a conversation with Father that led up to this remark: "Mr. Spiegel, I heard that this year your vishniak is better than ever." My Father, proud of his creation and reputation treated him and asked him to judge for himself. A little praise went a long way. Of course, I knew where it was and I treated my favorite friends with my Father's favorite beverage, anyway.

Where did one keep all these jars and, once in a while, a barrel with pickles? We had a pantry, the size of a small room, with shelves from top to bottom around three walls. In the apartment, into which we moved in 1935, we had a servant's room, beside the pantry. Since we had no servant, the space was used for the sewing machine and for provisions. It was a chamber of hidden delights up to 1940, then it turned into an almost desolate chamber, just like our lives.

How did one keep a house at the time before vacuum cleaners, washing machines and cars? Well, Mother had a big job running the house. A cleaning woman would come one day weekly to wax the parquet floors in the rooms, carry the carpets to the yard and beat them and brush them with vinegar-water. The windows were washed, the floor in the kitchen scrubbed. By the time she left the house was sparkling clean.

Every month she used to come for two days to do the laundry and the week after for a day of ironing. The laundry was hung up to dry in the attic. In the wintertime, it froze on the ropes and it took many days before it would dry. The frozen, white shirts of Father looked to me, as a child, like big, frozen birds- scary. Those odd shapes, stiffly frozen, seemed monstrous. Mother used to take us along to help bring down the laundry, for it had to be folded, sheets were rolled up, to be ready for next day's ironing. The frozen pieces could crack or break when they were completely rigid. Of course, the attic was bright but ice-cold. After the ironing, there were stacks of linens on the table to be stored in a cabinet, a special, large armoire for linens only.

Since this type of work was a real trade, there were armies of peasant women, who came from the villages to do this work in the big city. Most were Ukrainian women, who learned how to do house work from their mothers. It afforded them a living, or it helped the peasant families to make ends meet. It made city life easier, since women's work, at that time, was never done. What with daily food shopping, cooking, baking, darning, knitting and bringing up the children, of course. Most families were bigger than now.

However, when the hard times set in, no Jew could employ a non-Jew. The whole system changed; all of life, as it was known before the war, crumbled, withered, was gone. Most of the Jewish city dwellers were either deported by the Russians or later deported or killed by the Germans. The town that I knew until 1940 remained only in name. The population was either destroyed or the small number of survivors scattered all over the globe.

Chapter 2

The Teenage Years (1930-40)

By the time I was ten years old, in 1930, the older sisters and brothers had gone to America and Sali and myself remained at home. Suddenly we were a family of four, both parents approaching fifty and two girls of 14 and 10 at home.

The difference between the generations of parents and children always exists, yet, ours seemed very sharp. Religious parents, Father a merchant, closely involved with the synagogue and charities, fighting to keep a middle class home going - while the children were growing up under new and different influences. Of course, I looked up to Sali, who was highly intelligent and was part and parcel of a group of high school students, all moving in the direction of socialism. It was the time of the Weimar Republic in Germany, a time of social ferment, of industrialization, of inflation, of unemployment. I moved, unaware of the facts, into a similar direction as Sali. Many young people, who deemed to be progressive, subscribed to a lending library owned by a Dr. Bernfeld, in which the newest books from Germany, Austria and other Western European countries were available in the original German or in translation.

Before Hitler's advent to power (1933) the ferment of literary and social activity was almost physically felt in our town and I started to get pulled into that whirlpool by association. Sali's friends came to the house or met in the Habsburgshone - our beloved park - and discussed endlessly about politics and literature.

Most young people, who pretended to be thinking or were really aware of the critical times, were either leaning towards the left and internationalism or became Zionists and started to prepare for a life as settlers in Palestine.

My inclination formed very early and I took it for granted that I wanted to save the world, not just the Jews. Thus internationalism came before nationalism. I foresaw very little what strange contortions the world was going to go through in my own lifetime. How wrong my leanings proved to be. I was in a good company, when you think of the disappointments of Ignazio Silone, Arthur Koestler, George Orwell and millions of others, less famous, but not less disenchanted.

Instead of reading the equivalent of the Bobbsie Twins at the age of 12 or 13, I read "Mother" by Maxim Gorki or "The Death Boat" by Traven or the anti-Hitler books from Germany or listened to revolutionary songs of the anti-fascist movement. It felt like having stepped from childhood into deadly earnest world affairs and responsibilities. I really took a giant step from a child's world into adulthood, into the whirlwind, from which I could not step out for a long, long time.

My childhood was too short, I had no care free years, no innocent joys, no playful time, no teenage years of discovery - but a fall into a serious, dangerous, pitiless, turbulent world, which tossed me up and down, right and left without respite and for a very long time. I was all too soon thrust into a spot with responsibilities, which I had to fulfill - given no choices. As my parents were talking about the "War", their war, World War I, I was hurled into a turbulence, that started for me at 13, 14 and dragged on through my war, World War II and ended, when?

As for life from 13 on, its facets were: my school life, my home life and my developing social life. My parents did not interfere much with my activities.

They trusted that my good sense would carry me in the right direction. Now I think that they were too trusting.

School was very restrictive, demanding and often cruel. Although the lessons were from 8-1 p.m., six days a week, the subjects very diverse, so that no subject was taught more than three times weekly, yet the demands were extreme.

We had written assignments only in math, Romanian, French, Latin, German; the other subjects were just supposed to be studied. However, you were expected to be prepared for every lesson; tests could be given unexpectedly, any time. Those were called "extemporal" meaning: given at the spur of the moment- extempore. Discipline was rigorous: you wore a uniform, a black regulation dress, a white embroidered collar, a blue bow with polka dots and black stockings. On the right sleeve of the uniform and on the blue coat, you had the embroidered initials of the school L.F.2 (Girls'

High School No. 2) and your personal number sewn on. A navy beret with the embroidered initials of the school, too. Anybody who saw you in the street after 7 p.m. or at a movie or theater, which was not permitted to students, could call the school and have you expelled. Of course, one of the cardinal sins was to be seen with a boy in the street.

However, we circumvented many of the rules, but at a considerable risk. Fearfulness became a constant side effect. At all times, it felt like you were acting in a way that deserved punishment. The fact that you were Jewish was a chronic condition, which aggravated the situation. Very often, when a teacher found fault with you, she would remark something to the effect that "your tribe" or "your people" do not agree to conform.

Thus, in school, life was burdensome. Romanian teachers looked down at you; Jewish teachers tried so hard to be on the right side of regulations, that they often went overboard themselves. I remember as the most cruel of them all, my Latin teacher for four years Miss Camilla Kaul, a Jewish woman, whom one could easily mistake for Atilla, the Hun. In all four years, I had never seen her smile even once. After all, I am sure that the Romans had a sense of humor, too. My high school teachers could fill several horror shows, cruelty and lack of humor were their trade marks. Their judgment could never be questioned. In our police state, they were an extension of the police.

The summer before Sali went to America (1937), before my senior year in high school, the two of us went for a week to Campulung, a mountain resort in the Carpathians, in the Southern region of Bukovina. It was during summer vacation. She was already a student at the University of Czernovitz, while I was a high school student, 17 years old. During the summer months, I was not an actual student, but on vacation. The resort had a lovely swimming pool and both of us came in bathing suits, to enjoy the then modern set-up. Suddenly I noticed the principal of my school, with her family. I got scared stiff, didn't know what to do. How do you face your principal dressed in a bathing suit? No number, no insignia. Yet, vacation is leisure time. When the moment came to face her, she turned her head away. Perhaps she didn't know how to face me either, she was devoid of authority at the swimming pool, in the mountains.

Another incident, funny and unusual has remained in my memory. On my 14th birthday, my neighbor and admirer at the time, Arnold, surprised me with a portrait of myself, a drawing in blue chalk on white. Sali had been let in on the secret ahead of time; she had given him one or two pictures of me. On the eve of my birthday he came in and presented it to me.

It was flattering to be drawn by a young artist and next day, on the 10th of March, I took it along to school. (Arnold is to-day the cartoonist Ed Arno). Our lunch break of 20 minutes was the opportunity to show it to the girls. In all schoolrooms, above the blackboard, hung a framed portrait of the King. One of my classmates jumped on the desk and put my picture into the frame, covering up King Carol II. We all went to the rear of the classroom and ate together, laughed and joked and admired me for having a boyfriend, an artist. When the bell rang, nobody heard it. As the teacher walked in everybody ran back to their seats, I remained up on top, instead of the King. We were all scared, for that was real lèse-majesty, one strike against the dignity of royalty. Whether the teacher wouldn't have suffered a heart attack at the sight of my picture usurping the traditional spot of the King, who knows? I know that we were all relieved by the next bell and my demotion from that exalted position.

Arnold made portraits of me at 12, when I sat for it and at 14, as a surprise.

I lost both during the years when all our possessions were lost.

I still remember that at the beginning and at the end of each school day, we had to stand up, hands in prayer and one girl would recite the Lord's Prayer. The Christian students and the teacher - if Christian, would make the sign of the cross, the others just stood motionless. Everybody knew the prayer in Romanian, but when the first or last period was French, German, Latin or Greek, what then? The school decreed that there must be at least two students in class who knew the prayer in those particular languages. Why two? If one happens to be absent, there should be a replacement. After all, how can you end a German lesson and recite a prayer in Romanian?

Those who memorized easily volunteered. I learned the prayer in Latin; thus I was the one to say the Pater Noster. Of course, after all the years of hearing it, I knew it in all the other languages, except Greek. We never had it, in the two years of study, as first or last period of the day.

Greek was one of my least favorite subjects. Except reading and writing, I never really learned much. I think none of us derived anything substantial out of it. She would let us read, then she would translate the long passages and we would just copy them. Learning the translation by heart did not help either, for we didn't even recognize what text fit what translation.

Many of us loved poetry — Lamartine, Alfred de Musset, Alfred de Vigny, Victor Hugo, Verlaine. They sounded like music when read aloud by Miss

Agatha Grunspan, our French teacher. She inspired us, she taught French magnificently and made us love the language and the literature. I still remember a lesson on Flaubert, the author of Madame Bovary. She told us the story of Saint Julien l'Hospitalier. We were all spellbound, shivering with emotion. The textbook contained half a page about an author and two or three pages excerpted from a novel or short story. Miss Grunspan presented to us about an hour or two the author and his works. She led us through Victor Hugo, Voltaire, George Sand and Anatole France, just to mention a few. I am sure, none of us ever forgot her lectures. They were worthy of a forum at Columbia University.

In 1934-5 we studied all about Paris and, later on, the geography of France. We had no films, no audio-visual aids; we just had a fine teacher, who had been in Paris and described the sights in words, that depicted it all. When I came to Paris in 1947, so many years later, I recognized every important building. In fact, I knew, as I walked, that at one end of the Champs Elysées I'll see the Place de la Concorde and at the other end the Arc de Triomphe. She described the Louvre, with all its treasures and the Done des Invalides, where Napoleon is entombed, in such detail, that I knew the sight when I visited there many years later. Her enthusiasm for the beauty of the French landscape was infectious. I felt the tides rising when she described Mont St. Michel.

We used to think that the West was rich in thought and the cities and towns so attractive, we longed to see and experience those places. At that time travel was less accessible than today. One needed a passport and visas for every country. All the consulates were in Bucharest and it seemed so unreachable. That made the desire to see other countries even more burning. She opened an eye to the world of France.

As brilliant as she was as a teacher of the subject, as a disciplinarian she was even more efficient. Easily aroused to anger, any interruption or bit of noise provoked an outburst, like a sudden summer thunderstorm. Thus, as much as we loved the subject, we were scared to death of her. She was the fury in the flesh.

Grunspan was heavy, with an ample bosom. One day, she wore a blouse with a V neck and a strand of pearls. Suddenly the strand broke, dropping the pearls into her bosom. The class started laughing and she got red with anger. I thought she'd just burst.

No school reminiscences may exclude Martha Marini, our math teacher. With her tiny figure, big head with a mass of black hair and a very soft voice, she looked like a school child. She used to write formulas on the board; put one or two problems on the board and solved everything fast, by herself. Then she assigned homework. She never asked whether the class understood the new concepts in algebra or trigonometry. Nobody dared ask additional explanations. More than half of the class never understood the material. The result was that most of the students needed private tutors, at least part of the year. She looked like a scarecrow but she scared people. She was among the most feared teachers.

None of the teachers mentioned had ever married. Kaul, Grunspan, Marini and my history teacher Popovici - all were single, typical old spinsters, highly educated, lacking the slightest sense of humor or any understanding of the young. They actually terrorized the youngsters. That was a state school and they were the embodiment of a dictatorial system. Schools were run just like military regiments where the motto applied: Order must be executed and not discussed. Here it was: the information, the learning, the beauty and satisfaction of knowing, the awakening of interest in other lands and other cultures, the appreciation of literature and poetry - all this was offered and eagerly absorbed. The flip side of the coin produced intimidation, submission and resulted in fear and timidity.

I was so shy, so scared of all these authority figures: school and police. I never dared ask a question. I answered when asked and so did almost everybody else. I was a good student; I aspired to good grades, yet I was never competitive. It didn't matter to me to be mentioned for honors. I didn't want to cram day and night, as some did. Friends meant a lot and enlarging my intellectual horizon became of equal importance as school. The shyness resulted from years of intimidation in high school. The outside world was hostile- everybody feared the police and, of course, the antisemites surrounding us. From 1933 on, waves of anti-Jewish feelings were being felt all over Europe; it was Germany's highest priority export. It was translated into every language and propagated by zealots of the Nazi cause.

In spite of all the hardships, there were funny incidents that I can still remember to this day. At the age of 13 or 14, I was close friends with Lola. She used to play the piano and I used to sing. As they lived on the second floor, the windows were open in the summer, we would ask her older sister Erna, who was deaf-mute, to watch at the window every now and then, whether anybody stopped in the street to listen to us playing and singing the Schubert Serenade: Leise flehen meine Lieder... I don't think anybody did, yet we tried hard to be heard.

Their parents had a small furnished apartment on the first floor, which was sometimes rented, often empty. Whenever it was available to us, we would spend time there. The two sisters started smoking, I never did. They drew the blinds, for they tried to hide it from their parents, of course. Somebody would tell the parents that something fishy was going on, otherwise, why such secrecy? Thus, their mother came down and knocked on the door. We opened the window to let the smoke out. When we finally opened, she noticed the open window and suspected that somebody had left through it. Next time, when a similar situation arose, she came down with the maid: one posted herself outside, the other knocked on the door. It became clear — it was a matter of smoking.

The years 1928-1933 were a time of crisis and unemployment all over Europe an the struggle to survive - be housed, fed and clothed - was real. I did not actually understand, at the time, everything that went on around me, but struggling hard against financial difficulties and being Jewish, too, made for an on-going hard life.

For myself, life was hard because of sickness. At the age of 13 doctors diagnosed that I had a lesion on the upper lobes of the lungs, which caused a low grade fever. The cure, at that time, consisted in getting me fattened. They called it: "Mastkur" a fattening diet. X-rays were taken every month, in order to check whether the lesion was getting calcified. I had a tough time eating great quantities of meat, eggs, butter, cream, trying to gain a lot of weight. I was a very slim girl. By our standards of to-day, I looked great, but then, being thin and having a low-grade fever was a catastrophe. My parents were warned that it might be the beginning of T.B. — the scourge of the time, before the discovery of antibiotics.

Later on, at 15, I got jaundice, probably from a diet much too high in fats. Anyway, those were hard times from the health point of view. I was often absent from school, yet I did not want to lose a year of studies. In most subjects, I did my studies at home, on my own. Mathematics was different. My parents hired a tutor for me and I always caught up with the rest of the class. Thus I never lost a term.

My parents did the best they could to cure me of my ills and they never complained, never expressed any anger or pity or resentment toward me. I, on the other hand, being sick so often, didn't complain because I felt that I was one of the causes of my parents' many anxieties. We had a "live and let live" attitude in our little family circle. Everybody did the best he or she could, the rest was fate.

I can now understand why I rarely saw my Mother laugh. There were few reasons for merriment. She worked very hard and worried, too, yet she never spoke about it, at least, not to me. She stoically bore a heavy burden. The older children had left home and settled in America. First Eli left, just before going to the army. A three or four year stint in the service used to be a dreaded hardship, physical as well as financial. Soldiers were beaten and harassed. A Jewish soldier's tour of duty turned into a time worse than a prison term.

Some of Eli's friends decided to emigrate to Columbia, South America, he joined them. By that time I was four years old. About a year later Betty and Gertie left for the U.S.A. Uncle Morris, "the rich uncle from America" visited in Czernovitz and appraised the situation, at the time, as hopeless. he felt that the girls would have much better chances at a good life in America than in the small town in Romania. He was especially incensed when he heard about outrageous demands for a dowry, whenever a girl was supposed to get married. The groom's family used to insist on money for a business, or for a house, or money for the groom's sister's dowry. To Morris this seemed so old fashioned and also beyond my parents' financial resources. I was told later that he was also considering the nieces as the right girls to live with Grandmother. She was a widow, who certainly knew no English and needed somebody to share her apartment. Her son's devotion extended so far that he influenced my parents to let their daughters emigrate. Of course, they would have a large family in America and would, perhaps, also share in "the good life" in the Golden Land, so highly praised by people in Europe.

After a while Eli found life primitive and lonely in the town Santa Marta and moved on to Cuba and then to New York. Thus, all three older children lived in New York. They worked for uncle Morris, went to college at night and lived a life that was completely different from the one they had left behind. They were young and grew and developed in an American pattern.

In the summer of 1930, when I was 10 years old, Betty came for a two months visit. The expectation and excitement before her arrival were indescribable. Counting days was nothing, I counted the hours. How happy I was to see my oldest sister after five years.

A few days after Betty's arrival, I had my tonsils out. Father had taken me to the surgeon, who explained to me that I could either go to the hospital and have them removed under full anesthesia and come home after two or three days or have them removed in his office, under local anesthesia and go home after an hour or two. I wanted to know whether there was any difference and he explained that full anesthesia would slightly weaken my heart, while the other method might be more painful but have no lasting negative effects. Yet, I had to promise to sit very still. When I chose the latter method, he looked askance at my Father. Father assured him that if I promised, there was no doubting my word.

The operation is still vivid in my memory today. He removed one tonsil and showed it to me, while I was sitting in a chair, both hands strapped to the sides of the chair and a nurse was holding me head. I made a sign, pointing toward his watch and extending two fingers, telling him to give me two minutes rest before taking out the second tonsil. He did. The rest also went smoothly. Father took me home in a "Fiaker," a hansom carriage drawn by two horses, the equivalent of today's cab. Of course, I was looking forward to lots of ice cream, supposed to be good medicine as well as a tasty treat after the operation. The doctor saw me again soon and told me how proud he was of my behavior in the situation. Dr. Buchsbaum mentioned that a sixteen year old boy had had this same operation, with different results. He ran out after the first tonsil had been removed and refused to have the second operated. He suggested that I talk to the young man. I refused saying that a ten year old shouldn't have to tell an "almost man" what to do.

A few days later Mother, Betty, Sali and myself went to Gura-Humora, a lovely summer resort in the Carpathian Mountains. We picked berries in the forest, sat along the cold mountain brook called Humora, enjoyed a lovely Old World vacation. We picked flowers in the meadows, made garlands for my hair - it was grand.

At lunchtime, a woman would bring us a fully prepared kosher meal from a restaurant in the small town. Breakfast and dinner were served by our hosts: freshly baked bread, rolls, butter and cheese, from their own cows, fresh vegetables and fruits from their orchard. I still remember fondly the pastoral environment of the area, we stayed in a house, on a hill, overlooking the river Humora.

I remember Betty as an elegant, sophisticated young woman, telling interesting stories about America. However, as the end of August approached, I realized that Bubi (Bernie's nickname) was leaving with her. Thus, like in the song about the ten little Negro boys, when there was always one fewer left. Sali and I were left at home with my parents. Mother was sad, sullen, went about her chores in a very subdued way. Only the mailman could alleviate her gloom.

We were reading the letters, enjoying snapshots from New York. Bernie was a fun loving brother, a tall, good looking guy, with lots of friends coming to the house and now, we were left just the two of us, alone. We used to play cards with his pals, we used to joke, cheat sometimes, kibbitz and suddenly, all this was gone, changed overnight. I was not really aware how heartbreaking this change must have been for my parents.

In the course of the following years, I started to go out with boys. I had boyfriends and romances and crushes. In retrospect, I think I was a flirtatious girl, bright, precocious and critical of others. Some of the young men my age were not as well read as I and, perhaps, not as bright as I was. At any rate, there were girl friends, who were my equal or superior to me. They played an important part in my growing up years. It seemed that politics played an important role up to 1940. Some of my friends were deeply involved, more than I.

During the summer vacation of 1935, while I was with my Mother in the mountains, three girls from my class were arrested for illegal activities. One was my close friend L. The news hit me on my return home. My parents were struck by the news, as told by Sali. At the time, if a police informer caught somebody with a forbidden book, this constituted reason enough to arrest, beat and torture the suspect. By normal standards, reading books about Socialism or Communism does not constitute a crime against the state, but in Romania, in the 30s, if you looked the wrong way, you could be suspected of political illegality. If one's hair was curly and unruly, the teacher would call you a Communist. The term was used very loosely and in an accusatory manner. You could not question or doubt an opinion of a person in authority because that provoked a suspicion of Communism. Of course, there were Communists, in organized cells. When apprehended, they were beaten within an inch of their lives.

Coming back to the arrest of my three schoolmates, all three girls had older sisters, who were active anti-Fascists. It was really politics by family association. My parents were struck by the occurrence and talked to me very seriously, warning me that it should not happen to me because first, I was not very strong physically and could not endure the police beatings; besides, they could not pay hefty bribes to police commissars - every one of them had a price.

The three girls were released after two weeks and were expelled from all public school in Romania. One swam with her boyfriend across the Dniester river into the Soviet Union. Five years later, when the Soviets occupied our town, we found out that they had both been sent to the Far East, to

Siberia. The Russians believed that a real Communist was to suffer rather in a Romanian prison, continue fighting rather than escape to Russia, where the ideology was already a reality. The other two graduated from private schools.

They are my friends to this day; they reside in France.

In the summer of 1937, Sali went to the U.S.A. in order to study English for one year. There was great excitement during the weeks before her departure. She was going to stay for a few days in Vienna, where we still had some relatives and for a week to Paris, to see the World's Fair.

In September 1937, I started my last year of high school, the most difficult year of all. In order to graduate, one had to pass the matriculation examination called also matura. That was the monster at the end of the twelfth grade. How can one imagine to-day a comprehensive exam in almost all the subjects of the last four years? Students usually started to cram from January on. The exam was held at the end of June.

The preparations meant studying biology, zoology, botany, anatomy, geology - just for the natural sciences. Romanian literature, French, Latin, the history and geography of Romania, everything in all the details. As school was going on day by day, the reviewing of the text books from the previous years went on daily, late into the nights. There were discussions on how to keep awake. The accepted wisdom prevailed, namely, keeping one's feet in cold water. I never tried.

The students from the literary section had three written tests: Romanian, French and Latin; the scientific section needed math instead of Latin. Most of us had private tutoring in French and Latin for a few months before the matura. About a third of the candidates failed the written exam. The ones who succeeded took the orals. They were held in a large auditorium, at a high school and were open to the public. Five candidates faced a committee of eight teachers; the head of the committee was a university professor. None of the teachers were from our town. The orals took four to five hours, one group in the morning, another in the afternoon. The results were announced daily, late in the evening. The secretary of the commission posted the list of successful candidates. A great number of people: students, their families, friends awaited the results. Later, some were laughing and cheering, while others walked home despondently, they had failed.

I still remember vividly that before the dreaded exam I was feverish with fright. My close friend Rosl, who used to sit in class next to me, was on the school roster next to me, was at the matura exam in the same group and both of us passed. Needless to say, many who failed tried again in September or next June or September.

Since Romania was known for "baksheesh" — graft, there were often intermediaries who arranged a modicum to pass, but it cost a mint, about ten thousand lei. My Father had no money to throw around and, besides, he was certain that I would pass easily, the first time. He was right, I passed, but the anxiety was unbearable.

While we were preparing for that dreaded exam, Rosl's father told us about a bottle of champagne, that he had received years before and was waiting for a very special occasion to open. His daughter's success at the matura was that worthy event. The family and her friends, including myself, enjoyed the party and anxiously awaited the champagne toast.

We laughed and joked and danced and finally the long-awaited moment arrived, when all of us would be drinking champagne, for the first time and drink a toast to our future. Everybody held a glass, the father ceremoniously uncorked the bottle, poured for everybody some and we all exclaimed: Prosit and tasted. Well, the champagne had turned to vinegar. Nobody drank. That was an omen of things to come; we were lucky not to understand it, it was June 1938.

What was the importance of this exam? It enabled a young man or woman to study at a university, to go into a profession. My inclination was toward medicine but there was no faculty in town and there were no chances to be admitted in Bucharest. The faculties of medicine and engineering were practically closed to Jewish students. A strict "numerus clausus" assigned a tiny percentage to Jewish applicants, perhaps two or three percent of an incoming class. That left law and teaching as the only choices. The chances became remote that one could even teach at a state school, thus one chose to study languages, mathematics or law. In case of emigration, languages and math were useful skills. School became the outside world that hardened you for the years to come. I registered as a student of foreign languages: French, German and I started to study English. The idea of eventually leaving and settling somewhere, where English would be an asset, impelled me to begin learning a new language.

It sounds so dreary and oppressive and yet, young people found ways to enjoy life somehow. The pleasures were simple, yet genuine. Friendships were very close and deep. One sat next to one's best friend and the seats behind and in front, one tried to be among one's close friends. We used to study together, do homework together, if one lived in the same neighborhood. We lent books to one another, came to visit on free afternoons, knew each other's family closely.

When one went on vacation, during summer recess, friends wrote to one another. Telephones were nonexistent, so friends talked it over to meet, what movie to see, what books to read. Of course, boy friends became important, too. On weekends, on Saturday afternoon or evening, or on Sunday, groups of friends would meet. In spring or fall, we loved to walk and enjoy the city parks; in the summer we went to the Prut, swam or just spent the time talking, joking, taking pleasure in the give and take among friends, eating ice cream, drinking sodas, just living. The ice cream parlor has been an institution, in Europe, for a long time. We would go for an ice cream and sit and chat endlessly. We sometimes went on long hikes, to the woods around Czernovitz, a day's outing. Everyone carried a knapsack on the back, wore shoes with heavy soles and white, knee-high cotton socks. The girls wore a "dirndl" which consisted of a white blouse, a flowered skirt and a little apron, adorned with lace. It was the way the Tyrolians dressed, an old Austrian custom. Sometimes, we would sit in a meadow and one or another would read aloud. Paul Antschel, who later changed his name to Celan, loved to read to the group poems by Rainer Maria Rilke, in German, of course. Sometimes we'd read aloud H. Heine poems and sometimes we'd sing.

Life had its enjoyable aspects, too and we found pleasure and relaxation in company, friendship, romantic attachments as well as intellectual stimulation.

To be widely read, well informed on world affairs and to have a "Weltan-schauung" (an outlook on the world) an opinion on world affairs counted very highly. I am not sure that we competed with one another, but we encouraged and inspired one another and moved ahead, in spite of all the difficulties or because of all the hardships. Yes, we were a worthwhile generation. The lucky part was that we did not even have an inkling of what lay ahead of us. This entire group of bright-eyed, intellectually curious teenagers went into a future that splintered the group into all different directions. We would never meet again as grown men and women. The ones who survived live in different countries, under different regimes, speaking different languages. Our children are American, Israeli, French, German, Russian, Australian, Brazilian, Argentinean, English, etc. Whenever my generation of Czernovitzers meet, we still speak German among ourselves, our common language. We have a strong link with a common past and shared suffering, especially the years after 1939.

Home life proceeded rather peacefully, with a tacit understanding of live and let live. The outside world was hard to cope with and thus the home became a haven. We lived in a small apartment: a bedroom, a living room that served also as a dining room, a big kitchen and a spacious entrance hall. I did not ask for a separate room since it was unrealistic to expect it. When I was about 14 years old, I started to tutor, in order to earn some money for special expenses or for the movies. I earned my own spending money. It was taken for granted that the parents did the best they could and so the children tried to do their part.

When I was 15, we moved into a new building, with a separate bathroom, with a tub and a boiler, to heat the water for the bath. Up till then we bathed every Thursday evening in a big tin tub, which was kept standing against the wall, in the kitchen. Water had to be heated on the stove and poured into the tub by the bucketfuls. That same procedure followed when spilling the water. That was a very difficult way of bathing but since I had never seen a different system, it was taken for granted.

In the 30's new buildings sprang up and we felt very fortunate to move into a modern building, where life became more comfortable. Yet, one had to heat the water in the boiler, in the bathroom. Some of our relatives would come to visit and be treated to a bath. (In 1941, after the Germans attacked the Soviet Union and we were thrust into the war, one week later, the Soviets fled and the Germans invaded our town. I was a student and had a lot of Russian books, especially a full set of works by Stalin. What to do? We made a fire in the kitchen stove and also in the bathroom in order to get rid of the books. Paper burns slowly and we were tearing pages and throwing them into the ovens. Then, the water in the boiler ran out and the boiler cracked. Not only couldn't we dispose of more Communist texts, but we remained without a means of heating water for a bath.

Family life was close also by necessity. When friends came, we would sit in the living room, parents and young people. In the evening we sat around the big dining-room table. Father read the newspaper, I did homework or reading, Mother was sewing or knitting or embroidering or darning socks. Of course, Mother's day was never done. In the morning, she would go to the market for vegetables, fruits, eggs, butter, flowers. She cooked all the meals, from scratch. If you wanted to eat chicken, you bought a live bird in the market; took it to the slaughterer, cleaned the feathers, cut it open, koshered it and cooked it. That took hours. If you wanted cookies or cake, you baked them. The only ready made foods were bread and rolls. Everything else had to be prepared in the home.

You could buy shoes, winter boots, stockings and socks; everything else had to be bought: material for a suit or coat, lining, buttons and then made to order by a tailor or dressmaker. Life was absolutely different from what it is now. There were also so many different occupations that have disappeared by now.

If anybody would have told me of a way of life as it is to-day, it would have seemed strange and impossible, as a far out science fiction movie to-day. I still remember a cousin, who lived in a small town and came to visit, bringing along her little boy. He had seen his mother bring water from the well. In our house, he saw water from the faucet running into a tea kettle. He looked in wonderment and asked whether I could get a bucket full of water. I told him that I could fill two, three, four buckets full of water. Suddenly he burst out laughing and said: "Don't say that. Who has five buckets?" To him, life in Czernovitz was already science fiction.

In 1936 my parents bought a radio, a German manufactured, big apparatus, which needed a roof antenna. It looked similar in appearance to today's television. We heard broadcasts on long, medium and short waves and could enjoy programs from all over the world. A weekly radio program listed most European stations. On short waves one could hear programs from overseas. It was magic. We heard a Passover service from Jerusalem; we heard wonderful concerts from most big cities in Europe; news in Romanian, German, French and lovely light music from Sofia, Bulgaria. From 1934,5 we heard the raving and ranting of Hitler, the venomous speeches and the vicious Nazi propaganda, which made us cringe with fear and apprehension. From the Soviet Union, we were wooed with propaganda, in all the European languages. We were the first among our circle of relatives and friends to possess this magic box and did we have guests, no end.

Some came with special requests: to listen to German broadcasts from the U.S.S.R. On those programs, their lips were dripping honey and life there was described as the workers' Shangri-La. Of course, when we were listening to radio Moscow, every window had to be closed and one had to make sure to be among friends only. It was totally prohibited by law to listen to Soviet programs. If caught in the act, it was reason enough to be incarcerated in a Romanian prison. To be arrested on ideological grounds - Communism - implied torture and long prison sentences. Moscow propaganda fell on very willing ears in those years when the antisemitism of Hitler had poisoned masses of people in Europe. We felt so lost and hopeless, that we wanted to believe that there was hope for rescue.

Hitler's rise to power was not perceived as threatening as it turned out to be. He was thought of as an aberration. After all, how could a people, as "civilized" as the Germans, follow such a madman? Perhaps, even to-day, some young Germans may ask themselves the same question. European Jews, or perhaps all Jews have a long, historic memory. We knew of Haman, the Inquisition but those were far off in history. We knew of Bogdan Chmielnicki and his hordes, who slaughtered Jews in the 17th century, in the Ukraine. We knew of more recent pogroms, like the one in Kishinev (Bessarabia) in 1905, after which masses of Russian Jews fled to America. This was within my parents' lifetime.

There existed vicious Jew-haters in every land. In Romania, the Greek-Orthodox clergy and many intellectuals were fierce nationalists. Their logical conclusion was hatred of the Jews. The fact that they did not run the government and were not actually in power made life tolerable, for a while. They came to power in 1938.

I am aware, from my earliest recollections, that we lived with the feeling that the life of the individual or of the entire Jewish community was always in danger. Being born Jewish implied a way of life, a set of beliefs and traditions and a feeling of belonging to a community, a group, that faced the same uncertainties, was potentially the victim of persecution from any possible group or from the government, depending on political or social circumstances. When financial difficulties arose in the country, international crises, war, unemployment, a failed harvest - in short - any natural or social or political disasters that occurred, were often turned into antisemitic outbursts. That was the safety valve, they let off steam and we took the heat, bore the brunt of their anger.

The second half of 1937 was a great change for me. I had remained alone with my parents. At the age of 17, I felt like an only child, since all my brothers and sisters were in the United States by then. In December 1937, during the Christmas vacation, as a senior in high school, I travelled alone, for the first time, to Bucharest, for one week. My excitement knew no bounds.

My girlfriend M. was visiting her sisters and I was to occupy the room of a student, who had gone home on vacation. I took the school number off the sleeve of my coat, put on a small blue hat, instead of the beret with the embroidered numbers, and left by train on a Friday morning to arrive at six in the evening in Bucharest. My friend awaited me at the railroad station. As I got off the train, on that snowy late afternoon, I heard newspaper boys hawking an extra newspaper edition: Extra, extra, the new government of

Goga, Cuza. Death to the Jews.

That was my bone chilling, frightening reception on my first pleasure trip. King Carol II had called on Octavian Goga, a well-know poet and politician and rabid anti-semite and on Alexandru Cuza, a historian, professor at the University of Iassi, infamous for his incitement to pogroms on Jews in that town, to form a new government. Actually, it was a maneuver on the part of the king of Romania, who felt threatened by Ionel Codreanu, the leader of the "Iron Guard," known Fascists and antisemites, who were taking their orders from Hitler. The king felt less endangered by Goga and Cuza than by the young generation, who were looking at the German model. The Romanians had full fledged swastika carrying nationalists well before it became the rage of the 30s. Cuza made the Jews of Iassi tremble before Hitler came to power.

King Carol outmaneuvered the Iron Guard with one fast action: he copied the German actions faithfully. He had Codreanu and his clique arrested, led into a forest and shot them in the back. Next day's newspaper headlines read: They were shot while trying to escape. (Auf der Flucht erschossen), the typical Hitlerian method of disposing of political enemies. The king dared to destroy the Iron Guard, showing Hitler that he wouldn't bow to his dictates, yet he put a nationalist, antisemitic regime into power, one based on ethnic nationalism, without foreign models.

For the Jews of Romania, December 1937 was the beginning of a deadly pressure of their lives and livelihoods. One of the first measures, taken by the new government was the review of their citizenship, with the intention of stripping many of their rights. As a consequence of that measure, we lost our citizenship on a technicality. The second blow came in the form of a decree that all Jews must keep their places of business open at official hours and on Saturdays. Failure to obey the law was punishable by stiff fines and by revocation of the permit. As a result of this law, my Father gave up the store, for he would never work on Saturdays or on religious holidays. All this happened to us in the year 1938. We did not know what my Father would do in order to make a living and we realized that more drastic measures might follow.

In these circumstances, our lives had taken a sharp turn towards grave uncertainties. Sali, too, lost her citizenship and possessed no valid passport to return. In those times, only a fool would have considered returning to Romania. In the West, Hitler had started to engulf his neighbors: Austria, Czechoslovakia. Whoever could find a country of refuge left for faraway lands like Chile, Venezuela, Cuba and others.

We just lived from day to day, in the knowledge that a noose might tighten around our necks. The family in the U.S.A. wrote that we should try to emigrate, yet it would take many years to obtain an American visa. In order to go to Palestine, one needed a special certificate. The British, under Arab pressure, had issued a White Paper limiting drastically the settling of Jews in the Mandate territory. We felt powerless. Go to South America? Father was nearing sixty, had no real trade, could not envision what he would do there, no knowledge of the language, nobody he knew there. I was 18 years old and could not make any far reaching decisions. Thus we, like millions of European Jews waited for the storm to break over our heads. All the signs of a terrible tragedy became visible. Daily, newspapers carried tragic headlines: Central Europe's only democracy, Czechoslovakia annexed; Austria accepted its incorporation into the Reich with enthusiasm. The majority felt proud of their native son, Adolf Schickelgruber, now Hitler, who had made good in politics, in Germany. They also deserve the dishonor of having sent Viennese Jews to Dachau, the newly created concentration camp in a suburb of Munich, Bavaria. The brother of a close friend of my parents living in Vienna, was arrested and sent to Dachau and shortly after sent back to his family, in a sealed coffin. Later on they did not take that much trouble any more, people were buried in mass graves and afterwards they were disposed of in the crematorium.

Nightly, on the radio, we heard Hitler ranting and raving and screaming. He blamed everything that ailed the world on the Jews and he predicted that only their complete annihilation would save Europe and the world. On the radio were heard the German masses shout, as clear as if they were right around us: "Fuhrer, lead. We will follow." There we sat, listened and shivered and felt like cats trapped in a sack. That was exactly our situation: trapped.

One hoped for an assassin to kill Hitler; for a "Putsch," a political conspiracy to overthrow his regime, for intervention from the rest of the world. We know now that none of this happened. The French and the English bought time by letting Hitler consolidate his power, as they were trying to arm, way too late. They had all been caught unprepared for the awesome, destructive power threatening them. Even the United States had no army and discussions were engaging the public whether to intervene in European affairs or to remain isolationists.- In spite of all this war of nerves, we went through the motions of going to school, going to the movies, bathing in the Prut and waiting for something to happen, waiting for a miracle that never came.

Coming back to my beginning student life, as I registered in September 1938, in the department of literature and foreign languages. I took the usual courses in French and German, but in English, I was just a beginner. The faculty made provisions for two categories of students: beginners and advanced. People like myself had to endeavor to make giant strides and eventually reach the level of the advanced group. We had a Professor, an Englishman, sent by the British Institute. This was the first flesh and blood Englishman that our town had ever seen. He was tall, a trifle stooped, with ash blond hair, a drooping moustache and wore glasses. He dressed in plus-fours and tweed jackets. To-day, I would think this a disguise, but this was a real, live Britisher. Years later, I found out that he, as well as a Frenchman, sent by the French Institute, were both spies, sent by their governments to occupy positions at the university in Northern Romania, at a stone's throw from the Soviet border. That was in the fall of 1938. No wonder that Professor T. gave easy A's. After all, he endeared himself and his country to the eager local students. He became a local oddity, while the French lecturer found his way into the hearts and bedrooms of many a Romanian beauty, ready to practice French on different levels. I only hope that their political goals were as easy to achieve as their professional ones.

By the end of my first year at the university (1938-39), the history of art professor organized a trip for his students to be sightseeing in Turkey, Greece and Egypt. We were supposed to study especially the Hadjia Sophia Mosque in Istanbul, the pyramids in Egypt and the many architectural sights in Greece. The trip was supposed to take place in September, 1939. I had registered for the student trip abroad, in the company of friendly colleagues.

As a preparation for the boat crossings, I had a tailor make for me a rain jacket, with a woolen buttoned-in lining. We were supposed to travel by boat from Constanţa, a Black Sea port in Romania. That trip never materialized since World War II broke out on September 1, 1939. The only good that came of these preparations was the jacket, which did me great duty during the war years.

Chapter 3

Second World War

I remember September 1, 1939 very vividly, as it remained etched in my memory from that day on. It was a sunny Friday, a clear end of summer day, when all people would talk about was: "Will they give him the Corridor?" "They" were the Poles; "He" was Hitler.

Hitler had tendered the Polish government an ultimatum to cede to Germany the city of Danzig, to-day Gdansk, and the Corridor, a strip of land, of Polish territory, which separated East Prussia from Germany. The Germans wanted to unite East Prussia, with its capital Königsberg, with the Reich. That annexation entailed also a strip of the Baltic coast. It would have cut off Poland from access to the Baltic Sea and robbed them of their great port city Danzig.

For a few days, all of Europe was breathlessly awaiting the answer to the ultimatum. On Friday, that fateful day in September, Poland answered "No" and Germany declared war on Poland. The unthinkable has actually happened. The Polish reply did not come as a surprise. The appetite of the Germans seemed unappeasable; there was no limit to their demands. Hitler had avowed that agreements are only pieces of paper to be torn. When he was given the green light to annex the Sudetenland, a region of Western Czechoslovakia, with a predominantly "Volksdeutsche" (of German descent) population, the German troops marched in and occupied every inch of Czech territory. It became clear that he would demand the Corridor and would swallow all of Poland.

The Poles are proud people and would take a stand. Their tragedy through the centuries lay in a fact of geography, that they lived between the Russians, in the East, and the Germans and Austrians, in the West.

They have been buffeted by both before and it was to clearly follow after
1939.

France and England had a pact to protect the territorial integrity of
Poland, if attacked. On Sunday, the third of that fateful September of 1939,
France and England declared war against Germany.

Here we were, at the border of Poland and we saw that a great tragedy
was about to unfold. What can one do? Sit at the radio and listen to martial
music from Germany, call-ups of regiments from Poland and unmitigated fear
from one's insides. I looked at my parents and expected them to know what
to anticipate, what would follow. After all, for me it was my first war.

In 1935, Italy's fascist dictator, Benito Mussolini, attacked Abyssinia
(Ethiopia) and occupied that helpless African country. Their emperor, Negus
Hailie Selassie, was the first throneless, homeless head of state at the time.
(He appealed in vain to the League of Nations in Geneva, whose powerless-
ness as an international organization came clearly to the fore. At the end of
World War II and the defeat of the Axis powers (Germany, Italy, Japan), the
Abyssinian emperor was reinstated. Today Ethiopia is a communist country,
under Soviet influence and in deplorable financial straits). At the time, in
1935, we only read about that attack in the newspapers and heard about it
on the radio, but it was in a far away continent and thus of less immediacy.

Now, in September 1939, Poland was just a stone's throw from Czernovitz and the implications were bone chilling. Hitler had so far occupied
Czechoslovakia and Austria without any open warfare, yet Poland wouldn't
submit, wouldn't voluntarily say "Yes" to its extinction and thus, action in
grand style might follow. The situation looked ominous and we felt it, and
we knew it and we were completely defenseless.

Hitler became obsessed with the plan of isolating England and France
from a possible alliance with the Soviet Union and made the daring offer of
a friendship pact with the Reds. His scenario was written in the following
sequence: swallow Poland, defeat Western Europe, including England, then
turn against the Red enemy in the East.

In pursuit of his plan, he dispatched Joachim von Ribbentrop, the German
minister of foreign affairs to Moscow to confer with his Soviet counterpart,
Vyacheslav M. Molotov. The Germans were insistent in an almost non-
diplomatic fashion, as they feared to lose precious time before the onset
of fall, with possibly unfavorable weather conditions. On August 23, 1939
Moscow signed a non-aggression pact with Germany. This historic treaty
sealed the fate of Poland; it also meant a turning point in my life, in the

fate of the province, where I lived, it was the beginning of the unfolding of events never anticipated to happen, it gave Hitler a green light to invade Poland. The date September 1 had been decided by Hitler as the latest date for the attack in the East, before the onset of rains, before the roads became impassable in some of the marshy areas of Poland. He wanted his victories lightning fast - Blitzkrieg.

The Soviet Union had achieved an unusual boon through the pact. The Eastern part of Europe, from the Baltic to the Black Sea was declared as their sphere of influence. They spelled out by name the three Baltic republics: Latvia, Lithuania and Estonia - all three formerly, under the tsars, Russian territory. The two signatories included as part of the Soviet sphere of influence Bessarabia. Northern Bukovina had not been included in that sinister deal, yet Russia made its own decision to annex it, together with Bessarabia. They made it a kind of connecting bridge to Southern Poland.

Germany attacked and cut into Poland like a knife into butter. It was an uneven match and none of Poland's efforts had any chance of success. While the Western part was buffeted by the Luftwaffe and by armored German divisions, the Russians didn't need to waste a single shot. The Eastern part of Poland was taken over without resistance. It was clear, it went according to the deal that had been worked out together in Moscow, the previous month to the accomplishment of clanking of glasses of vodka.

That pact was signed with the understanding that Germany could concentrate fully on fighting the Western powers, without interference from the U.S.S.R. Both sides bought time for themselves.

In the late 30s, the Soviet Union was going through a period of internal bloodletting, as Stalin was fully consolidating his absolute power. Officially, the world found out about the 1937 show trials when Sinoviev, Kamenev and Radek, well-known political leaders, fallen into disfavor with Stalin, were tried and put to death. Among the victims of those trials were also top military men; some generals were sentenced to long prison stays in Siberia, in the Gulag. In fact, one of the difficulties at the beginning of the war against Germany (1941) was the fact that the higher echelon of the military had been disgraced, dismissed or incarcerated; some had been put to death. Marshal Konstantin Rokossovski was brought back from Siberia during the war. He brought great victories, distinguished himself as commander in the battle of Stalingrad.

Throughout the world, the non-aggression pact between Berlin and Moscow produced a gasp of horror. Since fascism was considered the deadly enemy of communism - here both united as expansionists, as occupiers of foreign lands and people - they signed a nonaggression agreement. France and England realized that what they had hoped for, wouldn't happen. They hoped that Germany would fight the U.S.S.R.

All over the world, liberal people, socialists, communists and all those, who sympathized with these ideologies, were stunned, shocked, hit over the head, disappointed with the Soviet Union to the n-th degree. At that time, writers like Ignazio Silone, Arthur Koestler, George Orwell and thinking people all over the world got their shock, the first of many to follow, about the reality of the Soviet regime.

In my own sphere, events precipitated so fast, one could not spend much time on political speculations. The events happened at such speed that every day brought new realities. The map of Europe changed daily.

Coming back to September 1939. The war brought about heavy bombardment in Poland. The German Luftwaffe was efficient, accurate, deadly. By occupying Czechoslovakia, the Germans had increased their air force through the acquisition of the Skoda works, that produced airplanes of quality comparable to their own Stukas. The Germans advanced at breakneck speed into Poland, with their heavy panzers, tanks and artillery. They bombed fiercely and disrupted trains, destroyed roads and bridges. The Poles had no chance against the German war machine. On September 8, the attackers had reached Warsaw. The world learned what Blitzkrieg meant. (lightning-war) Poland was defeated in 18 days. The Soviets streamed in from the East in order to occupy the Eastern half of that trampled country; that occupation started on September 17. The Germans mopped up the remaining army outfits; the Pole's didn't even try to defend themselves against the Russians. It became a fait accompli, Poland was dismembered for the fourth time in its tragic history. It was a full-fledged, independent country for 20 years, between the two World Wars. (1919-1939) On September 18, 1939 there was no more Poland.

As soon as the Russians invaded, the Polish regiments, in retreat from the West eastward, realized that they would fall into Russian hands. Tens of thousands of refugees from all over Poland, civilians, military and diplomats, masses of people spilled over the border into Romania. Suddenly our town was overrun by thousands of refugees from that defeated country to the North of us. There were some people, who had fled in such a hurry, some wore coats over their nightgowns. Women with babies on their arms; military people in uniform, completely armed. I saw for the first time in my life

Orientals, probably members of the diplomatic corps. Masses of homeless people brought the ominous reality of war into my consciousness.

At this point, Hitler proposed to talk peace with the Western powers, but it had become clear that Hitler could not be trusted any more and the West would not be fooled again. The prime minister of England, Neville Chamberlain, after his return from Munich in 1938 declared that he had secured "peace in our time" after that assurance from Hitler. The pact with Russia and the ensuing war and partition of Poland among the two showed that Hitler could not be trusted and that the Soviet Union was in the same category as fascist Germany.

In Czernovitz, our townspeople reacted in a humanitarian way by offering the refugees shelter for the night, a meal, a place to sleep. However, some Poles were such antisemites that when they realized that they were offered shelter by a Jewish family, refused to accept that humane gesture. However, within a few weeks, through the good offices of the Red Cross, the refugees were sorted out, some how. After reaching the capital, Bucharest, the diplomats returned to their respective countries. The military were gathered in several small towns and proceeded to Persia (Iran) eventually. There was organized the core of the Polish Army in exile, commanded by General Anders. The Poles formed a government in exile, in London. Some of their units fought later on in North Africa, on the allied side. Some Jewish refugees from Poland remained in Czernovitz and shared the fate of our community during the war.

Winter set in. The first few months of the war were called: the phony war or Sitzkrieg (sitting war). Not much happened on the Western front. Germany and the Soviet Union consolidated their respective occupation of Poland.

We knew that much more was going to develop, that it was the calm before the storm. The spring of 1940 set in with new events. Life in our family, by this time just the parents and myself, went ahead on a more or less even keel. I studied at the university, studied English intensively. My Father, having liquidated the store, had some merchandise left, stuff which he could not dispose of in such a short span of time. We had a "servant's room" and there Father stashed cartons of scissors, combs, needles, all imported merchandise from Germany. Knives, scissors, needles, razor blades- all these goods were manufactured in the factories in Solingen and started to get scarcer since the war broke out. We actually lived on the proceeds of this liquidation for some time. However, it was going to run out and no new way of making a living was in sight.

In the meantime, I started to teach English privately as there were many people, anxious to learn the language. Thus we got by, but times were uncertain and the future was troubling.

During the winter of 1939-40, the Soviet Union attacked Finland and met with stiff resistance. Yet Finland was no match for the massive attacking troops of the enemy. They eventually ceded some territory - the second largest city Vyborg and a few islands in the Gulf of Finland. The war ended in March 1940.

Soon after, the Germans attacked and conquered Denmark and Norway and by May 1940 Hitler's troops crushed Holland, Belgium and Luxembourg and invaded France. The English fled at Dunkirk, France was defeated. Paris was formally declared an "open city" and surrendered on June 16, 1940. Paul Reynaud, the premier of France, fled to Bordeaux and requested an armistice on the following day.

While the Germans kept busy occupying the Western Europe countries Russia took advantage of the turbulence. They occupied the three Baltic republics between June 15-18, 1940. The free Western countries, England and the United States were alarmed at the fast pace of events in the East, but the world was in such a disarray that nobody could stop it, especially since Hitler and Stalin had agreed that the Baltic republics and Bessarabia were in the Soviet sphere of influence.

Chapter 4

Russians Overnight

On June 26, the Russians gave Romania an ultimatum claiming Bessarabia and Northern Bukovina. Next day the territories were occupied. The former used to be Russian until 1918, but Bukovina was for hundreds of years Austrian. The Russians just rounded out the border line that ran through Southern Poland toward Bessarabia. The Germans must have felt relieved that Russia had not occupied all of Romania, because there was nobody to stop them. The Germans bought oil from Ploeşti (Romania) and would have been in trouble without that supply.

Thus, on June 27, 1940, we became overnight Soviet subjects, with all that it implied. It implied plenty. Unexpectedly, overnight, we realized that we were in a different country, with a new regime, a new language - a change that was supposed to mean a new stability. After all, the Soviet Union is a world power and we will be part of an egalitarian society. After all, instead of getting into the clutches of a fiendish, fascist regime, we had escaped the antisemitism of Romania and our life as Jews would be the equal to anybody else's, so we thought. Many Romanians fled overnight as did many wealthy Jews. On Friday, June 27, at about noon time, the first Russian troops arrived. Logically, I should have been overjoyed since my world views were in accordance with a socialist world order. However, the pact of nonaggression, the partition of Poland, the attack of Finland, the cynicism of Soviet politics had shaken my outlook. One did not know essentially what to expect. We had heard from some Polish Jews, who had fled from Galizia during the preceding year, that the Russian regime was cruel, oppressive and that prisons were overflowing with citizens who had not committed any crimes. The jails were filled with merchants, storekeepers or formerly members of political parties - right, left, center. The word "Siberia" crept in occasionally. As a result of these diverse strands of information, when the Russians came into our town, I felt some trepidation from the start.

Yet, all my friends were so overjoyed about our new situation, I felt that we had made a good change. After all, perhaps we'll be spared the war altogether. My parents felt very apprehensive about the political change - a very radical, revolutionary dislocation of system, government, language, way of life.

When I confronted them, asking them about the specific fears, my Father quoted a Jewish saying: "Never pray for a new king." Historically, when oppressed Jews would pray for a political change, for a new king, the new king would often turn out to be worse than the previous one. They applied the old wisdom and they were right. In fact, the Soviet regime was worse than the years we lived under the Romanian regime. Luckily, we did not fully comprehend, in those first weeks, what suffering we were facing.

The Russian troops, making their appearance that first day, were poorly dressed and shod; they spoke only Russian or Ukrainian. Some of them asked passers-by what time it was and grabbed their watches. Local communists and the ubiquitous opportunists started to occupy high positions, as initially, everything was improvised . Little by little, Ukrainians from the central administration in Kiev came in as civilian authorities, replacing most local people. We started to figure out the different uniforms, insignia and epaulets of the military. We found out about the thousands, with similar insignia-they were mostly N.K.G.B., later renamed K.G.B.

Since Northern Bukovina became part of the Western Ukraine, the official language was Ukrainian. The unavailability of dictionaries presented the great obstacle in learning the new languages. We needed Russian, too. I envied my Mother her knowledge of Ukrainian. Although she could not read or write it, she could make herself understood. We used to have cleaning women and washerwomen and they were all Ukrainians. She could talk about daily objects or about foods but not the terminology of grammar or the explanation of abstract concepts, about history or philosophy.

I learned to read and write in the Slavic alphabet from a single sheet. Then, I proceeded to make up my own dictionary using a small notebook with every page a different letter. An added impediment was the difference between these two Slavic languages. The writing presented also slight differences, also the orthography. All this added to the difficulties and the confusion, at first. The new, Soviet administration never thought of offering language classes for the new citizens. I still remember how bravely we learned to read the new daily newspaper "Radianska Bukovina" (Red Bukovina), just trying to make out the headlines and slowly braving to comprehend the articles. By the beginning of September, barely two months from the occupation, we delved into the study of the History of the Party, meaning the communist party, according to the direction of the Stalin line, the official party line. The teacher was faced with an unusual task, namely, teaching a class, at a university, where practically nobody understood him or the textbook. After every few sentences he stopped to ask: Sie verstehen, Genossen? (Do you understand, comrades?) This was the extent of his knowledge of German. Most of us just picked up single words and wrote them down in the improvised dictionary. It was unusual, but not funny at all.

The Russians changed the names of the streets and parks so as to wipe out the vestiges of capitalist decades. We used to call the streets by their old Austrian names after 22 years of life in Romania. We never got used to the Romanian names. Now, overnight, all the street signs bore names of Lenin, Stalin, Red Army and that was understandable. However, they put names to streets, names that baffled us. If a Russian would ask where Shevchenko street was, one did not know. They thought that we were saboteurs, anti-social elements.

Of course, I only realized the gravity of our predicament when instances of Soviet provocations occurred. A Russian would buy a small item in a store and pay with a bill, which people had heard that it was not in circulation any longer, was worthless. The new Soviet administration had heard or perhaps spread the rumors themselves. When the shopkeeper asked whether that bill was still in circulation, he was arrested on the spot for daring to question the validity of Soviet currency. The three shopkeepers that I know of, since one was my cousin, were tried within a few weeks, sentenced and sent to the "Far East" namely Siberia, for five years each. One of them survived and returned to Czernovitz. He was Leo Reiter, our cousin, an old time socialist, formerly a devoted sympathizer of the Soviets, who used to come to us to listen to the German broadcasts from the Soviet Union. After sentencing, the wife was told to bring warm clothes, as he would be sent away, to serve his five year prison term. She understood that he was going to "the white bears," to Siberia. When she brought a suit, a coat, shirts and shoes, the prison official gave her instructions to cut off all buttons, no suspenders, no shoe laces. These precautions were supposed to protect the prisoner, to prevent him from committing suicide: not to swallow the buttons and not to hang himself on the shoe laces or the suspenders.

That happened in August, 1940, less than two months after the Soviet takeover. It needs little imagination to understand how a person could shield himself from the frosts of Siberia, when he could not button the shirt or coat or lace his shoes. Instances of this nature filled our first months under Stalin's regime.

Everything was nationalized, everything became the property of the state. Thus the new administration was every citizen's landlord. They hired "house administrators" to run the houses and collect the rent. About every ten houses had one administrator, overseer. These officials were responsible to the local "militia" or police. They were spying on everybody. They provided a dossier on every family, on each individual within each family.

Every citizen had to have a so-called "passport," an identification booklet, issued by the militia, with all the personal data: place and date of birth, nationality (for us was the label Jew, not Russian or Ukrainian or Moldavian), occupation and place of work, data on military service. People were supposed to carry that passport at all times and anybody in an official uniform or secret police could stop you for identification. The word "passport" was a misnomer, for you could not travel any place on the strength of this identification. Nobody had permission to travel from one town to another. If sent by the workplace, one was issued a "propusk," a permit with the data and destination of travel. Once at the arrival destination, one had to register at the local militia (police). Thus, nobody could travel anywhere without a special permit, even if it were at a distance of 50 miles.

Suddenly I became aware that the citizen was a kind of prisoner, the individual was somehow in confinement, with very limited personal freedom. At that time we didn't think about crime in the streets, it was almost non-existent. Yet crime, on a gigantic scale, came not from the streets but from the top, from the Kremlin. Stalin and his most trusted man in power, Lavreti Beria, the head of the N.K.V.D. (to-day K.G.B.) and the rest of the Polit-bureau had a stranglehold on the entire population. They exercised such unlimited control over the lives of the entire, vast, conglomerate of nations that make up the Soviet Union. It is impossible, at this point, to figure out how many millions of people were annihilated by them, at their whim.

In the first week or two, it was hard to figure out the nature of that regime. I remember walking in the street with a girl friend and a soldier started talking to us. It was mutual - he could not understand us just as we could not understand him. Yet, he meant to be friendly, so he gave us a book, which he was probably reading. Here are Russians bearing gifts. Somebody, who could read Russian told us that it was Gogol's "Dead Souls." It was a book from a lending library in Odessa.

In the first week or so, they brought the Moysseiev Dancers, who performed in the Central Square of town, renamed "Red Square." They were magnificent folk dancers performing for the enjoyment of the newly liberated people, free people. Soon after came a group of outstanding Jewish writers, who delighted us with readings of their poetry and also sang some rousing, Jewish revolutionary songs. Within the next few years all these writers were put to death.

Of course, it reminds you of "pane et circensem" (bread and circus), the expression used by the Roman emperors 2000 years ago, meaning to give people subsistence and a little entertainment and they won't think of anything else, of what plight they are in. That was what we got, at the start. After the initial few honeymoon weeks were over, they clamped down on the population. It was probably the accepted philosophy from the Kremlin that they would rather be feared than loved. Actually love was given a very short chance, but fear grew and deepened and took hold of our beings, our lives, no doubt about it. Yet people were afraid to confide in others, did not dare to express their doubts.

Another facet of Soviet society, absolutely unsuspected by us, started to unfold. Some young military men, some handsome officers, began to court Russian-speaking girls. Quite a number of Bessarabian Jews lived in Czernovitz, some were students at the university. They spoke Russian and had an easier time handling matters. It didn't take long and a number of these men married local girls. Shortly after, it turned out that some had families: wives and children. They had been called on this assignment and left their homes. Some of them took advantage of the fact that we were ignorant of conditions in the Soviet Union. Some may have had their families thousands of miles away and figure that they may not see them in years. They had their mail sent to a post office box, not a private address and their families wouldn't know where they lived, just the town. Deceit and lying had become second nature, a means for survival. After all, in the Soviet Union, so many people spent time in prison and prison was mostly not for real crimes. There was a proverb coined under the Soviet regime, which in translation sounds like this: "Whoever was there won't forget it; whoever was not yet, will still be."

People started to look for employment. Until September, when the university would open - I was supposed to enter the third year of studies - I worked in a book store, where we were making an inventory of the existing stock. I found out that students who achieved all A's or A's and one or two B's, would earn a monthly scholarship of 150 or 125 rubles, depending on the grades. That sum was the equivalent of a clerk's monthly salary. That was what I was aiming for and I received the scholarship.

People started realizing that the Russians, who were heading all the enterprises, were helping themselves to the merchandise, right and left. Of course, food became scarce because peasants were afraid of controls on the prices of their produce. As a result, they brought less food to market. Anybody working in a food store or restaurant or bakery or yeast factory was doing very well, while I, who couldn't steal anything, except for a Romanian book or ink, was at a clear disadvantage. It takes experience to realize where to work in case of a communist take-over.

Well, I returned to school in September and tried hard to make sure to achieve top grades, in order to be the person, in our family, who had an income. University, organized on the Soviet system, was just like high school: daily classes from 9-2 p.m., daily written assignments; attendance strictly kept, no choice of courses beside the major. We studied Ukrainian, Russian grammar as well as literature. It sounds ridiculous, but we learned spelling in one lesson and had to read Pushkin, in the original text, next period. The same was repeated with Ukrainian spelling, grammar and also the reading of poetry by Taras Shevchenko. That was similar to learning the verbs to be or to have and read also Shakespeare. (Actually, that was how I learned English in 1938.)

The subjects that were most important: History of the Party and Dialectic Materialism. That had to be learned the way they explained it and no questions should be asked; no doubts were permitted. The history of the party had been revised several times, when Trotsky or others fell into disfavor and thus some pages or chapters had to be rewritten as heroes became thugs; as heroic revolutionaries became bourgeois lackeys. We had a teacher of linguistics who talked about language, meaning Russian or Ukrainian. Poor guy, young comrade Lysenko knew so little and felt so out of place when asked about romance or germanic languages. He looked like a bantam fighter, small and chunky. When he got drunk at the New Year's party, he, the comrade, kissed every girl's hand like a little comic figure.

Among all the teachers from the Ukraine, one became fairly liked and close to some of us. He was relatively young, about 30, thin, pale, reminiscent of romantic heroes who die young of T.B. He played the piano and recited poetry, to our delight. He dared recite Yessenin, a symbolist poet, a poet not accepted by the official line. Officially, we were supposed to admire Mayakovsky, who glorified the Soviet Union. I still remember our teacher reciting, in private, in a lugubrious voice this verse by Yessenin: "I wish, oh, how I wish to shit on the moon," debunking romantic poets. Whether this Russian teacher was truly critical of the party line or whether he was trying to play a game, initiated by the N.K.G.B., will forever remain a question in my mind.

The English teacher, Mrs. Koppelmann, was the best English teacher in Czernovitz. She was an excellent language teacher, a very decent person, but not really a scholar, not trained to be a university professor. The level of the university had dropped considerably, compared to what I experienced before, in two years of studies. Yet, we had a difficult time with the two new languages and also a course in military preparedness. All the students, men and women, had to learn military tactics and had to train in the fields, to become efficient shots. The training was done out-of-doors, in rain, snow or sleet. At every session, one was given three bullets. If you did not achieve a good score, you got a low grade. Fear of losing the scholarship made me try very hard and I lay so long on the frozen ground or soggy field, in order to do it right. In the end, in May 1941, I got very sick with pleurisy and just barely made it through the exams in June 1941, that fateful month when the Germans attacked.

Coming back to the quality of our lives during that year. The invasion of privacy became more and more oppressive, as the teachers were watching whether Jewish students were absent during Jewish holidays. I remember on Yom Kippur, in October, 1940, the teachers were especially paying attention to the attendance. Some zealous communists were even trying to find out whether anybody was fasting. That Yom Kippur was the first time I fasted, although I had to go to school. When I returned home, by 3 o'clock, my parents were in the synagogue. It was cold and rainy and I was shivering from cold, hunger and terrible disappointment with this cruel, petty regime that had no humane standards, no notion of freedom, no respect for human beings - a cruel, oppressive, invasive regime - where power was everything and human life was dirt cheap.

By this time, I presume, many of my friends realized what a bitter hoax Communism had played on decent people, what a deception, yet we feared to express our thoughts. We feared each other. Some were so anxious to believe and not waver, that they would deny the reality of our new regime. Thus everybody feared to open up in front of one's closest friends.

My parents and myself spoke freely to one another, especially after the tragedy that had befallen our relative, Leo Reiter. I had a boy friend to whom I did not express my opinions freely. My girl friends from high school and my colleagues at the university just didn't talk about the regime, for fear that somebody may possibly mention my name in front of a member of the Comsomol (Young Communist League) and one could end in prison. Since there was no third year, I studied English, in the second year. We were a small group of students, very much bound by close friendship. Martha, myself and Erich Einhorn would often study together. We spent most of our time either at the university or doing work together, after school. Erich was a close friend of Paul Antschel, who was in the second year in French. We shared most of the classes, except for the separate English and French courses. We often joked, made fun of everything except for political questions or judgment of the regime. We openly steered clear of that, but seemed to have similar feelings.

As teenagers, many of my friends had been part of anti-fascist groups, except for Erich. He was really a-political, but shared literary interests with Paul. During that school year Erich became a very dear friend. He had a keen sense of humor; was lively, witty and strong. We often studied together and enjoyed a kind of shorthand, the way we went over subjects, skipped the unnecessary, did not need particular explanations. He was as reliable and as decent as one expects a friend to be. Tall, broadsholdered, athletic looking, blond, with big, white teeth, exposed fully when he smiled or laughed. His was a hearty, loud laugh. Erich looked like a rather typical German. However, he was Jewish and could tell a good Jewish joke, too. Paul was shorter, slim, with dark hair and dark eyes, a handsome, poetic-looking man with a quiet, rare laughter. Erich's exterior showed a person, who looked people and events straight in the face, as if nothing could ever go wrong. Paul was rather reserved, with an almond-shaped face, darkly handsome, extremely attractive. His voice melodious and soft evoked a desire to protect and yet, to listen to this soft lilting voice. His humor was sharp, biting and often condescending.

Our sentimental attachments went into different directions. Erich had a much younger girlfriend. Paul focused his attention for shorter periods of time, on girls that were intelligent, loved poetry or on a girl, who possessed all these qualities and also looked a little exotic, like Tanja; for a while, he lavished attention on a pretty Russian student who looked very naive, childlike.

We all labored hard on the Slavic languages; we read Pushkin and Shevchenko and started to enjoy some more recent writers and poets like Yessenin, Mayakovsky and Madelstamm. The latter was persona non grata at the time; his poems were forbidden since he had dared to write a satirical poem about Stalin. He ended up in prison and disappeared. Most of us achieved a stipendium, went about our daily work and didn't plan too much ahead. All this lasted one full year.

It turned out to have been a stroke of luck that my Father had sold the store before the Communist take-over. Our house overseer registered that my Father had been a clerk. People, who had previously owned a house or an enterprise received a "passport 39" which assured one of a free trip of no return, namely to Siberia, as it turned out within the year.

I met Yuda in the fall of 1940, during the Russian school year. His Father fell ill with typhoid fever and was in quarantine in the hospital for infectious diseases. The family was not permitted to visit the patient. One of his friends was a nurse in the hospital. She told him that a young doctor in that department was a friend of mine. Thus Yuda came to me, introduced himself as a student of mathematics at the university and then tried to find out whether he could see the doctor. Of course, I tried to be helpful and asked him to wait for my friend. For about ten days he came daily to find out about his Father's recovery. That was how we met, surely unaware that we would share the rest of our lives.

The Russians settled in and learned a lot about us in the process. They realized that we were better educated than their own students, who only went through ten years of schooling before higher studies. They wondered at the difference in our housing, our customs, our food. Russians occupied vacant apartments from people who had fled to Romania and from Germans, who left officially for Germany. At the start of their occupation of Northern Bukovina, a delegation of German officers came to Czernovitz and were received as friends and allies. They registered all Germans who desired to leave for Germany. A number of their apartments became available.

There were stories, told about Ukrainians, who had never previously seen toilets. They washed their feet in the toilet bowl. Others bought fish and kept them alive in the bath tubs. They were faced with another problem. They realized that many people had radios and could hear news from all over Europe. In the Soviet Union they only had loudspeakers at every street corner and they played marches or propaganda from Moscow. At home, the population could enjoy a kind of news box (tochka-spot) which transmitted the same program as the loudspeakers. The length and breadth of that entire vast country everybody heard the same thing: propaganda. They were really cut off from the rest of the world and were indoctrinated to think that theirs was the best country in the world.

There happened instances, where Soviet students asked us whether we were rich.

They had been told that in capitalist countries only the rich went to school, while the children of workers and peasants remained illiterate. When we told them that school was free and compulsory for six years, they realized that there was something wrong, somewhere. It took them time to become aware that their regime had lied to them all along. We understood that serfdom had been abolished all over Europe after the revolution of 1848, yet in Russia it was still prevalent, not only for peasants but for everybody - save the party. It was a bitter pill to swallow.

Among the ways to indoctrinate and also to entertain the population were big parades on holidays: May Day and November 7, the celebration of the October Revolution. Participation at the parades was compulsory. We had to come to the university, where attendance was taken, and march in a group with pictures and banners. On these holidays, as well as on New Year's eve, were big parties in school, with dancing, food and drink. On New Year's eve was a masquerade ball, dancing and drinking all night.

At that same time, the war raged in Western Europe; German u-boats were haunting all shipping, yet we knew little about the rest of the world. True, we could listen to the radio, in our homes, but were afraid of being found out. One could not talk about it since it was forbidden. The only newspaper in town continued to be "Radianska Bukovina" (Red Bukovina), a Ukrainian daily, which praised workers and peasants, glorified the party and Stalin.

In May 1941 the N.K.G.B., secret police, the ones with light blue epaulets and little red squares on them, descended one night into a great number of homes and deported many local families to Siberia. They came with an open truck, gave the family an hour to pack a few bundles, put them in the truck and they were gone. That same thing happened on two consecutive nights. A few thousand Czernoviters were deported, destination not mentioned, yet understood - Far East, Siberia.

In our apartment house, they deported a couple with a ten year old daughter. The man had owned a small furniture store, which had been nationalized by the government. Across the street from us, they deported a family, whose son and daughter had been known as communists. The father, Mr. Ippen was a socialist, the son had volunteered to fight on the Republican side in the Spanish Civil War and was killed in Spain. It became known that the entire family was non- grata because the son was supposedly a Trotzkyite. The daughter and son-in- law were communists, but since they lived in her parent's apartment, everybody in the house was taken away. They then sealed the place and a commissar or an officer moved in and inherited the entire household.

In May, at the time of these dread occurrences, we came to class in the morning and looked around to see whether anybody was missing. Since many of the Russians took part in these "actions," they knew that we knew about the night deportations, but nobody mentioned a word about it. I was aware about the disappearance of my neighbors; others had relatives among them and nobody knew when it would stop. Many Russians considered it a fact of life that people would disappear by the favor of their government. They had suffered through these spasms of their police state, at different times and now they saw the local population go through this baptism of sheer despair. It is, by no means certain, but it was said that if the war had not broken out in June 1941, all of us, local people, would have landed in Siberia, in gulag.

In that same blessed spring, I fell ill with pleurisy. Since there was no medication available, I lay in bed for six weeks, was told to sweat until the liquid on the pleura receded. Those were harsh times from every point of view. My poor, devoted Mother was told to feed me vegetables juices, which are rich in vitamins. She would grate carrots and beets by the kilos, squeeze the mass and feed me the juice. My parents did whatever they humanly could to see me on my feet again. Finally, I got out of bed, in May; suffered the scare of the deportations, passed the exams in June and on June 22, 1941 the Germans attacked the Soviet Union.

A few days before the actual attack, the English supposedly warned the Soviet Union that Germany was massing troops on the Eastern frontier - from the Baltic Sea to the Black Sea. Day by day, Stalin was supposed to be informed, but disregarded the warnings as English propaganda, as an attempt to thrust a wedge between the two allies: Germany and the Soviet Union.

On Sunday morning, June 22, a few days before the first anniversary of our "liberation" by the Soviets, Germany staged a surprise attack all along the German-Russian border; they bombed the entire length of the frontier. Since Czernovitz was on that line, our small airport was attacked, all planes on fire in the first hour of the first day of the hostilities. On that Sunday, as people got up in the morning, rumors started about war. After a few hours the radio broadcast the official acknowledgement of the German attack. The first reaction of a well seasoned population was: "Do we have water? Do we still have electricity?" As these were still intact, one had to buy bread, flour, yeast.

It took no time to witness the panic that set in among the Russians. Some tried to leave right away, to go home, wherever home was. The military were going hither and thither in their trucks. Within two, three days it became apparent that they were not even trying to hold the line and a stampede Eastward started. Panic set in. Officers and their families ran away; any official, who could put a hand on a truck, loaded it with all they had acquired in such a short time and fled. In different sections of town, the military stopped young and middle aged men in the streets, loaded them on trucks and took them into the army. Those men just disappeared, they were not granted permission to say good bye to their families. Yuda's only brother, Michael (Muniu) was snatched that way. He had got married a few months previously to Sonia, with whom he was reunited 10 years later. They waited for one another. Yuda saw him just once more, in 1971, in Israel, after 30 years. That was the only time I had occasion to meet my brother-in-law. At that reunion, the heartache was so visible on everybody's face. They knew that they were the closest blood relatives and had been apart for most of their lives. They knew that they were brothers, yet they were in essence strangers, molded by completely different conditions. Both had gone through inhuman hardships, but in different places, in different surroundings. That was the only time spent together with this frail, thin, soft spoken man, a collector of dolls. He passed away in September, 1982.

Coming back to that last week of June 1941, people were petrified at the imminent arrival of the German troops. Many, who had openly avowed to be communists, were afraid of being denounced to the Germans or Romanians; others were in fear of retribution from some who held grudges against them. They tried to flee with the Russians, to be evacuated into the Soviet Union, escape Eastward, escape coming battles or bombings or pogroms or all of these.

As soon as the war had broken out, the Russians decreed, in the interest of national security, that all private citizens had to deliver their radios to the authorities, at the building of the former stock exchange. The threat, in case of non-delivery was so severe, that nobody would have dared to be found in possession of one. On the day, before the abandonment of the town, the building with the radios was set on fire. Not a single radio was left in town. Before the retreat, they also destroyed the electric utility station, the railroad bridge as well as the pedestrian bridge over the river Prut, the post office and the stocks of arms which they could not evacuate. Of course, we were left without electricity; no water pumping station. Those were inconveniences; we were left in a much more desperate state, unsure of our lives from that day on.

The Russians were gone within 8 days. They offered no resistance against the German troops. The students, at the university, were offered to be evacuated, together with the Russian teaching staff and with the Soviet students. I had a knapsack packed from the second day, like almost everybody else that I knew.

My friend, the doctor, left with the hospital staff. When he said good bye, he asked me to take care of his parents and sister and her child just as I would of my parents.

Next day, when my long time friend Martha came, with her knapsack on her back, asking me to come along with the students at the university, I looked at my crying Mother and my destitute Father and I realized that they would be lost without me. At that moment, I threw down my pack and said: "I'll stay. Whatever happens to them will happen to me." Martha left. The die was cast. I chose to share my fate with my parents and I never regretted it.

Chapter 5

German Occupation

Two days later, the Soviets had left and the Germans had not yet come in - the town was in no-man's-land. Nobody dared step out of the house for fear of looters, bandits, drunkards. In fact, before the Russians abandoned the town, they emptied the liquor stores and cosmetic stores in search for alcohol. Whoever was not lucky enough to find vodka, took denatured alcohol or eau de cologne; they drank anything. Many drunken soldiers lay in the streets and in the gutters and were taken prisoners, while drunk; some were shot on the spot.

Some war record for glorious red soldiers.

Peasants, in the villages around Czernovitz, massacred the Jews in their communities. In town, looters broke into apartments, that had been left by the Russians as well as by those who had fled with them. In a day or two German troops came and hastened further East, for they routed the Soviet army in an unexpected way.

The initial Russian defeat was due to the element of surprise, of disorganization and partly because many refused to fight and deserted in droves and greeted the Germans as saviors. They had hated communism all along. My professor of Russian at the university and his daughter, who was the leader of the comsomol (young communist league) stayed behind in Czernovitz. They, like many others, hid during the evacuation. Soon after the Romanians occupied the province, the Ukrainian and Russian sympathizers of fascism opted to go to Germany. They wanted to insure themselves to be far away from Soviet territory in case of reverses of the war. How they fared, I do not know. I know that thousands remained behind and later on many joined the Bandera bands, who fought on the German side against communism, murdered Jews pitilessly in Galizia and Bukovina.

The Germans imposed a curfew from 7 p.m. to 7 a.m. In the first week shooting went on at random. The targeted victim was the Jew. At first nobody went out for fear of being killed in the streets. We only found out later that the Jewish inhabitants of small towns and villages had been massacred. With no radio and no newspapers, we lived in isolation from the outside world.

The Romanians took over the administration of the conquered formerly owned province. In order to repair the damages caused by the retreating Russians, they forced all able-bodied men to do the necessary repairs. Jewish men worked in the hurried reconstruction of the bridges, they cleared the rubble in the post office, repaired the electric utility station, cleared the devastation from the many explosions. Yuda, his uncle and cousin worked on the bridge; Paul Antschel at the post office. Of course nobody was paid for the work. Once in a while the soldiers, who were supervising the work, would give half a loaf of bread per person, to be taken home. Yet once in a while the soldiers would hit the older men when they could not work fast enough. Yuda told me how his uncle was beaten in front of his son and his nephew. The pain and the shame of the father beaten and the son who could not protect him. A few days after the German-Romanian occupation they burned our beautiful Temple. During that night, they summoned the rabbi, Dr. Mark and the cantor Perlstein, forced them to open the Temple, then the Germans set fire to the Temple. Dr. Mark and the cantor were taken to Rosha, a village nearby with German population. Both were shot there. That night we stood at the window of our apartment and saw from not too far the flames lashing out all night against the clear summer sky. Next morning we saw that disaster.

The Jewish population was ordered to sew on a yellow star, of a prescribed dimension, on every garment worn outdoors. We were permitted to go out in the street for two hours only, from 10 till noon; that was for the purpose of buying food. Those who were doing hard labor at the bridge or the electric station received a permit to go to and from work, at those particular hours.

Whoever went out to purchase food soon found out that most peasants refused to come to market to sell produce. Thus daily life in the summer of 1941 became a matter of grave difficulties. First, the exchange of money into Romanian currency was almost impossible. In case one had dollars, one could exchange them for lei. The fact was that practically nobody had dollars and even if so, where to look for blackmarketeers?

The administration was handed over completely to the Romanian military, General Calotescu became the chief administrator. Some of the former Romanian inhabitants of Czernovitz started to return. However, life was tough, food hard to come by. We could not buy bread, bakeries did not function but we still needed food. We had flour, but could not obtain yeast. Mother tried to make a sour dough and make it rise. The baked result was as hard as a rock. We ate beans with oil, the hard bread, rice and not much else. Slowly, slowly the peasants started to bring some food in exchange for towels or shoes or whatever they bargained for. Little by little people started to sell valuables: a golden watch, a bracelet, rings for Romanian money. Yet, as bad as times were, as limited one's movements, we knew that it could get worse, we had found out about the massacre of the Jews in the small towns and villages. We only hoped that we would be left in our apartments. Homelessness and hunger were the worst fears and soon autumn was going to set in.

With all my friends gone, I went to see whether any of my former classmates had remained behind. Dorothea (Duschka) Altneu, with whom I did not associate much before, became a new friend. She was highly intelligent, an outstanding student, but never among my group of friends. Lutza, a close friend from former years, married and pregnant, had remained in town, with her husband and family. I had seen Paul Antschel in the ruins of the post office. He lived in a different section of town. Since I could leave the house for two hours only, one could associate only with people, who lived nearby.

I felt like I had been robbed of everything. At the age of 21, alone with my parents, practically no friends, surrounded by enemies, almost under house arrest and all around - vultures; the beginning of a different type of existence, everything bleak. The past-gone; future-none.

At this point, 44 years later, I try to understand how I continued an existence that hopeless. One lived day by day, every day a challenge for survival, as each day was one day nearer to the end of the war. We, the Jews, took it for granted that Hitler would be defeated, that the evil of Nazism and Fascism would be eradicated but whether we would live to see it was problematic. So we tried one day at a time. Property became unimportant, clothes became only important if it could be sold or exchanged for food. The values changed radically. Every day was one day less to the end of the war. It took four long years to that hoped for day, and six million of our own never made it.

We were cut off from the outside world for years. One could buy a Romanian newspaper and read about the German victories. The truth was that the Soviet armies were retreating and the Germans were conquering immense territories. Although we hated to believe in their astounding victories, yet they were frighteningly true. Here and there some Romanians told about the news heard over the B.B.C. and the news travelled incredibly fast, through the grapevine. However, since information was whispered as it spread by word of mouth, it often turned into something different. Some people went out during the allotted two hours just to get news, from an "unimpeachable source."

The war was only three months in its unfolding, when rumors started spreading about a "Jewish Solution." What are they going to do about the Jews? that became the burning question at the beginning of October. In the villages and small towns around Czernovitz all the Jews had been murdered. In Bessarabia there had been devastating pogroms. It seemed that the authorities were not going to leave us untouched. On Simchat Torah, October 11, 1941, on a cold, windy Saturday morning, there appeared notices, ordinances, pasted on buildings and lampposts, to the effect that every Jew was ordered to move into a certain section of town, formerly mostly populated by poor Jews. That section was designated as the Ghetto. By 5 o'clock on that afternoon, no Jew was allowed to reside in town any longer everybody had to reside within the confines of the Ghetto. Noncompliance was punishable by death, execution on the spot.

My Father came home from the synagogue with the news. On the most joyous holiday in the Jewish calendar, we received the most horrifying order. (We found out, after the war, that this order had come from Berlin, from the highest German authorities. Yuda and I saw the document in the Jewish Museum in Amsterdam.) I ran out in the street to read the ordinance and saw the awful instructions.

Anybody who knew a family in that section of town just went there. We put some clothes, bedding, shoes into bags, pillowcases and carried the stuff into the apartment of Mrs. Schachter, whom we had known for a long time. They had a store next to my Father's. Her husband had been imprisoned by the Soviets on a trumped up charge and he was somewhere in Siberia. Her son and daughter were with her. By the afternoon barricades were built up to lock in the Jewish Ghetto, to seal our fate.

The situation was mind boggling. In every apartment were ten times more people than could be accommodated. In the two rooms and kitchens, where we had found asylum were 45 people. A few older persons slept in the two beds, the others stretched out on the floor, with the legs under the beds, some were sitting, some on the tables, under the tables. It was just inhuman to be crowded into staircases, corridors and plainly on the sidewalks. The electricity had not yet been restored; some apartments had no running water. It was an unmitigated disaster. My Father said that we will all die of typhoid fever or some other disease will decimate the population in the Ghetto.

Two days later soldiers came into the Ghetto to spread the news that next day certain streets would be evacuated, the people re-settled in Transnistria. Everybody in these streets should be ready to move next day. First we could not figure out what "Transnistria" was. It was part of the conquered territory of the Ukraine, across the river Dniester, East of the river, Soviet territory.

Next day two or three thousand Jews were chased out from two streets and they were walking, taking along what they could carry on their backs. They were chased toward the rail road station. Romanian soldiers chased them to hurry, to fill up the cattle wagons. By the evening, the trains fully packed, sides bolted - they were on their way to concentration camps. On that first day, my friend Lola and her entire family left, among so many others. As we had our knapsacks ready to go, we went to a different location in the Ghetto, because next day was our turn to leave for Transnistria. As we had seen on the first day what was happening, we three decided that it was better to try to leave later. Thus, we made up our minds to go from place to place, maybe a miracle would still happen.

We moved four times, to different locations. In one place, in an attic, there was such terrible fleas, they tortured us all night. We went from place to place with only one sack each, for that was all we could carry. After ten days of deportations, the Romanian administration changed their plan. The town was paralyzed without the Jews. There were no people to run the services after the destruction left by the Russians, the Romanians had not returned yet in any numbers and without the local Jews, the town was paralyzed. Besides, there were Romanian-Jewish intermarriages and the affected families intervened with the government in Bucharest. There may have been some intervention from abroad, but that is not proven. As a result, the general issued a decree stopping temporarily the "re-settlement" of the Jews. By that time three quarters of the Jews had been deported to Transnistria.

There had to be guide lines concerning who was needed, who would be allowed to stay. Since the Jewish community could not figure out what was intended or who was needed, they started registration of specialists. My former elementary school was within the Ghetto area and registration took place there.

Everybody was desperate and lists were made for any kind of specialty. I registered where ever they would accept my name. You did not have to show a document, that would come up later. I was on a students list (who needed students?), on a chemists list, nurse, anywhere. I put Father's name on all kinds of lists, Yuda was in the same situation, although we had no contact at that time. He also registered on all kinds of lists and he got a certificate to return home as "factory foreman." The deportations stopped temporarily.

In the meantime, October neared its end, the weather got colder, rains made it very hard to stand for hours and listen for the names of people, who received the permit to return. I went daily to that military station, where the lucky ones received the reprieve from concentration camp. Those returned to their apartments in town and those who remained behind felt more and more desolate. In the meantime the Ghetto shrank because as soon as some went home and tens of thousands had been deported, the area, where we could stay became smaller. They moved the barricades, enlarged the town and shrank the Ghetto. Well, after about 2 weeks, we still had no permit and we became fairly despondent. We had decided that in case only the parents received the permit and not me, they should stay home and I should go alone. If only I could remain, then we should act the same way. If one remained in town, that one could help the person in Transnistria.

One day, the soldiers chased out everybody in the street where we were "Yudengasse" (Jew Street). My parents and myself took our sacks to go to the rail road station. While we were going with the rest of that day's contingent, half way to the station, a woman walked by and said: "They called your name at the certificate station." On the spur of the moment, I said to my parents: "You continue going. I am going back, get the certificate and will take you out." Nobody would have let all three of us go back without a permit. Of course, it was easier said than done. The military watched all along the roads and they said that Jews can go only one way - toward the rail road station, not back. I was a young girl, 21 years old and desperate to go look for that elusive piece of paper. I promised each one money on my way back, some I gave a few lei and I ran toward that building, where the military were giving that life giving piece of paper. On my arrival there, I asked insistently whether anybody had seen the certificate for Spiegel, somebody said that a blond woman had taken it, intending to give it to my Father. She was the daughter in law of the people, where we had stayed. She knew that we were on the way to the deportation. Since she could not go any further to look for us, for she would have been swallowed up by that mass of humanity, she gave it to a man, who was going as a deportee and told him: "If you see Mr. Spiegel, he is a man with a beard, give it to him."

When I heard that the certificate was taken to the railroad I ran again toward the station, without the paper. I arrived as the trains were ready to leave. My parents were in a cattle car, some people, were still drinking a last gulp of water at a pump. Almost unable to shout any more, I ran from car to car, asking whether anybody had a certificate for Spiegel. A man called from inside a cattle wagon, asked me for the first name and gave me the certificate for Markus Spiegel. I frantically ran and called my parents' name and as the trains were about to leave, I got them out. A few minutes later the train left and the three of us trudged back to the Ghetto. We could hardly walk those one or two miles, yet we dragged ourselves back to the ghetto, into the house in the Yudengasse. The house was deserted, they had taken the Feuer family in the afternoon. Mrs. Feuer was the sister of uncle Morris partner, in New York. The entire family perished in Transnistria. We three had almost come back from the grave. On the return from the train, I showed the guards, along the road, our certificate to prove that I had not lied to them. They had, probably, not seen anybody go back.

The house, where we spent the night, after such a nightmarish day, was eerie. We were the only people in the entire street, everybody had been deported on that day. On looking at the permit, it was made out for my Father only. Next morning I went to the military where the permits were handled, forced myself into the colonel's office. I explained to him that my Father had a wife, so he added "and wife"; then I said that I was the daughter. He angrily turned to me and asked whether there were more sons and daughters. I said: "No, I am the only daughter." Thus he added "and one daughter."

Next day we left the Ghetto. The gates had been moved again to shrink the periphery of the Jewish section. We walked about fifteen minutes to our apartment, with our knapsacks on the backs. I had fever blisters all around my mouth. The day before was hell on earth, but we escaped as if by miracle. When I think of that day, I paraphrase Winston Churchill, and say: it was my finest hour. In our apartment, a few windows had been broken, it was bitterly cold and damp on November 11, 1941. We had spent a harrowing month in hell, I mean, in the Ghetto, in Czernovitz. Two more Jewish families had returned to the apartment house: an elderly couple and a widow, the mother of two daughters, the older my former schoolmate. Both had got married during the year under the Soviets and they fled, with their husbands, to the Soviet Union. The old couple, a second marriage for both, formerly widowed; she had a son my own age, he had a married daughter, whose husband had been grabbed in the street and taken into the Russian army. Since we were under house arrest, with only two hours a day permission to spend outside, we were thrown by necessity to spend considerable time together. When one returned from outside, we exchanged information about political news or rumors. We also encouraged one another by dreaming of plans for after the war. Actually, none of us really believed that we would survive.

The old neighbor had a number of Yiddish books by Sholem Alechem and I.L. Peretz. He and my Mother would take turns reading aloud. That was the time when I learned to understand Yiddish very well. My Mother used to read beautifully.

In the apartment, the windows were fixed, we bought some fire wood, food became more easily available. We could not afford to heat the kitchen and both rooms, so we moved the parents' beds and my sofa into the living room- dining room. It was more sheltered than the bedroom, that had three windows- a kind of bay window, too much exposure and too costly to heat. We lived in one room and a kitchen.

About a week after our escape from the Ghetto, the military stopped issuing permits to return and there remained about 3000 Jews in the confined area. The mayor, Dr. Dori Popovici, a decent man, who had lived all his life in Czernovitz and was friendly toward the Jewish population, got the consent from Bucharest to dismantle the Ghetto and everybody to receive a permit signed by him. It later turned out that we, who had permits signed by the governor, were in a different category than those, whose permits were issued by the mayor. At the time we did not know that the Popovici permits would turn out to be almost a death warrant.

We had barely settled in when, by the end of November, the governor issued a decree, summoning all permit holders to have them reviewed by a military commission, to have everything documented. That threw a new scare into everybody, especially those whose name was not exactly the same as on their papers; the profession was not correct, names added, like on ours. Since life depended on a signature, many people were scared to go, for fear that they may lose that valuable permit.

The commission was made up of officers, each one reviewed one or two letters. There arose people, who knew officers whom they could bribe. The bribe assured the signature and thus the validity of the permit. I looked for an influence peddler, who could get assurance that the officer, who examined letter S would pass us. I could not find a way. We decided that we had to go by ourselves because they may stop the procedure altogether. On a Friday afternoon, without any possible help, I asked Father to come with me, to have the paper validated. The paper was in his name; Mother's name and mine were added.

My Father knew no Romanian and by that time I had become the mover and shaker in our family. I took along a Waterman fountain pen, covered with silver filigree, which Uncle Morris had left us on one of his visits to Europe. That was intended as a "thank you" for an officer, if needed. All the way from home to City Hall Father was mumbling, talking to himself. When I asked what he was saying, he said: "Nishmas" (Hear, oh God ... an appeal to God to hear his prayer in this hour of need.)

We came into a big hall. About 20 officers were seated along a table. The officer at the letter S looked through the identification papers of all three of us. As I was showing him what he was asking for, I tried to talk lightheartedly, to cover up my fear. Without asking many questions, he signed the certificate, stamped it and wished me good luck and added: "You'll need it."

As we were walking home, on that moonlit, clear, cold, bright early evening, Father said: "God answered my prayer." We returned home elated. Mother was standing at the window and saw me wave my muff, as if in triumph.

Next morning, the commission announced that they would stop reviewing the Jewish permits. Everybody, who is in town, will reside in Czernovitz on the strength of a paper signed by the mayor, Dori Popovici. In July, 1942, the Romanians deported on one night, from Saturday to Sunday about 2000 Jews with permits signed by Popovici. During the night, the military took entire families for "resettlement." Horror spread among the rest of us, since nobody knew what criterion they were considering. Everybody packed a knapsack and held it ready. The following week the same thing happened. We realized that they took only families with Popovici permits. Paul Antschel and his parents were in that situation. After the first deportation, he hid on the weekend in a factory building, which was closed of course, on the weekend. The Romanian owner gave someone the keys for the purpose, while his parents remained at home. His parents were deported and were killed within a few months. They did not want to live in hiding, while Paul never gave up trying to save himself. He was a devoted son, especially to his mother. I think that he could never forgive himself not having insisted that his parents join him in hiding on that fateful weekend. That pain followed him to the day in April 1970, when he ended his life in the Seine river, at age 49.

Coming back to the events of the summer of 42. Those deported were sent to the area along the river Bug, further east of Transnistria, an area administered by the Germans. Out of a few thousand deportees, a handful returned to tell the story of that utter tragedy. Friends and neighbors of ours found their bitter end there. Selma Meerbaum-Eisinger and her parents, two young girls, students of mine, granddaughters of the Gottliebs and their parents, all met a most horrible death there. Some were shot as they were too weak to work; others weakened from starvation, died of typhoid fever, others who almost survived, were mauled and killed by dogs let out by the Germans, so that nobody should survive to tell of these horrors. My friend, who had asked me to take care of his parents, could not foresee, nor could anybody envision the horror that would take place. His family died there, too.

The beginning of December, less than half a year from the start of the Russo- German war, the Germans were deep inside Russia. Thousands of prisoners of war, entire regiments, armies were encircled. Some regiments openly surrendered to the fascists, in the vain hope that their lives would be spared. However, the Germans despised the Slavs to such an extent that even when they deserted, professing their hate for communism, it did not endear them to the conquerors. Prisoners of war were mistreated, thousands killed, their golden teeth pulled out, their uniforms and boots stripped and their bodies left to rot in the fields.

Here and there a person from Czernovitz returned, helped along by a German or by a Romanian, since all local people spoke both languages. Whoever heard these stories from a returning soldier became despondent, thinking of one's own husband or father or brother, who was in the army or had fled and may have been caught.

Our neighbor's daughter became extremely disturbed about the news, her husband was in the Russian army. On December 7, 1941 famed Pearl Harbor Day, the young woman jumped out of the window of their fifth floor apartment. It was a frosty Sunday evening. My parents and myself were eating dinner, when somebody hammered at our door. When I opened, Mr. Nachman carried his daughter into our place - we lived then on the first floor

- and put her on my sofa. She looked asleep, but she was dead.

That scene, to this day, makes my heart race. An hour before, she spoke rationally and in a controlled manner; her despair was never openly expressed.

We all seemed to be in the same desperate situation, yet most of us kept going being each other's support. She must have expired on her way down, there were no signs of injury. Her Father heard the scream. He saw the open window. No doctor came. They carried her upstairs. On my sofa remained a spot where her head had lain. Next day was her funeral. There were just a few people. Nobody was openly crying; some must have envied her peace then. At the end of the war, her husband returned and married her younger cousin.

Next day we heard that the U.S.A. has been attacked by the Japanese. This event seemed to complicate the war situation even more, to spread to other continents: America and Asia. We could not receive mail from the family even before, but now it would become an impossibility. We could not know whether Eli, Bernie or anybody else in the family was affected. We only knew that we, ourselves were in a hopeless situation, with no end in sight.

The winter of 1941-42 was severe and we suffered great deprivation. Mother had a gold chain and rings, Father always carried a gold pocket watch and a chain. Every now and then we sold a piece of jewelry in order to buy food and pay rent. Bread was often hard to get and yeast, for bread-baking, not easily obtainable. We consumed a lot of beans and peas and potatoes and waited for the elusive salvation to come.

What kept people in such circumstances going? First, we never tried to realistically appraise the plight we were in. Magic thinking took over. Miracles were expected imminently. What if Hitler got killed? What if the Russians reorganized their troops and started routing the Germans? What if the Western powers revived their strength? The United States entered World War I in 1917 and a year later, the war was over and the Germans defeated. Perhaps, the involvement of the U.S.A. would shorten the war. After all, the U.S. was an ally of the democracies and at war with Japan, an Axis power. From day to day we lulled ourselves into believing that a miracle might still happen, as it did often in our own history.

While the Soviets proved to be a grave disappointment and the month before the outbreak of the war brought such despair with the deportations to Siberia yet it made us long for a return of the Russians. They sent you to

Siberia but they did not outright shoot you. It seemed like the lesser of two evils. Thus, we hoped for German defeats and Russian victories. We learned geography daily - Orel, Gomel, Dniepropetrovsk were lost or held or about to fall. They crossed or, didn't cross the Don or Dniepr. The same went on with North African geography. The fate of Tobruk or Tunis or Bizerta were bandied around daily.

When our elderly neighbor, Mr. Nachman, went out at 10 a.m., we hoped that he would bring the newest battle reports from the synagogue. I will never forget that at one juncture in the war, the two fortified cities Tunis and Bizerta were critical for the fate of North Africa. General Rommel, the famous desert fox, brought Germany victory after victory. Strategists considered the recapture of these two cities from the Germans as critical, otherwise, if the Germans broke the allied defenses there, they could advance all the way to Cairo. One Saturday morning, Mr. Nachman returned from the synagogue, knocked on our door. When I opened, he said "Both" and rushed upstairs to tell his wife. I knew that Tunis and Bizerta had been recaptured from the Germans.

In 1942, a Romanian family, who had taken over an apartment from a deported family, on the fourth floor, demanded to swap flats with us. We could not object, we could have been sent to Transnistria, on their say so. We moved up to the fourth floor and had to climb 100 stairs. Later on, when there was no water, we carried pails of water from about ten blocks away and up the 100 steps. Life was an unending string of hardships. Yet we were glad that we could still remain in the same house and sleep in our own beds.

In the summer of 1942, since nobody could figure out how long deportations would continue or start again, everybody kept a packed knapsack, in case. About that same time, a Romanian informer reported to the police that we are in possession of a radio and that we listen to the news. One day, two men came to our house: one tall and lanky, artistic looking, with longer hair, worn by poets or actors. He was about 30 years old, mannerly. He showed his badge, he was from the Siguranta (secret police). The other man accompanied him.

The commissar looked around, saw the knapsacks, looked at the books, saw German, French, English and Romanian books. At his request, I explained that I had been a student of languages and literature. After looking around everywhere, he asked Father to come to the chief police station, at five o'clock. I told him that I would come along, since Father didn't know Romanian. He gave us a summons to appear that day. We were greatly alarmed as it was during the deportations.

Although we were terribly scared, yet my optimistic side thought that nothing could happen, since we really had no radio. My optimism was a kind of defense, a negation of the evil that loomed all around. On the way to the Siguranţa, it was a very long walk, Father was saying his prayer. I took again the Waterman fountain pen, in case of need, as a small bribe. The commissar, Mr. Andreescu arrived after five (they enjoyed a siesta from 2-5 p.m.), called us into his office and told me that he would write a declaration, which Father should sign. I told him that, in case he would write that we have a radio, he won't sign. The commissar told me to let him write it and if I don't agree, then I should write another one. It sounded good. He typed a statement and handed it to me. In it Father declared that he had never had a radio. When I told him that we had had one, but the Russians had confiscated it, he retorted: It is better to say that you never had one.

Greatly relieved by the outcome of the confrontation with the Secret Police, I asked him who the other gentleman was. He told me that the other man was an informer, who came to report to the police that in the evening we pulled down the shades, proof that something unlawful was going on. Of course, if a crime would be discovered after an investigation, we could be deported and the informer could claim the apartment and the household within. Mr. Andreescu told me that he knew right away that it was a false charge, because people, who live with a packed knapsack next to their beds would not try anything that dangerous. He said that he saw my books and asked me whether I would teach him and his wife English. I thought that was an entrapping offer and I replied that I would gladly teach them German. He insisted that they would rather learn English. I offered to teach them as soon as he and his wife were ready.

Father and myself walked home elated. He did not understand the long conversation, however, he realized that it was a very friendly chat. We got rid of a threatening charge and we even made a friend in the Secret Police, for he had warned me of that informer. Should that man try to threaten us, I should get in touch with him and trouble from that source would stop.

We came home and shared the great news with Mother. Besides, Father and myself had taken such a nice walk through the town, on a pleasant summer day. The house arrest had been going on for over a year. Except for two hours daily, we spent all the time indoors. We pulled down the shades, for we used to sit around the table and one or the other were reading aloud Jewish stories. The informer lived across the street, in the Ippen apartment, vacated when they were sent to Siberia.

As fall approached, Jewish men were taken to labor camps, run by the army. It became apparent that in every family, at the very least one person had to work, in order to be entitled to remain in town. Yuda, whom I did not see much at that time, was sent to dig trenches or hew stones in a quarry in Paltinoasa, Alexandreni or other locations in Moldova. Every few months he would come home to his mother. Then they would call him up for a different assignment, at a different location. During one of those stints in a labor camp, his mother died of a stroke. Her daughter-in-law, who shared her apartment, was with her. Yuda came home way later. I never knew my mother- in-law Esther, but I know that the last few years of her life were pure hell. Her husband died on the operating table, during that fateful last week in June, 1941. Her older son Munju (Michael) was somewhere in the Soviet Union and Yuda was in labor camp. She didn't live to know that both her sons survived the war and the holocaust.

The call-ups to labor camps was the work of the Jewish Community Council. The military would request a certain number of men, to be sent to a certain location. Within a few days the Jewish Council provided the number of men. As soon as a group returned, some weeks later they would be sent again. It was hard labor, but people were not killed there.

Rumors spread that everybody would be deported within the next few weeks. The chances of survival were uncertain from day to day. It was assumed that those who converted to Christianity would be spared. Here and there news spread about a pastor, in a certain church, who would give a certificate of baptism if one went a few Sundays to church and then approached him about the matter. Whether he knew that it was just a paper to save one's life or whether he considered it a genuine conversion - I don't know. Talking to the only friend I had at that time, Duschka, we decided to talk it over at home. Neither her parents nor mine objected to our trying that road. For my parents, to know that I went to church to seek baptismal papers was no light issue, yet they would not stand in my way, if that could save my life.

One Sunday morning, the two of us walked to the church, without the star, with hats on. When we came to the yard and were supposed to enter the chapel, we looked at one another and both of us could not do it. I could not lie to the pastor and I could not stay behind in case they would take the parents away. The same applied to my girlfriend. We walked home, sure that this stratagem was wrong for us. When my parents saw me return and I told them that I did not even go into the church, we all had tears in our eyes.

There was also another incident and chance for change for me, yet I could not do it. When I was a student in the first year (1938-39), I joined a sports club, where most of the members were workers. We were a liberal group of students, who tried to make contacts among workers and help educate them. I was teaching two girls and a non-Jewish worker French. That young man, Andrei, was a very handsome, athletic Ukrainian, who became part of the student group. He started to court a former classmate of mine, the daughter of a Hebrew teacher. She was deported from the ghetto. Later on Andrei started to come to our house once in a while. He was an artistic fellow, played the balalaika well, sang, was a terrific sportsman and a very decent person. In the winter of 42-43, I remember him coming on a winter evening and he brought me an orange. During the war it was an absolute rarity and very expensive. We sat down, I peeled the orange and offered to share it with my parents. Since it was a present for me, Andrei refused to taste any. I ate a half and my parents a quarter each. Well, this man proposed to marry me and take me along to Romania and thus escape the imminent danger, Just as before, I could not try to save myself and leave. It seemed that the day when I said the fateful words "what happens to you will happen to me" that had decided the course of my life for the duration of the war. I had become the active one, the doer. My conscience has never bothered me in that respect. I refused Andrei's offer. He understood.

Since somebody in the family had to work, I volunteered to labor in a big workshop, which employed about 200 women dressmakers, a few tailors and upholsterers. No Jew received any pay for their labor. All the clothes confiscated from the deportees were cleaned and remade into children's coats, smocks, etc. Capable professionals did the cutting and others did the sewing.

A student, of course, was not needed anywhere. My cousin Silva, two of her friends and myself pretended that we could sew. The real dressmakers made us feel like intruders, like cheats, but it gave me a "work paper" and a card showing the times when I could walk to and from work. The shop was almost an hour's walk from home. In the winter, I left at 6 a.m. in order to start work at 7. The place was poorly heated and we labored hard for ten hours. Of course, nobody received any pay or food. I worked there for ten months.

The dressmakers looked down at a lowly student, who needed her help when setting in a sleeve. Once, one looked at me and asked with scorn: What are you? Not one of us, a student, a no-good. She felt it below her dignity to accept a student within the "needed" workers in the needle trade. That same woman, Miss Lenz, made a living as a fortune teller, yet she didn't let on about it in the shop. People knew that she was reading palms, tea leaves, cards. Every end of the week, fear spread about deportations on Saturday night to Sunday. We used to work six days. On a particular Saturday rumors persisted about the approaching night. This woman whispered into my ear the question whether tomorrow would be a calamitous day. I looked her straight in the eye and asked: "Are you asking me?" with emphasis on the you. She looked at me and answered: "Aha, you know" meaning that I knew that she was predicting the future, for money, yet she knew about the future as much as anybody else - nothing.

The winter of 1942-43 was the coldest winter of the war. The Germans will never forget that winter either. The defense and siege of Stalingrad and Leningrad are highly documented historic chapters of the war. The fierce winds and diabolically low temperatures plagued all of Eastern Europe. That was the winter of our deepest despair. The people in Transnistria died by the thousands, be it of starvation or frost or sickness. Once in a while Romanian soldiers or civilians came from there and brought news from the desperate Jews. Some Romanians would accept, for remuneration, to bring some clothes, or money or food from relatives in Czernovitz. Some had no relatives left in town. In some villages, they could not find anybody who would take a message to relatives. They succumbed to typhoid fever by the thousands.

The governments that inflicted such inhuman existences and deaths on defenseless people, those same governments inflicted great suffering on their own soldiers by forcing them into a war, a no-win situation, far from home, in frigid weather. All of Russia became a mass graveyard for soldiers on both sides and for tens of thousands of defenseless deportees, whom they sent to their deaths. The intention was to let them expire, without Germany spending money for bullets. Prisoners of war suffered similarly, for Jews and Slavs were considered by them as sub-human "Untermenschen."

The conditions at work were tolerable but the real dressmakers made our life unpleasant, because girls like myself could not fulfill the quota; we could not keep up with the majority. Nevertheless, they did not betray us for our shortcomings. After about 6 months I transferred to the bookkeeping, where three older men, accountants, had chosen three former students to help out. That made the circumstances at work easier.

In the meantime, in order to survive, we sold anything that had any value:

a good coat, all the jewelry, a nice woolen dress, some linens, a warm house-coat - anything that could be sold. Since little merchandise was available in the stores, because of the war, Romanians bought whatever they could buy cheaply from desperate Jews. I remember, I had a Japanese long house dress, with a zipper. That was a very exotic-looking dress in Europe. I had worn it at the masked ball on New Year's eve in 1940-41. Yet during the war years that was sold too, we needed food daily, we needed fire wood for cooking and heating.

Before working in the "Consiliu de Patronaj," where I spend 12 hours daily, I used to tutor Jewish children during those two hours, when one was permitted to leave the house. Parents were afraid that their sons and daughters would miss too many years of education. Thus Erna and Sidi Gottlieb, Mrs. Gottlieb's granddaughters, came to acquire some education. All too soon, the two girls took theirs to the grave. Others came once a week for an English lesson. All the remaining hours, I used to knit sweaters or mittens or scarves for Romanians. It was almost impossible to buy woolen winterstuff. The Romanians bought roughly spun wool from the peasants in the villages and had Jewish women like myself knit for them. Although it did not pay well, yet we needed that bit of money desperately. When I came back from work around six, I would eat and sit up till midnight knitting. Sometimes, the wool was so rough, it would cut into the skin and bloody my fingers. That winter, we had no electricity and the knitting was done by the light of an oil lamp.

In 1943 the curfew was partially lifted and Jews could walk in the streets for longer hours. One day I met Yuda in the street and during the conversation I asked him to come to visit. He really came up and visited more and more often. We became quite friendly but he was summoned to a labor camp again. He promised to write. In the meantime, the situation on the Eastern front changed and he never returned to Czernovitz. After the Russians came back, a friend who worked at the post office found in a sack of mail a card from Yuda to me, where he expressed his deep affection for me. About two years later I found out that he was alive, in Palestine.

At the end of 1943, the Romanians became aware that their German protectors were slowly approaching defeat. The siguranta commissar and his wife came to our house and requested me to teach them English. I used to go after work, for an hour, to teach them. They turned out to be intelligent, well-meaning people. His sister was married to a Jew, in the Old Kingdom. (The two original Romanian provinces were: Muntenia with the capital Bucharest and Moldova with the capital Iassy). These two provinces were called the Old Kingdom or Regat. All the other provinces were attached in 1918, after the defeat of the Austro-Hungarian empire. The Andreescu family had always had dealings with Jews and had few prejudices.

Somehow, the captain, who was the head of the Consiliu de Partonaj, where I was working, found out that I was a foreign language student. One day, when I was called to the main office, to see the captain - my scare knew no bounds. Once there, he asked me to teach him English. As much as I advised him that German would be more helpful, he insisted on English. I taught him just a few times and then, they began to evacuate the enterprise and he was busy with his own problems.

At the beginning of 1944, the fate of the war seemed to be decided. Romanians started to send furniture back to the Regat. High officials, who had enriched themselves by robbing and stealing all Jewish property, wanted to insure and secure their ill achieved gains. Once we saw them panicking, we knew that another upheaval was ahead of us, namely the abandonment of the territory by the Romanians and Germans and the return of the Soviets.

Nobody could foresee whether the Germans would defend the area or abandon it, once the Russians advanced North of us, around Lvov On March 10, 1944, on my 24th birthday, the siguranţa commissar Andreescu and his wife came to congratulate me on my birthday. They brought me a bottle of French chocolate liqueur. It was a matter of weeks before they would run away and the Soviets would return. They offered to take me along to Romania when the time for evacuation came. I thanked them for their thoughtful concern for me but I declined. We were three people and we had nowhere to go in Romania. We embraced and I never saw them again. That bottle of liqueur played its part later on.

The panicky Romanians left and German troops filled the town. They suddenly descended like locusts: masses of gray uniformed men, endless trucks, tanks, cars. We were petrified by what was going to happen. We had made sure to prepare bread, candles, gasoline for the petrol lamps, some food and wait for the convulsion. Again, like almost three yeas before, one power would leave, another take over. Nobody could foresee whether the Germans would hold the line, whether the Russians would bomb, whether an artillery battle would take place - everything was fate.

The Germans gathered to reorganize their units, on the flight Westward, after crossing the river Dniester. They did not resist along the river Prut, but fled. We were again in no-man's-land for a day or two, until the Russians

returned. We survived a second time the retreat of the defeated army and
the return of the soon to be victors. On April 4, 1944, the town had a red
flag atop City Hall instead of the swastika and the Romanian tricolor: blue,
yellow, red. At this juncture, the German army was in retreat, but by far
not yet defeated. The Russians were advancing but by far not yet victorious.

Chapter 6

The Russians Are Back

We were facing a great number of uncertainties and dangers. First, whether the Russians would treat us decently, us who had lived through the German occupation; whether the survivors from Transnistria would come back; how many had survived the retreat of the Germans; whether our friends and relatives in the Russian army and those who had fled voluntarily would come home; whether any of them had survived the almost three years of war; whether we'll have food to survive.

The Russian military, in pursuit of the retreating Germans, were angry, aggressive and contemptuous of the local population. The ubiquitous question: Why did they kill all the other Jews and left you alive? That thought implied that the survivors were all collaborators of the Nazis, whether they were Jewish or not. The antisemitism of the Russians surfaced glaringly. It soon became all too clearly apparent that the liberators hated us as much as the Germans did. On the other hand, they needed personnel everywhere: for the army, the coal mines in the Ukraine, workers for the Northern Territory of Murmansk and Pechora, where the lend lease help from the U.S. arrived. Just as in the first week of war, in June 41 when they grabbed men to the armed forces, now they did the same and they took women and girls to go to the Donbas - the coal mines along the Don river, in the Ukraine. This was a very frightening time.

Some of the survivors from Transnistria started to drag themselves to return home, to Czernovitz. Cripples, beggars and some in reasonable shape returned. Most had their wretched bodies covered with tattered clothes, their legs and feet wrapped in rags. Most had no home to return to. We had a cousin, a woman Mother's age, Mrs. Kreisel, who came to us, since her husband had died of typhoid fever during the first winter, her daughter and son had not returned yet. She was an absolute cripple, just hardly dragged herself up the stairs to our apartment. I gave her my bed and slept with the parents.

I started to work for the railroad, telephone and telegraph section, as an assistant to the personnel manager, who was a party official. My assignment consisted in obtaining bread ration cards for the workers and their dependents. Workers received larger daily portions than their children. When a worker was deployed from one station to another, from one village to another, I was supposed to provide him with a militia (police) permit to travel and a bread ration card for that particular location and for those certain days. The lines at Town Hall, where they issued ration cards, were long and unruly. People were pushing and shoving and squeezing and stepping on one's toes; it was a daily stampede. Russians; military, militia, N.K.G.B. - all these people claimed that they did not have to stand in line, only the local people had to. Their ideas of democracy were such, it would have been a good joke, but the joke was played out on me, a local person. I with my knitted sandals, I had bloody toes every day.

The worst part of the job proved to be getting a 30 day bread ration card for a worker. I knew that when he was summoned to the central office in Czernovitz and my boss ordered me to get him a 30 day bread ration card, he would be put on a train to Murmansk or Pechora. It would take him 30 days to reach the location - an Arctic port, where American ships arrived and provided the Soviets, at that time allies, with military materiel, clothing and food.

The people in charge of each railroad division in the Soviet Union had to provide a certain number of workers to the Artic Railroad. Thus each section picked scapegoats. Some were sent to the North Pechora Railroad, an area in the tundra desert, a frozen waste land in the Russian Arctic, where the government endeavored to build a net of rail connections to the Kara Sea, an arm of the Arctic Ocean. Geographically, the latitude corresponds to Northern Siberia, except that it is West of the Ural Mountains, on the European Continent. The railroad was meant to be used as a supply line for Russia's interior, when goods at the time could arrive only through the arctic sea lanes, north of Scandinavia. The Pacific Ocean was the American-Japanese theater of war. Russia was fighting in Europe, thus the help was needed on the European side of the Soviet Union.

When a worker from a village arrived in our town, he had no idea that he would be sent ten thousand miles away. Had he known, he might have run to join anticommunist bands in the woods. Who could imagine that a man who came for a day to the central office would be sent to the Arctic, without even saying good bye to his wife and children. He was given a bread to take along and a "propusk", a permit to travel. The peasants were illiterate; even if one heard destination Archangelsk, Murmansk or Pechora, a railroad worker wouldn't know where those towns were. The viciousness of the regime was such that they sent a barefoot man, in a thin pair of pants and shirt and tricked him into going to the Arctic, with little chance to survive. Suddenly I realized that I may be sent to that same place any day, since every section had a quota to fulfill.

To try to influence my superior, a young woman party member, not to put me on any list to the North, I brought her my only good woolen pullover as a present. She liked it and asked me to help her with her hairdo, to look more attractive. I did that, too, while I saw lice crawling on her head. But I was scared to go home in the evenings, a regiment of Don Cossacks, who had come to town, came into homes, at night, and took able-bodied women into the army. A bookkeeper, an elderly man, which whom I had worked compulsory work during the Romanian occupation and was also working for the railroad, offered to let me stay inside the office during the night. He had keys to the office. After work, I went up. He left me inside and locked the door. Well, in June, if you sit all night in a chair and shiver with fright - life is awful. After two nights there, my parents and I decided that I would hide at home.

The first night, while I stayed over in the office, Cossacks had come to our house, in the middle of the night, and poked with bayonets into the beds; made crippled Mrs. Kreisdel stand up to see whether she was fit for military service, then left.

We had a storage closet, for winter clothes. It had a door, which was painted the same as the walls. A piece of furniture stood in front of it. We decided to leave the door accessible and if anybody knocked at the door at night, I would hide in the closet and the dressing table, with its high mirror would be put in place.

However, the situation deteriorated drastically for every able-bodied person. When I came home from work one day, I found a call-up from the army and another to go to the Donbas (Don Basin coal mines). Actually, the tug of war went on, I was called in three directions: the army-West; the coal mines- East; Arctic Pechora-North. How could I manage to remain in town

until university would open in September? That summer of 1944 became a
very desperate time. The Soviets let students in the third and fourth year
finish their studies, while the first and second years were closed. I was a third
year student, but the few months until September were endless. It turned
into a fierce battle for survival.

I brought the two call-up notices to the office and showed them to an
elderly colonel there. He admitted that they really needed me at the present
job and promised to accompany me to the two different authorities. I mentioned that I had something special for him. Thus he followed me home,
waited in front of the house. I went up to take the bottle of liqueur, that had
been given to me, on my birthday in March, by the Romanian secret police
commissar. When I came down with the French liqueur, he was beaming
with delight. He achieved my release in no time, from both places - the army
and the Donbas - he made me look very important in front of the authorities. Fine, I was saved again and continued at the Railroad Telephone and
Telegraph station.

All through the summer, the curfew went on. At 7 p.m. nobody was supposed to be outdoors, all windows were blacked out, since the war proceeded
in full swing towards the West, through Poland, Romania and the Baltic region. The Russians kept the town informed about the course of the war and
their advance in Western Europe, by issuing every evening a military report
direct from Moscow. It always started the same way: the national anthem,
then the victories of the day and the praise of the supreme commander Iosif
Visarionovich Stalin. That same daily report was heard all over the Soviet
Union.

The Soviets expressed their displeasure about the Western allies and their
lack of cooperation, namely by not starting a second front. They called the
landing "dessant" (descent) and complained daily about the delay. By the
time the landing happened, on June 6, 1944, the Russians made very light
of its importance, just as they rarely mentioned the fighting in Italy and
the considerable allied losses there. They minimized the contribution of the
Western powers toward victory. In fact, all the other war news was almost
disregarded and the population had no way of getting any other news reports,
since radios were unavailable.

My Russian boss, for whom I prepared all the lists and bread ration cards,
was a blond, slim Northerner from Leningrad. When sober, he was distant
and quite proper; but when he was drunk, one had a hard time fighting him
off. He was very demanding and we were forever writing. In the entire section

there was not a single typewriter. Everything was written longhand. The bookkeepers were using the abacus, the only available calculator. Paper was extremely scarce, to the extent that we were writing on newspaper, between the printed lines.

At the end of August, I told my boss "the nachalnik" in Russian, that I would go to the university, in September. He could not officially prevent me from leaving, but he insisted that I did an outstanding job and was hard to be replaced. If he had only told me that sooner, I would have been spared so much aggravation and fear.

What happened to all those people who had gone to Russia, voluntarily or involuntarily? Many of the men, married or unmarried got involved with Russian women. They heard all along that the Germans had killed all the Jews in occupied territories. Many men had great difficulty surviving and were glad to find a woman, who would let them into the house and feed them. They were willing to accept the kindness and sometimes the responsibilities that followed. Many Russian men were at the front and morals during wars are low. As for myself, I am at peace with myself because I never compromised my morals, in no situation, all through the war.

Many of our Czernovitzer women, who survived, found out that their husbands were either married or lived with a Russian woman. There were untold tragedies, complications. Some would come back and couldn't decide whether to return to the former wife or return to the new one in the Soviet Union. Some found out that the wife had saved his parents during the war and he got himself a Russian replacement.

One such example was a cousin of mine from Poland who was married and had a six year old son. He was called up to the army, where he fell in love with a Russian woman. His wife survived, their boy had been killed. When he returned, he found himself with two wives. His predicament was not enviable. He divorced his first wife who consequently married his best friend, a bachelor. Yet I know that the consequences of that entanglement were never completely resolved, although never mentioned to outsiders. At his funeral, I saw the grief on the faces of both women.

Many perished miserably at the front, others returned and found no family alive. The time of resolution impacted everybody differently. Besides, new situations were created by the fact that many men became separated from their families because they were in labor camps, in Romania. Their families remained behind in Czernovitz. Yuda, like many others in the camps, remained in Romania. Some tried to get to Palestine on small, illegal boats.

Yuda and his younger cousin Leiser were together in a labor camp and were frantically trying to reach Palestine. Leiser's older brother Arieh had volunteered, as a parachutist with the English forces, to be dropped over Romania, behind the German lines, in order to help in Allied war effort and also to contact Jews and give them aid and comfort, to show them that they had not been forsaken by their brothers in Palestine. Arieh had been apprehended by the military near Ploeşti and was handed over to the Germans, as he was in the uniform of an English captain. He spent the rest of the war in a prisoner of war camp in Germany. At the end of the war he was released and he returned to Kibbutz Beit Oren in Palestine, where his wife Yaffa awaited him. Leiser was favored to leave on the first available boat from the Romanian port Constanţa, to reach Palestine. He left on the Mefkuere for the short trip through the Bosporus and Dardanelle Straights and on to the open Mediterranean. There the small boat was torpedoed by the Germans and sank, no survivors. When Yuda arrived in Bucharest, he found out about the good news about his cousin's departure and soon after of Leiser's tragic end at age 21. He had spent the last few months of his short life together with Yuda.

A few weeks later Yuda set out on his way to Palestine. He went through a harrowing experience from the port Constanţa to Constantinople, on a boat that was taking water and almost sank. From there the refugees continued on by train through Turkey and Lebanon to Palestine. He intended to settle in Haifa, where he had an aunt and her family. Arieh had already been home from his prisoner of war years. The family mourned together the tragic fate of Leiser.

Coming back to my life in Czernovitz in the fall of 1944. I went back to the university; I received the scholarship, to which I was entitled for earning top grades and I tutored some Russian students in English. However, life was joyless, food was scarce and whatever was available was intolerable. By the end of September, after Rosh Hashannah, Father got sick with pneumonia. Since he suffered all his life with asthma, pneumonia was a dangerous disease. Penicillin was a new drug in the West, unavailable in the Soviet Union. There was sulfa but only for people with special privileges like party members or military personnel. We were neither.

An acquaintance of mine had returned from the front as an invalid, he had shrapnel bits lodged in his lungs. An invalid could possibly obtain the sulfa, on prescription. He went with me to the Polyclinic and demanded to have the prescription filled. Any rare medication could be obtained only if the director of the Polyclinic affixed the round stamp on it. Any bigshot who could use a round stamp at his discretion, used to carry it in his boot, for safety reasons. My invalid acquaintance knocked at the door of the "nachalnik", walked in with me and started yelling. His future father-in-law has pneumonia and he is entitled to get the round stamp on a prescription. I, the supposed fiancee stood by the whole scene. He got the stamp affixed, I received the drug within an hour for the sum of one ruble. On the black market it would have cost one hundred.

Father recovered slowly. On Yom Kippur, he was still so weak that he consented to eat and drink. He said that it was proper, to save his life. Mother asked whether she should ask the rabbi, Father explained that he did know what was proper and saving one's life went before the fast.

Except for bread, which was rationed and available, everything else was scarce and if available, people stood in line for hours, sometimes days. The bread was baked from a mixture of grains and maize and the cobs ground in. A kilo bread (over two pounds) was a small loaf, heavy as a rock. You could not bite the bread, only gnaw. Nobody would eat that in normal times, but there was no alternative. Father suffered so, he could not digest it. We were hungry most of the time. If clothes or shoes were available, one had to stand in line for days. We didn't. We made do with whatever we still possessed. That summer, I wore a pair of hand made sandals. The top was crocheted of thin string and attached to a sole. The hand made front of the sandals was tied to the ankles with shoe laces.

My boy friend Sasha had survived; he had spent the three years in the military service. I could give him no explanation why his family was not alive. He too thought that everybody had survived, except his own. I could not give him any exact date, since I did not know where they had been deported to and what exactly had happened. They had a Popovici permit and were taken away in June 1942. Thousands had dropped by the roadside, dead from sickness, hunger, cold or plainly shot by the Germans. That was the fate of those taken across the Bug river. That locality was called "Cariera de piatra" (Stone Quarry) and most of the deportees lost their lives there.

I could not accept any responsibility for their tragic end. Even a situation like ours was rare. Parents and a daughter alive, still in the same town as before, even in the same apartment. The survival was achieved at great cost, with a lot of suffering. I had also become resentful. He and his sister and brothers went along with the Russians, to save themselves; none was willing to stay behind and try to help the parents. It surely was not my responsibility. Eventually, the correspondence stopped.

I remained burdened just facing every day with its new challenges and trying to go on. For years we received no mail from the family in the United States. The Red Cross may have functioned in some places, yet not under the Germans and the Russians in Czernovitz. We almost did not expect to hear from anybody until the end of the war.

In February 1945, we received a letter from Bernie. It had been sent a year earlier, on the occasion of his marriage to Connie. It was an invitation to the festive luncheon at the Waldorf Astoria. The menu sounded like fiction: meat, vegetables, wines, desserts, liqueurs - all this just French and American names. We had not seen any of these foods in years. The name Waldorf Astoria did not mean anything either. We did not know at the time that my sister Betty had given birth to a daughter Frances in 1942 and that Sali had borne a son Allan in 1943. My parents were not aware that they had become grandparents of two new off-spring.

The winter of 1944-45 continued to be bitterly cold; it was hard to acquire enough kindling wood to heat the apartment. Besides, when it was stored in the cellar, we had to carry it up 100 stairs. Life continued to be brutally hard, sullen and joyless. We had been cut off from the family for years. Life after the liberation offered little chance for improvement. Father's family had been wiped out in Poland. We knew it from a reliable source, from a Jewish partisan, who had fought in the underground, in Galizia.

When this man, with a little red flag in the fur hat, came to look for us, he gave us all the bitter news that one could comprehend. My Father's step-mother and some of her children and grandchildren were hidden in a bunker, in the ghetto in Kolomija. After the deportation of the entire community, the Germans suspected that there were some Jews hidden somewhere. They burned the entire section of town and the last survivors died by fire. After listening to the elaborate report, Father said: "I don't think that I will every laugh, for the rest of my life." I don't think he did.

The winter of 1944-45 found us also exhausted and demoralized, after years of daily wrangling for survival.

The war went well for the allies in all the theaters of war. People started to think about an end to this ongoing horror, which had started in 1939. There was an uncertainty as to the future of our province - whether it would remain Russian or would revert to Romania. That seemed to be on the minds of the politicians in the Kremlin, too. The rumor spread that once the war was over, the allies would demand a decision by plebiscite. In that case, the population would decide the future of Northern Bukovina, which had never been Russian in its history, up to 1940.

In order to insure that the plebiscite would result in the favor of the Soviet Union, the Soviets decided to let people apply for "re-patriation". As soon as these people would leave, the Soviets would bring in Russians, to fill the town. In case of a plebiscite, in the near future, the votes would go in their favor.

When the news first spread, that people could apply at the militia, to leave for Romania, many careful people could not believe it. They feared that it was a ruse, a trick, a way to show up people as unpatriotic. They feared that if one applies to leave for the West, they would put you on a train going East, to Siberia. The very careful ones are still in Czernovitz.

My parents and myself talked it over and decided to register right away. There was no certainty that they would not send us all to Siberia, anyway. In case we are really lucky and leave, we may one day be united with the family in the United States.

In that year 1944-45, the second time under Soviet administration, all my fears and disillusionment with that regime became fully defined. I harbored no doubts about my dislike of life in that society. My boy friend seemed to have a woman friend, a nurse, an assistant in the same regiment. They were not married and he wrote that he would definitely return to Czernovitz. Yet, he was a member of the Party and sent me a picture in uniform, proudly displaying his medals.

By the time he left, in June 41, I was a 21 year old girl. At this time, after almost four years of a tough school for survival, I was different; I could judge in a more detached manner. First, he would not leave for the West because of his political affiliation. If I were to stay, the parents would not depart alone, so they would be stuck, too. Their hopes would all be dashed. Also, the fact that his family had been lost would remain a dark shadow all along.

Thus, I did not let him know that I applied to leave. If I could live without him for four years, I'll be able to do so for the rest of my life. I preferred to leave, without meeting again. I had made a clear, clean decision. I wanted to make sure to leave before we may meet again, for in that case, I was not completely sure of myself. As for life at the time, it was pure hell: the regime, the conditions of life and the hatred of the Soviets for surviving Jews, in particular.

In March, 1945, my Father and myself went to the militia, to apply for a permit to be re-patriated to Romania. I knew that they could immediately expel me from the university, yet I didn't mind taking the risk any more - life was insufferable. They put a stamp on our identification papers right then: Applied to go to Romania.

As soon as the official had registered us, he asked whether he could take our apartment. "Of course", we said. "The sooner you issue our papers, the faster you will get the apartment." He came next day to look things over. That was a good omen, they intended to let us leave. It took one month to receive the permits, we were among the first to leave Czernovitz.

An endless number of Russians wanted the apartment and it made no difference to us who would win in that tug of war that developed. We had to leave the furniture, the entire household, anyway. One could not sell anything; one could not take along anything, they took everything for free. The widow of an officer tried to get the apartment; the militia official tried for it; an N.K.G.B. officer made great efforts. We didn't mind if they would fight over it, which they did. Later, we found out that two parties shared the apartment; they divided up the bedroom, namely one took a bed and a nightstand - the other took the other pieces; two families remained in the place, sharing the kitchen jointly. What they did with the dining room, I don't know or care.

In the middle of April 1945, we paid for three spaces on a truck, that would take a few families to the border. The night before we left, all three knapsacks ready, we looked around the house: the furniture in the dining room and bedroom, all brought by the parents from Vienna, the beautiful grandfather clock that had to be wound once a month - all these were part of our lives. Father, without saying a word, opened the clock, cut through the spring, took the two beautifully engraved, gilded weights and threw them in the garbage. He did not want anybody to enjoy that clock, that was brought from Vienna in 1918 and was chiming the quarter, half and the hours for our entire life, in good times and bad. It was the only spiteful act that I ever saw him perform, this quiet, gentle man.

My dear friend, Luta, came to stay overnight with me. We talked and cried all night. We knew that we'd never see one another again. She felt the loss so keenly, as she remembered that my Father showed great sympathy for her and her family, when her parent passed away. They had only recently moved to our town; her mother was left with five children. Father made the arrangement for his funeral and for a week, he came daily to conduct mourning prayers, at their house. Luta and her family remained in Czernovitz to this day.

What happened to all my friends from my youth? Of the ones, who were deported to Transnistria, very few survived. The ones in the Soviet Union, all survived; some came West in the last ten years. I saw Martha and Malzia in Israel in 1983, after more than 40 years. We were 21 years old when we were scattered with the wind. We met again as women in our 60s. Rosl lives in Germany and visited me once in New York in 1982. I correspond with some to this day.

By the time we left Czernovitz, none of those friends had come home and thus, there were few people to miss - just my youth and my familiar surroundings from the day I was born, the memories of years of war and suffering. When we left, I was 25, my parents aged 62 and 65.

Chapter 7

Refugees In Romania

The three of us shared a truck with a number of people. We were left in a field, at the ruins of a small border town Herţa, near the Romanian border. It was April 1945. There was no building, no official border markings - nothing. Hundreds of people arrived and we were all looking for a shelter for the night. The town Herţa was burned to the ground and completely abandoned. There were some walls, perhaps of a hall or movie house, but no roof. Hundreds of refugees sat on the ground, leaning on the knapsack, the only possession left to a person, after a lifetime of work and toil. All of us were homeless and penniless and stateless; we had the proverbial shirt on our backs, no more.

Just before we left, we had heard that President Roosevelt had died. We did not know who was going to follow and what consequences to expect. We knew that the war was approaching finally its end and that the Axis powers were defeated. We did not have any family in Romania and had no idea where we would stay in the immediate future.

We finally saw a few Russians, in uniform, approaching the refugees, us. They knew nothing about the border crossing. The border was supposed to be only a few miles away. A young woman from Bessarabia was sitting on her knapsack, next to me. The two of us started a conversation with a middle aged officer and explained to him where we were supposed to be going - to the West. He told us how fortunate we were to be permitted to leave. As it got dark and we could not really see his face, he talked all evening and confided in us about the misery of Soviet life; about his wife, who was suffering of tuberculosis and about the constant fear of persecution and of the dread of prison and of Siberia.

We were stunned at his confessions and said so. He averred that he could only unburden his heart because next day he would not be there and we would not either. How fortunate a group of people we were, he stated again. Imagine, none of us had a home, none of us had more than our bare lives, yet he deemed us so lucky, so fortunate, so privileged. Only if one has lived under Stalin's regime and tasted that bitterness and constant fear can one understand that homeless and penniless was preferable to life in the U.S.S.R.

Next day was cold and rainy and nothing happened, no trucks in sight. That girl and I decided to walk to the border, perhaps they did not know that we were supposed to cross into Romania. By the time we arrived at the frontier, there was one house where a family ran an inn, probably for the border guards.

We were informed by the innkeeper that we could not talk to anybody until next morning. Nobody every crossed that border, anyway.

By that time it was too late to walk back to where the refugees were waiting. They let us sit indoors overnight. It was eerie and cold and we were hungry, but lucky that we were permitted to take shelter. Next morning the two of us walked towards the border tower, which was quite a distance, and were told that they had been advised of a group of people, who would go to Dorohoi, Romania. The two of us started walking back. My parents and the others awaited us impatiently. Finally trucks arrived and transferred us across the frontier. By that time it was late Friday afternoon.

Romanian peasants with their oxen-drawn carts were waiting on the other side.

It took us about six hours to make the few miles to Dorohoi; it was late Friday night. What could a religious man, like my Father, do? He could not remain in the fields, on the Russian-Romanian border. Thus, he rode in an ox cart on Friday night and was brought to a synagogue, where we spent the rest of the night, sleeping on the synagogue floor, after three nights in a roofless ruin.

The life of a refugee, which we opted for, after years of deprivation, was plain misery. We had not washed for days, we had hardly eaten anything. Some Jewish community representatives came to see who these refugees were, where they came from. A day or two later, we were allowed to settle in an empty hotel building. We all slept on floors, but the place was clean and empty. We could wash ourselves and some of our personal laundry, while in the synagogue we stretched out under the benches.

We had taken along a winter coat each, a few things to wear and a few items of religious importance: Mother's brass candle sticks (the silver ones had been sold long ago), Father's kiddush cup, the filigree spice box for Saturday evening Havdalah, the Chanukah menora which I am proud to possess and a Pessach plate. Each of us had a piece in the sack. I took along an English dictionary, a volume of Shakespeare and a pronunciation dictionary.

Before we left Czernovitz, Father took a loan of one hundred dollars from a woman, with the proviso that, if we survived and got in touch with the relatives in the U.S., we would return her double. Agreed. We returned it to her in the Bronx, in 1947. In Dorohoi, we exchanged some dollars on the black market, bought some food and starting thinking what to do next.

We found a "furnished" room for the parents, in Dorohoi. I intended to go to Bucharest and try to get in touch with the family. The small town, a typical "shtetl" of Eastern Europe had no running water in the houses. I had never seen this type of town. A water carrier came by daily, rang his bell and people would come out with a pail or two, to buy water. A little mule pulled a barrel which was mounted on a stand, on wheels. The spigot would release a thin stream of water that slowly filled the pail. The water carrier was a colorful personality and anxiously awaited, because often people would run out of water for cooking or for tea. Of course, an outhouse was in every yard, in the back of the houses. We were used to a more modern way of life, but that was only an interim, we hoped.

By the time the parents were settled in that shelter and cooking was done on a kerosene lamp, in a corner of the room, I got ready to go to Bucharest. Some people had relatives in Romania, usually in Bucharest. They wrote letters and expected to be able to settle with relatives, for the time being. We had no family in the Old Kingdom. All our relatives in Europe used to live in Poland and they had all been taken care of by Hitler.

I had the address of my girl friend's two sisters in Bucharest. Their father survived the war years alone in Czernovitz and used to come to us daily, to "smell Martha smell". The lonesome old professor knew Latin and Greek to perfection, but was so absent minded as to almost burn alive, in his own bed, when he fell asleep with a lit cigarette falling off his lips and setting his bed on fire. He asked me to see his daughters, if I ever came to Bucharest. He left our town half a year after us.

A family, whose daughter I used to tutor a few years before, lived in Bucharest. I knew that they would be helpful to me, I just did not know exactly where they lived. Trusting my luck or my instincts, with next to no money, I set out on my journey, to try to get in touch with the family in the

U.S.A. The war was still on, but further away, West, in Hungary, Germany, Belgium and, of course, in the Far East. We knew next to nothing about the battles in the Pacific, about the U.S. - Japanese War.

I joined a number of people in a freight train, headed toward Bucharest. A journey that should have taken normally about six hours stretched into two days and a night. We arrived at the North Railroad Station on the first of May, in the evening. Romania, being already partially occupied by the Soviet troops, celebrated May Day with loud music on the loudspeakers.

I had no idea how to get to the people, whose address I had. Thus I and many others sat through the night in the R.R. station. Next morning I finally arrived at the place. The two sisters had already left for work, but the landlady of the pension admitted me into their room. I fell asleep with exhaustion. By late afternoon, when they arrived, they were more shocked than elated about my presence.

They took me within an hour to a coffee house, on Lipscani Street, where many Czernowitzers congregated. Sure enough, I met Jancu, the uncle of my former student Vera. He immediately took me with my belongings, to his family, to his parents. They were the warmest, friendliest people imaginable. Vera's mother was happy, because now, she thought, Vera would pass the grade, with my help.

The Kronenfelds did not mind me sleeping in their crowded apartment, one more did not matter. They started looking for accommodation for me somewhere near them. A Romanian woman, who owned a beautiful private home, rented me a corridor, between one part of the house and the other. There was just a bed, a tiny table, a chair and an entrance door, no window. She warned me right then that no guests were permitted into my "room". If anybody would want to get in touch with me, the person would have to wait in the street, but not call my name either. Even if I could find students to tutor, nobody was allowed inside. Since I had no alternative, I took that "room".

One week after my arrival in Bucharest, on May 8, 1945, was Victory Europe Day. The Germans had finally been defeated, war was over after almost six seemingly endless years. I felt badly not to share that day with my parents, my former neighbors and old friends, people with whom I had so valiantly struggled to survive.

Bucharest was the first big city, where I was to spend over two years. Throngs congregated in Piaţa Victoria (Victory Square) people hugged and kissed and whistled and danced, with abandon. The only military around were Russians and they kept to themselves. Life was supposed to return to normal, but it never did for Romania any more. In over a year, the Communists took over and life there was steadily deteriorating.

I had housing trouble all along, all through the over two years of my life in Bucharest. I changed addresses about six times. Inflation ate up the value of the currency to an extent that, as soon as I rented a room and agreed on a rent, that sum was almost worthless next month. Since the landlady could not raise your rent every month, she just chased you out under one pretext or another. Bucharest had been bombed several times during the war and therefore housing was in very short supply. Many refugees converged on the capital and it turned into a nightmare.

Food became a critical issue, it became scarcer by the day. Even when one had money, one could hardly buy any. I remember that, at the time I used to eat the main meal of the day in a pension. It was on the second floor of an apartment house and you were lucky if they served you. After about half a year, a new manager took over. He knew me and told me that previously all the veal dishes were really prepared with cat meat. Now, that was the reason that the meat tasted so sweet and soft.

When I came to Bucharest, I knew the reason why, yet I could not foresee the manifold hardships ahead of me. I wanted to get in touch with the family and also finish the studies at the university and finally get a diploma in languages and literature. However, nothing could be accomplished if I could not make a living. All three challenges were hard to fulfill. I did them all, but with an enormous effort.

How did I support myself? First, the Kronenfelds tried to get me a job. Jancu's brother-in-law, an engineer, had extended connections among the Romanian high bourgeoisie. He knew a former cabinet minister who was planning to open an export business. Gabor recommended me as a secretary, since I knew all the languages that they could possibly need, yet I could not type. Mr. Lupu paid for a typing course for me prior to starting work.

One day, on the way to the secretarial school, I met a former classmate from high school, who had been sent to private school in Bucharest at age 16. In her early youth she strongly sympathized with the "downtrodden" but among the daughters of the very rich she realized that she would rather join them than fight them, as was her earlier inclination. She forgot all about politics and after starting to work as a secretary, she married the boss. When I met her, on that hot June day in 1945, she was married and had an infant daughter. We were delighted to see each other. I had only been in Bucharest about a month.

She invited me to her house for lunch next day. They lived in a most luxurious high rise building on the sixth floor; the office was on the second. The apartment was exquisitely furnished; they had a cook and a nurse, for the baby.

When I came up, I could not believe what I saw. In the baby's room, the walls and the bed were hand painted by an artist, with characters from children's stories. We sat at a table, in the dining room and when a course was finished, Blanka rang an electric bell, under the table, and the cook came to clear the dishes and bring the next course.

She had sent her parents to Palestine and paid a considerable amount for it. Her only sister, a doctor, was living in China. Thus, she herself was fairly lonesome. Her husband's family had been deported from Hungary to Bergen Belsen and out of a large family, only one brother and one sister had returned. She was not very comfortable with the newly-met sister and brother-in-law. She became greatly attached to me and thus, I came for lunch daily after the secretarial school. That was about a month after my arrival in Bucharest.

It was a hot summer, air conditioning did not exist in those years. Blanka intended to rent a house in the mountains for the season. She trusted me so fully that she asked me to go to a resort and rent a villa for the summer, which I did. She thought that my liveliness and optimism were so admirable, that I could accomplish anything. Essentially, she was a pessimistic person, and my forward looking attitude felt like a tonic for her. The business, that Mr. Lupu and the great Malaxa had in mind, never materialized. I never learned to type well either.

All through the summer I stayed with Blanka, the baby daughter Tamara and the nurse, in Poiana Tapului, in the Carpathians. That was my first summer in Romania. We went through some very unusual days and nights in that two story "chalet" that I had rented. It was an unfriendly house. The upstairs bedrooms were connected to the downstairs living and dining rooms by a very intricately carved wooden staircase. Whether the stairs had dried out or the window frames had creaking frames, suffice it to say that, during the night we heard lots of strange noises. It happened every night. The old nurse was petrified, she ran out of the room, which she shared with baby Tamara, crossed herself and invoked all the saints. Sometimes Blanka and myself were scared stiff; we didn't know what to do: oil all the hinges or stuff our ears. It was as near to a haunted house, as I'll ever come.

We also lived through some nice adventures. We were bored to be sitting in the sun and all three watch the baby. One day I proposed that the two of us should take a ride to Sinaia, where the royal castle was, about two hours distance, by car, from Poiana. We told the nurse that we'd return by late afternoon. Once in a while, one could see a taxi pass by and we intended to hire one. We were 25 years old, both of us and fairly nice looking. On the main street, the road North-South, a car with three gentlemen stopped. They asked us how far we wanted to go, two were going to visit their families in Predeal, the third was headed for Braşov. It was exactly in the direction we intended to go. We got in, started to converse and before you knew we were already in Braşov, a beautiful town high up in the Carpathians, the Alps of Romania. The gentleman had a reserved room in a hotel, went to confirm his reservation and then proceeded to show us the town. That town was magnificent.

We saw the last German outposts in the mountains, before they finally gave up defending Transylvania. By 4 o'clock, we went to the railway station but there was no more train going South. The gentleman was a genuine gentleman, if I ever saw one. He gave us his room and he sat overnight in the lobby. Blanka was beside herself: no telephone in Poiana, to tell the nurse about coming home next morning; no pajamas for the night, nothing. Won't the nurse be in a panic? Next day, Saturday morning, her husband was supposed to come to visit. What if he arrived before us? Next morning we went to the R.R. station, got into a train and arrived an hour before her husband. The nurse was so happy to see us back, she told nothing. We did.

I never forgot that adventure. In fact, when Blanka was so frantic, I said that we will eventually think about it later on and be amused by it but while it happened, it was not funny. I am still in contact with Blanka. The family lives in Paris. She and her husband visited us here and we stayed with them for five days in 1968, on our first return to Europe. Eytan our son met their son Robert a few years ago when he was a graduate student at M.I.T.

Getting back to the main reason for my being in Bucharest. I soon found out that there were neither consulates nor embassies of England or the United States in Romania. There were small military missions and no services to the public. I went to the U.S. military mission and explained that my brothers were in the service and our entire family was in the U.S. We were newly arrived refugees and our relatives did not know of our whereabouts. I proposed to the sergeant, at the reception, to accept to send a letter of mine to my family in New York and forward it with his return address. There was no regular mail going overseas. He agreed.

The letter that Sgt. Andrews sent to the family was the first one received by them in years; it was not only a sign of life, it also notified them that all three of us had survived the war and that we were in Romania, had left Czernovitz.

Lucky for me: I gave him Blanka's telephone number and as soon as a letter arrived for me, he called and I came to the mission to pick it up. I actually did not know from month to month where I was going to live next, so her address was the constant one. For over a year, the contact with the family continued through various members of the military mission. We started to get letters from Eli, who was stationed in Germany. We found out about the birth of Frances, Irving, Martin, Allen and Judy, the new grandchildren.

When the sergeant was about to leave, I asked him to introduce me to his replacement and he did. The last contact was Sgt. Leo Castelli. Eli wrote to us from Germany, where he was stationed. He came to Europe with the first troops that had landed in Normandy. Later, he acted as a translator in his military outfit. Ulm, in the South of Germany, was the town where he spent a few months, before his demobilization. Bernie was stationed in Staten Island all through the war. He was part of the medical team, checking the eyes of those about to embark for Europe. The family in America and Eli, in Europe, informed us about everybody. In fact, Irving and Martin were born in June, 1945. I received the first photos of the twin sons in one of the first letters through the military mission. After about a year, normal mail service resumed. The Hias opened an office in Bucharest and documents were sent through them.

The refugee years in Romania were highly eventful. An interesting incident occurred. In Western Europe the price of gold coins was much higher than in Eastern Europe. Some of the gold coins, from tzarist times, affectionately called "little pigs" were about half the price in Bucharest and were therefore eagerly smuggled to Paris, for fat profits. Since my friend's husband knew that I had an "American connection", he suggested that I ask "my American" to take a roll of one hundred "little pigs", they were the size of dimes, sell them in Paris and bring back the money in dollars and make some money. Not afraid of anything, I asked my connection. "Of course, I am going to Paris for Christmas." He was willing to accommodate my request. My friend gave me the roll of gold coins, just on trust. It was worth a lot of money, which I could not possibly repay, in case it got lost. He trusted me and I trusted the sergeant. We were supposed to split the profit half, and half, my friend's husband and myself.

The sergeant stayed away about six weeks, much longer than I expected. I felt awkward in the situation, kind of afraid, yet optimistic that, in the long run, things will turn out right. However, my friend's husband, my partner in the deal, was a real businessman and a real gentleman. He waited for me to tell him of the result. Finally, the sergeant returned, some money was made and the deal was never mentioned again. A few months after the transaction, the sergeant told me that he was being discharged, was about the return to New York. He gave me his address to call him if I ever came to the U.S. After my arrival in New York, in 1947, I asked Eli where that address would be. He said that it was such a wealthy section of New York, I should rather forget about it. I called before Christmas. The housekeeper mentioned that the gentleman was in Paris, for his Christmas vacation. Imagine, exactly one year before, on his Christmas leave, he had done our joint "gold coin" venture. To-day, he is one of the most famous art dealers in New York. When I saw him once on T.V., about 25 years later, I didn't recognize him anymore.

In the summer of 1945, after spending July and August with Blanka in the mountains, I returned to Bucharest. I found out about a room, to be rented out by a German family, in their beautifully situated private home. Dorzia and I had decided to share a room. We went there together, to negotiate. They let the room under one condition: in case their two daughters, who had been deported by the Russians recently, were to come back, we would have to vacate the room within a day or two. This was a rare case in Romania, but it seems that they were known as Nazi sympathizers. Since we knew that once people were deported, they didn't come back, we agreed and moved in next day. It was the beginning of September, 1945. We shared one bed and ate, wherever we could, for we had no kitchen facilities or privileges.

Dorzia worked in a jewelry business and I was running around tutoring privately and going to university, too. I was forever riding on overcrowded streetcars. I used to come "home" in the evenings tired, with sopping wet shoes. They felt like heavy weights, dragging me down. They had to dry overnight, so that I could put them on next day.

In the night of New Year's the two daughters returned. We were told to vacate within the promised two days. Dorzia moved to her sister. I moved, too, yet I had no room. My friend Blanka let me sleep in their office. I had to leave the place by 7:30, in the morning, because they opened for business at 8. My suitcase was upstairs, in the apartment, on a higher floor. That was the arrangement until I got a room.

The refugee years in Bucharest were quite eventful. While the parents stayed in Dorohoi, I studied and tutored and finished the full course at the University of Bucharest and graduated. That was no mean feat.

In that first year away from Czernovitz, in September 1945, the parents felt very lonesome and asked me to come to them for the New Year and Yom Kippur holidays. That trip turned into a memorable journey. The trains functioned badly, were overcrowded and you knew when you left, but not when you'd arrive.

Not really fully aware of the situation, I took a train to Jassy, which was supposed to take about six hours and then a connecting train to Dorohoi, about two hours. I left in the morning, on a train that was as crowded as a subway car in rush hour. One could not go down at any station, since it would have been impossible to get on again.

Since the train stopped many times, some passengers from Jassy told me that the train would arrive in the evening and there would be no connecting train till next day. They also mentioned about a strictly enforced curfew because of drunken Russian soldiers roaming the streets at night. None of them offered to let me stay overnight in their home. There were no hotels available, at all. I had the telephone number of a Czernovitzer friend, who was living at the time in his brother's house. Thus, from the train, I went to the Central Post Office and tried to call, but to no avail, no answer. The clerk looked up the number and saw it was a business phone and it was already 8 o'clock at night. The post office was going to close at 9 p.m. and I was advised to leave the building. I explained to the clerk that I had no place to go and "how could I spend the night alone in the street?" Everybody knew about the drunken soldiers. I proposed to them to let me stay in the building overnight. They locked the building with me inside, in a back office. They let me out next morning, after a scary night. Next day, at noon, I arrived at my parents.

The parents lived in one room with one bed; I slept on the table. To the few girls that I knew in Dorohoi, three former classmates of Sali, I seemed like a girl from the capital, the metropolis, with interesting stories to tell, an interesting life. In Dorohoi, the only event of the day was a walk up and down Main Street. By that time, we received some funds from the U.S. and the parents did not depend financially on me any longer; yet in every other respect, they were helpless without me.

Returned to Bucharest and the university, I registered for a very heavy program. I took courses in French, English, German and history. German was unimportant to attend if one bought the lectures. I could not attend all the lectures, I did not have the time. One day, Gaber (I forgot her first name), a girl from Czernovitz, alone, like myself, who could not afford to buy the course, told me about a girl - Eva Bleier - who had bought it. Gaber suggested that we try to persuade Eva to let us study with her for the exam. I met her and she agreed to share the lectures with us. Once in a while we went to her house, to study together.

Eva was the first survivor of the concentration camps Theresienstadt and Auschwitz. It was about four months after the end of the war, yet we had never heard of other places than Transnistria. Jewish communities had been so isolated during these years that every group had been tortured in his own torture chambers, without being aware of any particulars of other communities.

Eva had returned alone from Auschwitz, where she had lost her mother. She was the first person to mention the name of Mengele. She was the first person, that I saw, with a number tattooed on her arm. An uncle and aunt, living in Bucharest took her in and treated her like their own daughter. We became friends at that time and remained so to this day. She lives with her family in Manhattan.

At the beginning of 1946, I moved into a room near the Opera, a place I was forced to vacate after four months, due to the rapid rate of inflation. The next room, in a residential section, was unfurnished. I thought that I would be luckier, if I brought my own bed and table and chair. That did not last too long either, due to different circumstances.

In July, 1946, after finishing all my exams, I was near exhaustion. I was studying late into the nights, food was scarce and of poor quality and the heat became oppressive; I did not even have a fan. One could hardly sleep at night for that was before the availability of air conditioning or refrigeration.

I remember going to my last exam in history, on the Fourth of July. The professor asked me what disaster befell the English on that day. He was thinking of the loss of the American colonies. When I walked from my place to the university, on a blisteringly hot day, I felt a pain on my scalp, my head.

When touching the head, the hair pin was so hot, it burnt my touching finger and my scalp.

I decided to go to Câmpulung, a small resort in the mountains of Bucovina, stay there for a week and then go to my parents. I had a friend Mimi, who was living at that time with her married sister a long time resident of

Câmpulung.

She recommended me a private home, where I got a room and full board. In my state of exhaustion, the owner woke me up for breakfast and I went back to sleep. I slept almost continuously through that week. Feeling more refreshed, I went to Dorohoi. There I found Mother quite upset. She had a growth on her lower lip. We decided that Mother would come with me to Bucharest to see a competent doctor. Father felt despondent with both of us gone.

Our troubles were manifold: the owner of the house, where I had rented the room hated the idea that instead of one person there were two. Besides, my Mother was first in a hospital, then at home. The treatment took a long time, since the chin did not heal. The medication, a powder that was supposed to be applied, smelled badly. The owner threatened to throw us out. He had rented out a room, he said, and now he had hospital smell to endure. One day, when we came back from the doctor, the owner, a retired Romanian officer, had put a piece of furniture in front of my door. He had locked us out. We had to go into the room through his kitchen - an impossible situation. I had to find another place to live, an apartment, and bring Father to Bucharest.

The officer had one son, a doctor, married to a Jewish woman. I remember talking to her and asking her whether she could not talk to them and make them understand our situation and not pressure us so insistently. She claimed that her in-laws couldn't understand what it meant to be homeless. Then I asked her whether they could understand what it meant to be sick. She shrugged her shoulders. I remember telling her: You know, I'll find a room; they will be rid of me and I of them - but you, you won't get rid of them that easily; they are heartless people.

I finally found a place near the North Railroad Station, a workers' district. It was a bombed out building, barely repaired. We moved in. Father came from Dorohoi, we were again together. It took quite a while to get Mother in better shape. She needed a skin graft, a new procedure at that time. It was innovative surgery. For a long time she had difficulty eating, since the lip had not healed properly. I remember with great gratitude the kindly Jewish surgeon, Dr. Brochovici, a man of real compassion and of great capability.

In all this hardship, we had some luck. At the beginning of my stay in Bucharest, in May 1945, the Bickel sisters recommended me a lovely girl to be tutored, since she had lost years of schooling during the war. That bright girl, Elika, was living in an uncle's house. As I started to come there, a friend of theirs, a lawyer, used to visit daily. That was Dori Scharf, who had a high position in the Ministry of Commerce, had a car and a chauffeur - in short: the good life: Dori liked me a lot and we became very good friends, nothing more.

When Mother got sick and needed to go long distances, to doctors, he would sometimes send his car to give her a ride. Also Jancu Kronenfeld was very helpful; he sometimes took us to the doctor.

We lived in three lousy rooms, on the third floor, with windows like little portholes, under the roof. It became unbearably hot in the summer, Bucharest was dry and intensely hot. When Mother's health improved, we started to concentrate on plans to leave Romania.

The parents were entitled to receive first preference visas as parents of American citizens. I had no right to any special visa. Thus arose the idea of going to study for a master of arts degree in America.

The HIAS (Hebrew Immigration Aid Society) had been helpful to Jewish survivors after the First World War. This same organization opened offices in Bucharest, in order to facilitate communications between families abroad and the various survivors: Romanian, Polish, Hungarian, Russian Jews, who happened to find themselves in Romania at the end of the Second World War. People had been displaced in so many ways: Hungarian Jews who had been taken into the army and fought along with the Germans on the Russian front; Polish Jews, who had remained in Romania, after their flight from Poland in 1939; people like us, who had fled from Czernovitz; survivors from Transnistria - in short, a variety of homeless people. The expression D.P. – displaced person – had been coined later.

The services of the HIAS extended to all the capitals of Western Europe. The documents sent by relatives from the West were handled by them, money for train and ship passage was sent through them, too, and handled by them. They helped obtain visas and bought tickets.

I started my trek to the HIAS as soon as their services became available. Getting a Romanian passport was possible. However, in the meantime, the Communists took over the regime and the bureaucracy almost came to a halt. The new regime could not decide whether to let people emigrate and under what guidelines. Finally, it was decided that based on a visa from a Western country, a person would be granted an exit visa. Under these conditions, a passport was not enough.

The greatest obstacle in this entire process was the fact that no South or North American country opened any consulates, at the time, in Romania.

Consequently, visas to the U.S. or Canada or Chile or Brazil had to be received in Paris. The French government was reluctant to issue transit visas because they were afraid that many Jewish refugees would flock to France and perhaps stay. In that case, the French had no place to deport those unwanted newcomers. An exit visa was a one-way departure; the person became stateless.

The French transit visa became a grave obstacle for most. The problem became acute, since people had a passport, valid for only one year and the delays with the French transit visa and the Romanian exit visa - all this led inexorably towards the running out of the one-year validity of the passport.

By the time the parents received their passports, my Father started to feel poorly. He felt nauseous, he lost appetite, he even lost the capacity to enjoy the prospect of finally leaving. The doctor, an old friend from Czernovitz, found nothing essentially wrong. He thought that after all these war years, Father was just worn out.

Finally, after great efforts, the parents received the exit and French transit visas and were ready to leave. It would have been more reasonable to go to Paris by train, but times were abnormal, to put it mildly. One could not go through all those countries with no well defined borders, no regularly scheduled trains. Thus, they embarked on a ship, in Constanta, a Black Sea port in Romania. The boat trip took two weeks, stopped for a day in Haifa, one in Palermo and finally landed in Marseille. Through the HIAS, the parents had tickets all the way to Paris. The expenses had all been covered by the family in U.S.

In the meantime, I had received admission to New York University and to Columbia University to start on a master's program in September, 1947.

My parents left in June, 1947. I took them to Constanta, saw them leave in the company of a number of other older people, who like them, were going to be reunited with their families.

In the meantime Yuda and myself had got in touch somehow and found out each other's address, his in Haifa, mine in Bucharest. Thus, I let him know when the parents would land in Haifa, for one day. He awaited them at their arrival and since the cousin from Nahalal, Mr. Schleien, had not yet come to meet them, he took them on a tour of Haifa, up to Mount Carmel and then back to the boat. It was the last time my Father and Yuda saw each other. Of course, Father never knew that he would be his son-in-law. At the pier, the cousin had arrived in the meantime. He was one of the early settlers, one of the founders of Nahalal, the first moshav in Palestine. The father of Moshe Dayan was his next door neighbor.

The Schleiens gave the parents a very cordial reception and tried to persuade them to remain in Palestine. For my parents there was only one aim in life, one desire: to see their children, their grandchildren, Mother's brothers and their families.

On their arrival in Paris, the HIAS set them up in a hotel near Porte Maillot, where they remained for almost four months. The hotel was in the immediate vicinity of the Bois de Boulogne, a world renowned, magnificent park. The parents wrote to me that they had found a lovely park, almost as nice as the Habsburgshöhe, our beloved park in Czernovitz.

When I returned from Constanta, I remained alone in my "palace" in Bucharest. Soon Mrs. Kreisel's married daughter moved in with me. She and her husband had been eager to come from a provincial town to Bucharest, in order to take steps toward emigration to Palestine. It took them fifteen years before they were permitted to leave Romania. Manja was a kind person, a woman five years older than myself, but her husband was a tyrannical, stubborn man. I felt sorry to have accommodated them immediately after my parents' departure. Among the mistakes that I made in life, this was a minor one.

When I applied for a student's visa at the American consulate, I was congratulated by the American official for qualifying for Columbia, but they wanted me to guarantee that I would return as soon as my studies were over. I told them that I was engaged to be married and would surely return. Well, Dori Scharf went with me to a notary public and gave a declaration that we were engaged and by the time I achieved my Master's degree, we would get married in Romania. He signed, the notary sealed the document and the consul eventually granted me a student visa. By that time, Dori had already left Romania on a mission to Italy and he never returned again.

I remember, when I came to the HIAS and showed my visa, the news spread like wildfire and the crowd looked at me in disbelief. One man came by, looked at me and exclaimed: "This is not a girl; this is a Cossack."

In the meantime, my parents settled in Paris, got used to the hotel and found out about the Jewish section, where they went to eat in kosher restaurants. Many other refugees did the same. In fact, the hotel Maillot catered exclusively to refugees, referred to them by the HIAS. However, my Father was not well; he could hardly eat.

One day, a man from Lille came to Paris on business. He inquired in that kosher restaurant whether they had met any refugees from Czernovitz.

The owner brought them over to my parents' table. He was the son of a longtime friend of my parents, Mr. Stark. It was a mixture of joy and tears. he had settled in France years before the outbreak of war and had fought in the Resistance. His family in Bukovina had not survived. Mother confided in him and asked him whether he could recommend a doctor, to whom they could talk - be it in German or Yiddish. Mr. Stark had a cousin, Dr. Falk, an internist in Paris. In all that misfortune, finding Dr. Falk was a blessing. He treated Father as if he were his own parent. He diagnosed that my Father had cancer. The doctor's wife took him to have x-rays taken; she picked up the results; she drove them back to the hotel. They were angels.

When Dr. Falk realized in what desperate situation my parents found themselves, he wrote to Bernie in New York and to me, in Bucharest. He told me about the seriousness of his condition and that somebody had to come and arranged for them to go to the U.S., otherwise, as his state of health worsens, he would not be able to leave anymore; he may not be granted an American visa. When I received that letter, in August 1947, I was absolutely distraught.

I can not remember ever crying as hysterically as I did, after reading that letter. My hopelessness and helplessness in the situation was so extreme, I felt like tearing my hair out. There I sat, in a hot hole, under a burning roof, in Bucharest, with the knowledge that I may or may not be able to finally get that exit visa. My passport would expire in a few months and then, I'll never get out. How could I get there to help them? The parents sat in a hotel, in a strange country, alone, Father so desperately sick, Mother trying her best and not being able to get through the bureaucracy, to get tickets on a boat to America. That was really the only condition to be fulfilled in order to receive the preferential visa. HIAS in Paris called the Cunard Line and they claimed to have every berth booked to the end of the year.

Finally, after years of effort to solve the many problems, when the parents left, it seemed that the solution was in sight. We were struggling to get out of the wilderness and like Moses, Father looked from far to reach the Promised Land. When that letter arrived, everything seemed to collapse. My chances of leaving were 50-50. Their chances of getting out of Paris were getting slim, since Father's condition was deteriorating.

At that same time, the Communist regime let the inflation run its course and then, devalued the currency. They issued a new kind of lei. Everybody could exchange 80,000 lei for 20 new lei. The day before the exchange, I had 2 million lei. For that amount, I bought two pairs of hand crocheted summer gloves; there was nothing else available. I would have preferred to purchase a kilo meat, but that was out of the question, unrealistic thinking. The authorities stamped everybody's identification card, namely that money has been exchanged. Everybody possessed the same amount of cash, everybody started a new life, under Communism, with a total of 20 lei.

In the meantime my French transit visa had been issued and I applied for an exit visa. However, those were harsh times, politically. One was frightened to apply under the strict new regime, but it was the only thing for me to do. The exit visa was issued fairly soon. I obtained a train ticket through the HIAS, to go to Prague; from there to Paris and to arrange for boat accommodation there. I left Bucharest on September 10, 1947. My good friend Jancu saw me off at the Northern Railroad Station, a few blocks from where I lived. The day before I said good bye to Evi and promised her to try to find some way of getting her a visa to any South American country. Her uncle in Paris would pay for it, but he knew no way to get a connection. She had little hope of going to the U.S.A., where her father had been living for many years.

Why could the parents not get their visas, since they were available at the consulate in Paris? They could not get accommodation for passage on a boat to the U.S.A. Presumably, the Queen Mary and the Queen Elizabeth had been booked for months in advance. The American consulate issued a visa only if the applicant had a reservation for a ticket.

Father was languishing in the hotel and they knew no way to get out of that bind. The HIAS had the money for the tickets but when they called the Cunard Lines, nothing was available, officially. Hundreds of prospective travellers to Canada and South America faced the same dilemma.

If you have to be stuck, Paris seems to be a good place. Not in 1947 and not when one is terminally ill. Food was very scarce, it was rationed. You could buy "baguettes", the long, thin French bread, without ration cards; everything else was rationed. Camembert, on rations, was available, yet my parents would not eat it. Besides, Mother could not prepare anything in the hotel room.

The Hotel Maillot, where they resided for four months, had French personnel and Jewish customers: Polish, Hungarian, Romanian refugees. Everybody was waiting for a visa - all displaced persons, everybody clinging to a hope, a piece of paper. In the yard of the hotel, red-cheeked peasant girls from Bretagne washed the hotel laundry. They also cleaned the rooms, scrubbed with rags and brooms. When the cleaning girl would come in and see Father in bed, she would say: "Monsieur shlooft" (Monsieur is sleeping, in Yiddish) and would come later. The only pleasant aspect of that time was the proximity of the Bois de Boulogne, which reminded my parents of home, of the Habsburgshohe.

They watched children playing and the boats on the lake and there they spent hours upon hours. They hoped that one of their children would come to rescue them from that exile - Bernie or Pearl.

Chapter 8

Bucharest

What did this span of almost two-and-a half years turn out to be? So much happened politically around me and in my own life, I find it hard to appraise.

The war had ended finally; I lived alone for over a year, for the first time; I met a lot of new people in this new environment; I worked harder than ever before or after; I finished the studies at the university at an enormous effort; made a living; made all the preparations for emigration. The anxieties because of the political change-over to Communism - the second time in my life - galloping inflation and Mother's sickness and two operations and finally the departure of the parents and three months later my own departure to Paris. My desperately sick Father was waiting, hoping for me to finally make their passage possible.

During the years 1941-1945, we lived in constant fear for our lives, much of the time confined to the house or at work, feeding off our slowly dwindling possessions. From the age of 21 to 25, I had not heard a concert, seen a performance or read any new book. We were cut off from the rest of the world and from things of the mind, from art, from literature. While in previous years the radio offered news and musical entertainment, it was taken from us in June 1941.

During the years 1940-41 and 1944-45, under the Soviet regime, every performance was blatant propaganda; every dance or play glorified the happy peasants or workers and the lies were too transparent to be ignored. Thus, in Bucharest, a window to freedom of art had opened to me as well as to other refugees. Of course, this last burst of artistic freedom ended in 1947. It was a short but sweet interlude.

Bucharest was a vibrant, lively, big city with great numbers of theaters, cabarets, musical comedies, opera, recital halls, all at affordable prices. It was an ideal place to come in normal times. In December 1937, when I visited there the first time, it impressed me as a metropolis with lots of traffic, broad avenues, richly stocked stores, elegantly dressed people, a tempo and rhythm of life pulsating visibly. The Jewish section of the city, named Vacaresti, was famous for endless streams of people coming and going, its restaurants, the well known "carnati" and broiled, spicy meats on "graţar" a kind of barbecue. Everywhere one could hear gypsy violins, even in the smallest eating places. Of course, Romanians love to sing and dance and get sentimental, as soon as they have consumed a bottle of wine.

At this time, after the war years, the glitter had tarnished. The food and drink, so lavishly exhibited and indulged in, had slowly dwindled. People were less elegant, the illuminations a little dimmer; life a little poorer and drabber. Bucharest looked like a dowager, who had fallen on poor times. Yet, it was still a lively town with great numbers of theaters, movie houses, an opera, concert halls, cafés. I took from it whatever I could. Prices of admission for students were very low, easily affordable. I started to go to the theaters with a vengeance. It didn't matter that I sat in the last row balcony, but I could savor plays, which I had previously not even known about. In Bucharest there was a sudden burst of artistic creativity. After the restrictions imposed by the fascist government of General Antonescu, during the war, there came a relaxation, a thaw, a sudden opening of doors to new plays, to Western literature and art.

The theaters mounted productions of Eugene O'Neill's "Mourning Becomes Electra" with the great actor George Vraca; "The Lady of the Camelias" was produced in two theaters during the same season, one in modern dress, the other in traditional decor and dress; "A Midsummer Night's Dream" with the Mendelsohn music; a dramatization of Alphonse Daudet's "L'Arlesienne", with the incidental music by Bizet, a hauntingly beautiful suite, a favorite of mine ever since. I saw "The Voice of the Turtle", which was then a hit on Broadway. I saw Jewish performances and a few operas.

I remember the opera performances quite clearly, to this day. The hall was unheated and the opera lovers sat all wrapped in coats and mufflers and gloves - the place was frigid. Yet, the performers sang and the public disregarded the discomfort. A performance of "Lakmé" by Leo Delibes remained very distinctly in my memory. The hall was cold, the public wrapped in winter coats and poor Lakmé, dressed in flimsy rags, sang in an Indian market.

That coloratura sang her heart out (not so well), all those trills, all those high notes. I only hope she survived that evening without catching pneumonia.

I saw for the first time a movie with Rita Hayworth "Gilda" and was enchanted to see dancing and singing and all those beautiful people on the screen. The spoken English delighted me, too.

Bucharest was a throbbing city that had come on hard times: food was scarce, the electric street cars always overcrowded and often jumped the tracks. The resources strained to capacity, the upkeep of the transportation system practically non-existent. There were tens of thousands of refugees.

Every type of newcomer met at a different coffee-house with people from one's home town. Thus, the Czernovitzers used to frequent Café Elite on Lipscani Street. It was an unofficial meeting place, where one could get information about who came from over there, where he or she lived and worked. A few thousand had come, like ourselves in 1945 and another big group one year later. People helped one another, recommended a room or a place to eat, informed about a possible job or whom to contact about a visa to go abroad.

Having left home, that became a replacement, an information center, a place to keep in touch. The time in Bucharest built my confidence, showed me that I was not lost, I had friends, contacts. Some wanted me to teach their children, some wanted to learn English prior to emigration. Thus I tutored and supported myself. I also made lasting, enduring friendships: Jancu, Dori, Evi. We remained friends for the rest of our lives. Those hard times brought out the best in people. I remember Mimi, who had worked with me in the "Consiliu de Patronaj" in 1942-3. She moved in with a married sister in Câmpulung, after leaving home. One day she realized that he teeth were loose. She was then about 21 years old. The local dentist recommended her to see a doctor in Bucharest. Of course, she came to me and shared my room for about two weeks. In Bucharest she was told that her condition was a result of poor nutrition, lack of vitamins.

We walked in the street, looking for a place to eat. The restaurant had only malai (bread made of maize) and brinza - a very salty cheese. Both of us ordered two pieces of malai and brinza. That tasted awful: cold and heavy on the stomach, yet there was nothing else we could buy. She returned to her town in the mountains, where she could probably get a little bit better food.

The city was surrounded by woods and lakes. Once in a while one could take the streetcar to the end of the line and spend a few hours near the lake. People everywhere used to discuss, gesticulate, exchange information. We would sit at a café, drinking Turkish coffee and spend hours talking - spending the equivalent of 25 cents. Bucharest broadened my horizon, showed me what a big city can offer.

My thoughts went ultimately toward emigration, America. Actually I had not thought out to the end what would come next. I gave no thought to marriage, I considered Bucharest an interim, a way station towards a different place, a different life. Good bye Europe and all the hardships of the years from 1939.

The other side of the coin - most refugees suffered exceedingly because of the greed and prejudice of landlords. Nobody actually slept in the street, since there were always people who would offer you a bed temporarily, even if one slept on the floor, but one was not completely abandoned, ever. That was at least my own experience.

asterisk.

Once, when I was looking for a room, I came to a widow, who refused to rent her vacant room to me because I was Ashkenazy. That was my first encounter with a Sepharady person, a Jew of Spanish background. I suffered plenty of discrimination, but from the part of non-Jews; but to be told by a Jewish woman that she does not accept in her house a person of my background, an Ashkenazy, shocked me. I later found out that many of them considered themselves superior to our brand of Judaism[1]

.

Of course, the officer who harassed me to move out of his house, because he refused to be inconvenienced by the fact that my sick mother came to share my room - he was just like any landlord, at the time: greedy and heartless. The fact that inflation made his pension, probably, worth very little impelled him to let a room in the house to a stranger. However, he and his wife showed no humane feeling toward me, a refugee, who found it even harder to keep going. They probably charged higher rent to the next tenant. Landlords were nasty, irrespective of religion.

Yet in my personal relationships with people, I made friends easily and

---

[1]Ashkenaz means Eastern, sepharady means Spanish. Spharadim originate from the Jews of Spain, who were chased out during the Inquisition, in the 1515th century. While their vernacular, called Ladino, has a Spanish basis, our Yiddish is of Germanic origin. Our common language is Hebrew, which both groups share in the synagogue, for prayers or for studies of the Bible and other holy texts. Their home language and ours are entirely different, incomprehensible to one another.

suffered few disappointments, at that time. I tried to be as forthcoming to them as they were to me, friendship being a two-way street. Being a realist as well as an optimist, I expected things to be tough, but that they would work out in the long run. This philosophy of life carried me over great hardships, actually to this day. I just took care of things, one at a time, and trusted my luck. Since my expectations seemed to be fulfillable, the disappointments were not such that they should lead me to despair. The other ingredient toward survival was my sense of humor. I retained my capability to be amusing and amused. I could still tell a joke and be delighted by the sense of levity of others. I think these attributes made me into a survivor.

After all, how much more could I lose? I had already lost my home, my familiar surroundings, a boyfriend for whom I cared deeply and all my friends from before. How much more could I lose? All I had left were my life and my parents and that I struggled to keep.

Chapter 9

Prague, Paris and the Journey to America (Fall 1947)

On September 10, 1947, I left Bucharest by train, headed for Prague. The Hias sent about ten people on that same train - eight oldsters, myself and a young woman, my age, who was supposed to go to the U.S. to marry a cousin, whom she had never met. The two of us were supposed to keep an eye on the entire group, answer any questions about documents at the borders or whatever else may occur. Mary, the other young woman, came from a small town in Transylvania; she spoke Romanian and Hungarian; for the rest I had to step in.

It took about 36 hours to arrive in Prague. None of us had any foreign currency - we had no money in any currency, since it was against the law in Romania to take money out of the country. Somebody from Hias was supposed to await us at the Wilson Railroad Station in Prague. We had left on Friday and arrived early on Sunday morning.

The train filled up in Hungary and in Czechoslovakia it was overcrowded. I sat next to a Czech, to whom I spoke about all kinds of matters. He was a train conductor and was going home, to Prague, for a few days leave. He offered to show me his city, but I did not know where I would stay and for how long. We made an appointment, like the "good soldier Schweik" at noon, two days later, at the statue on Wenczeslaw Square. He said that everybody would be able to tell me where it was.

By the time we all got off the train, all ten of us, nobody awaited us. Since it was Sunday morning, there was no answer when we phoned. I had been advised, ahead of time, to ask directions in Russian. If the person would not understand me, to ask again in German. The Czechs hated the Germans so bitterly that they would not answer any foreigner who spoke German to begin with. Yet, at that time they sympathized with the Russians, who had liberated them from the German fascists. The strategy worked, they explained to us, Mary and myself, how to reach the Hias. The older people stayed behind, at the Railroad station. But we had no money for the fare on the street car. According to the instructions, we were supposed to take two street cars to reach the address. We told the person that we did not have the change for car fare, since we had just arrived from Romania. The second person, whom we asked again offered us the car fare. Soon after we arrived at the Hias, somebody came to the office. There was a cable instructing them to pick us up at Wilson Station. We reached the others and were eventually put up at a hotel, where we also took our meals and were told that we would leave in five days, on a direct train to Paris.

I met the gentlemen on Wenzel Square. Mary had come along with me. We admired the many beautiful bridges across the Vltava (Moldau) River. We saw the Hradczani Castle, situated across the river, on a high hill - but only from the outside. They told us that it was closed for the day. Later, we found out that on that particular day, in a communist "putsch" - conspiracy, they threw the foreign minister out of the window and declared to the world that he had committed suicide. The foreign minister was Massaryk, the son of the founder of the republic.

We spent the few days in Prague enjoying this historic city, with its unusual sights from the Middle Ages: the oldest synagogue in Europe called the Alt- Neu Synagogue (Old-New Synagogue), with the cemetery in back of the house of worship. The legend of the Golem of Prague originated from there. Rabbi Loew, known in Jewish scholarship as Rabbi Judah, the Maharal, wrote a famous commentary to Rashi. Among the legends told about him is the creation of the Golem, who on instruction from the Rabbi saved the Jewish community from persecution. As soon as the Golem had fulfilled his mission, the rabbi returned him to his lifeless state. I went to this house of worship on Rosh Hashannah, the Jewish New Year. It was a most moving experience. Since few Czech Jews had survived, the crowd was made up of remnants from the survivors of different Jewish communities. The books, the torahs, the cemetery - everything, at that time, was in complete disarray. It was the most moving experience that I ever had in a synagogue.

I also saw and admired the square where Huss was burnt on the stake. He was the Czech reformer, who wanted to translate the Bible into the national language and was burnt to death by the prevailing Catholics, who judged him as a heretic. The old, historic town fascinated me no end. The medieval houses, with fortresslike portals, the waterwell in the courtyards, the crossover walks from one side of the street to the other, at the third or fourth floor level for escape, in case of attack; the walls around the area. It all brought the history of the city alive; it brought the Middle Ages alive.

Besides, Prague is famous for its many churches with gold-leaf covered domes. In the sunshine, Prague is golden. I fell in love for ever.

At the end of the five day stay, the entire group boarded a train for Paris. Although my parents knew the time of my arrival, they could not travel on the train that far because of Father's illness. An old gentleman, a former neighbor of ours, the one whose daughter had committed suicide and was laid out on my bed, this Mr. Nachman awaited me at the station. By that time he was already an old hand at travel in Paris; four months of residence made him an oldtimer. Well, he said that he loved the city, he regretted to have come so late in life.

The reunion was very emotional; Father's appearance was changed. He looked drawn, pale; his voice weak, his eyes lustreless. Yet, my parents hoped that a resolution of their hardships was in sight. They wanted to show me off to Dr. Falk and his wife, two wonderful, helpful people. Next day I went to visit Dorzia in the Rothschild hospital. She had left for Paris before me and resided with her married sister, in Paris. The recurrence of pleurisy forced her into the hospital. Since the Metro in Paris works like a dream, it took me no time to be able to commute.

A funny little incident happened on my way to the hospital. It was the day before Yom Kippur. Mr. Nachman visited my parents and when he saw me about to leave, he bade a hasty goodbye and left with me. After about three stops on the metro, he had to change trains. Just before leaving, he embraced me and kissed me on the cheek, which he would never do otherwise. Only after he had left, did I realize why he was sorry not to have come to Paris 50 years sooner. So many couples were kissing on trains and he had missed all this enjoyment, all this life. At least, this time, he kissed a girl on the metro; he used the opportunity, at least once.

The refugees in the hotel were of different ages, from different countries, intending to travel to different destinations, with different intentions of building a future. Basically, they had in common their homelessness, their rootlessness, their great losses of family, friends, homes. They could not communicate with the people around them, except with each other. Some were waiting for months, others would be waiting for years for a visa to Canada or Australia or New Zealand or Chile. They were hounded by the French police when their transit visas expired and had to be renewed again and again. In the meantime, people had no more valid passports and remained stateless - in possession of a piece of paper with name, address, age and country of origin.

Coming back to my parents and their plight. After a long conversation and clearing up what the stumbling block was, next day I went with Mother to the American consulate on the Place de la Concorde. It was a palatial building, with many people working at reception desks, information - all civilians. As we were sitting there, I noticed a young man in uniform coming and going, talking to the American personnel. I had the impression that the man was Jewish. When he came out again, I approached him and asked him whether I could ask him for some advice. I told him that I was in possession of an American student visa, but that my parents desperately needed tickets on one of the boats: Queen Mary or Queen Elizabeth, in order to get their preferential visas. He introduced himself as Mr. Ungar and thus the contact was established. He gave me his telephone number and asked me to make an appointment to see him in the Hotel République, on Place de la République. He assured me that in case he was not there, his wife would make the appointment; she spoke Yiddish.

I came to his hotel next day and everything became clear. For double the price of a ticket from Southampton to New York, we could get tickets on one or the other boat. Of course, it had to be paid in New York to his brother in Williamsburgh, a section inhabited by Orthodox Jews. We wrote to New York and waited for him to get a signal from his family that double the amount of money had been paid for three tickets. It took about ten days for him to receive the proper letter; we got tickets for the parents on the Queen Mary for the first week in October and for myself, on the Queen Elizabeth, one week later.

As soon as the consulate saw an approval for passage by boat, they issued the parents their visas. I wanted to leave one week later because of the immigration authorities. Had they noticed, in New York, at arrival, that the parents came as immigrants and I as a student, they may had made great difficulties. I didn't realize at the time that I would encounter complication on my arrival, anyway.

Before I left Bucharest, I had promised Evi that if I could find some connection to get her a visa to a South or Central American country, I would let her uncle in Paris know about it. When I met Mr. Ungar, I realized that he could get anything in Paris, for money. I talked to him about it and he got a visa for Evi, paid by her uncle in Paris. Such a visa was good as a basis to receive a passport in Romania, an exit visa and a French transit visa. Evi got her paper, arrived in Paris and lived at her uncle's for several years, before going to Mexico and eventually to her father in New York.

When Dori Scharf found out through friends in Romania that I was in Paris, he went there from Milano. By the time he arrived, they told him in Hias that I had left for the U.S. He settled later in Brazil, where he lived for 20 years. He resides now in Israel.

After the parents left, I spent one more week in Paris. The Falks took me out one evening to a restaurant to see a new American movie "The Best Years of Our Lives," a top film about World War II. His cousin, Mr. Stark had come to Paris soon after my arrival. He had fallen in love with me and wrote me silly cards from Lille. He even came to Paris to see me off all the way to Southampton. He really spoiled that trip for me. He was well intentioned, but a terrible bore. Besides, he argued with everybody on the train ride, from Paris to Calais. Whenever one opened a window, he wanted it closed. He insisted everything different from anybody else, a real pain.

Mr. Ungar had bought a ticket for another woman, who spoke only Polish and Yiddish. She had a son in New York and she was going to marry a rabbi in Williamsburg. He asked me to be her companion; he put her under my protection, since she could not communicate with anybody on the train or on the boat. We slept one night in London, then took the boat-train to Southampton, to embark on the Queen Elizabeth.

The trip from Paris to Calais was uneventful, except that I could see the utter devastation of the region North of Paris, the area of fierce battles after the landing of the Allies in Normandie: the rubble in Boulogne, the wrecks of planes and trains strewn all over, battlefields not yet cleared. I had seen similar devastation on my train trip through Germany a month before. The train had stopped in Nurenberg. All you could see then were bombed buildings and shacks covered with cardboard roofs.

The short passage by boat from Calais to Dover was stormy, the boat was rolling and shaking and I felt seasick. Yet, the white cliffs of Dover were clear to see on that sunny, windy October afternoon. The queasy feeling on that short trip was a harbinger of things to come, of a week of stormy weather on the Atlantic.

As for my impressions of Paris, I spent three weeks there, not as a tourist.

There were important matters to take care of, there was a mission to fulfill. Lucky for my parents and myself, it was accomplished successfully, but with great anxiety, I spent one week alone in the Hotel Maillot, after the parents' departure to New York in the room where my parents had spent four months.

I went to see the Louvre - a unique experience - and Versailles. The palace was completely empty since the French had hidden all the treasures during the war. The palace itself and the gardens were grandiose, but no flowers in bloom, no fountains in action. I went to see the tomb of Napoleon, in the Dome des Invalides. It was that day of the week when the building was closed.

I went to see the places that my high school French teacher, Miss Grunspan, had described.

Coming out of Bucharest, Prague was on the same scale, by size, manageable to walk around and see the Old City, its grandeur and history. Prague was also a revelation, since I did not know what to expect. It surprised and enchanted me, for I had not foreseen such beauty, such panoramas along the Moldau River (Vltava in Czech), the Castle on the hill, such bridges with statuary on them.

Paris, a much large metropolis, on a different scale from the cities seen before, was overwhelming. I could easily make myself understood, I recognized many streets and buildings and squares from my high school studies. It felt somehow as if I had seen it once, long ago.

The look of the people, their uninhibited behavior, their open expressions of tenderness - that I saw for the first time in my life. While in Romania, where I grew up, people flirted and loved just like any place else in the world, yet people acted very discreetly. Kissing and hugging occurred only in complete privacy, expressions of tenderness were hinted at - in Paris people kissed wherever one looked: in the streets, in the Metro, under street lights. People stopped you in the street, if you walked alone, and started flirting, talking, in a non-threatening way. It seemed like the most natural thing to do. As I went alone to the Consulate, to visit Dorzia, to see Dr. Falk, to see Evi's uncle and to Mr. Ungar, I was travelling and walking all over the city. First I did not know how to handle people, who started talking to me. Then I decided to answer only in English - I don't understand French. One young man started up a conversation, as I was walking down Champs Elysee, in the morning, at about 10 a.m. When I motioned that I didn't understand and continued walking, he tried to express himself, like a mime and said: flirt, flirt. The French have love on their mind the moment they get up in the morning. We grew up so repressed, while they expressed themselves so openly and innocently. That was a revelation.

Another revelation was the way of getting our tickets. It showed me that corruption was everywhere. How Ungar divided up the sum of money with the people from the Cunard Line, a British company, I don't know. Yet without the graft, things did not move, no way. It taught me that the Romanians were not alone in accepting "baksheesh" (bribe). They did the same in the West, with a vengeance. That corruption bothered me, too. Later, my brothers told me that when they came to the gentleman in Williamsburg, to pay double for the tickets, he would not give them a receipt.

He said that this transaction works "on trust." It cost $1500 instead of $750 and that was a lot of money to hand out in 1947, without being sure that they were not a couple of swindlers. Yet they paid, they knew that it was imperative for the parents to leave. The man gave the signal, the tickets became available.

The sadness when meeting my ailing Father and distressed Mother threw a pall over everything at my arrival in Paris. The thought that had one of their sons come to Paris in July and perhaps eased their trip to America sooner, perhaps he could have been saved; perhaps Father's life could have been prolonged; perhaps their lonesomeness could have been eased. One could see that Father was dying. In that situation, I could not really enjoy Paris. Besides, going to America was an unknown for me. At Columbia University, the semester had already started in the first week of September and here I was, in the middle of October. I arrived in New York on October 17, 1947.

Crossing the Atlantic took one week. Most of the passengers were Americans of English, Irish or Scottish descent, who had visited their families, for the first time after the war.

The food on the boat consisted mostly of fish, all kinds of seafood that I had never eaten before, that I knew only from reading and from dictionaries. Whether it was turbot or cod or hake or even salmon - everything was boiled and tasteless. To make matters worse, the ocean turned very stormy and I could hardly eat at all. The passengers could not place me, where I came from. I spoke English but differently from the Americans or the English. They found it hard to believe that anybody, coming from the Balkans would speak English, anyway. My room mate, the future "rebbetzin" was so seasick, she feared to get out of her bunk, in our cabin.

The night before our arrival, the storm was so severe that the boat anchored in the middle of the night and practically everybody came out of the cabins because of the commotion. As it stopped for a few hours, we could not arrive with the tide, in the morning but 12 hours later, in the evening. It was the first time that the Queen Elizabeth came in 12 hours late. That was the headline, in all the New York newspapers.

Everybody was excited, full of expectations and trepidation. We saw the Statue of Liberty, from afar - an impressive sight. The woman, who was travelling with me had not seen her son in years, had lost her husband during the war and was going to meet her intended new mate. I was going to see my family after so many years. When Eli left, I was five. Betty and Bernie saw me last when I was ten; Gertie when I was fourteen and Sali had left home ten years previously. I was 27 years old but had gone through troubles that could count for a hundred. Of course, there were uncles and aunts, in-laws, nieces and nephews, cousins.

The arrival turned out to be as complicated as everything that had preceded that event. Only the parents remained in the Bronx, where they were staying with Bernie and Connie since their arrival the week before. Father was too sick to travel; everybody else waited at the pier. When all had disembarked, I was left on the ship - the only passenger out of 2000 not to be allowed to disembark.

My family was told about difficulties with my documents. Somebody should come to the boat next day at ten, when the Immigration would take me to Ellis Island. The reason for not admitting me was my Romanian passport. It was valid for another three months only. Romania had turned communist lately and the immigration officials did not know how to proceed. They told me that, at that point, a passport had to be renewed or extended for another year, otherwise I would have to return on this same boat, back to Europe.

The ship, that was so elegant and animated when in use, looked like a death boat, at night. The crew took off all bedding, all the tableclothes and dishes, glasses and silver. It was dark and quiet and enormous; you heard some creaking noises at night.

Next morning, at 10 a.m. an official from the immigration called me to come down the gang plank. I looked around to see whether anybody from my family was there. I recognized my brother Bernie. When he saw me walk down, he approached us. I asked Bernie whether he had a car. When he affirmed, I asked the immigration officer whether he would mind going with me to the Romanian consulate, for I was sure that they would renew my passport right away; if not, he could then take me to Ellis Island. I made a sign to Bernie not to say anything. First the officer was surprised that a newcomer could speak English, then it seemed like a logical step to take. Bernie looked up the address of the consulate, then he drove there and I, flanked by an immigration official and my brother, asked the Romanian officials to extend my passport and they did, right on the spot, for six months.

We said goodbye to the immigration official and there I was, with my brother, in his car, going to the Bronx. Bernie called Connie to tell her that we were finally on the way home. There was no big reception for me as expected the day before, everything complicated, as usual. However, in the long run, things worked out.

Chapter 10

New York

It was the middle of October, 1947 and I finally arrived at the hoped for destination. I first met Bernie and his wife Connie and their 18 month old daughter Judy. In the afternoon and evening of that first day Eli and my sisters and their husbands and children came - sister Betty and her husband Nat and Frances, five years old and the twins Martin and Irving, two and a half; Gertie and then husband Jacques and Esther, the oldest of the next generation, seven years old; Sali with Willie and Allan four and Susan, a baby six months old. Eli was not married yet. My uncles and their wives: Max with Marge and Morris with Syd. That evening they were supposed to meet the family of their son Jack's fiancee, Rae Lynn. There were endless cousins all from Mother's side. They had all come the week before to meet my parents; now most of them came to see me - we were the event of the year, the survivors of the Stadler and Schleien families. Sad, but true, that so many never made it out of Europe alive.

The seriousness of Father's illness set in right away. Bernie took Father to the Sloan Kettering Hospital or Cancer Memorial, as it was called then. The diagnosis made by Dr. Falk in Paris was confirmed. After exploratory surgery, the well-know surgeon, Dr. Peck, decided that it was too late to operate successfully, that the cancer had spread too far, it had metastasized from the stomach to the liver. The best we could hope for was six months. My Father lived exactly seven months longer, a time of intense suffering for him and for us.

However, life in America began to take shape. Since we came soon after the end of the war, there were many people, who wanted to hear from an actual survivor, what had happened in the Bukovina. Bernie was approached by Mr. Eisenberg from the Bukoviner Society whether I would be willing to talk to some "Landsleute" about what had happened during the war years, in their old home. I agreed.

A few days after my arrival, he came to pick me up, accompanied by Bernie. We went to Manhattan Center, a hotel in New York City. I did not realize that a meeting of the Bukoviner Society had been called and hundreds of people showed up. I was completely unaware that so many people would attend, eager to hear about the events that had taken place in the part of the world from where they and I originated. The difference was tremendous - they were sheltered during the war years, while I could tell them only about a holocaust in their former home. The unusual attraction seemed to revolve also around the fact that the "green" one spoke English.

Although I was not prepared to deliver a speech, yet when asked to say anything I wanted, I spoke to them for over one hour. You could hear a pin drop. I don't remember exactly what I said, the gist must have been the events in Czernovitz during the years 1940-45. People came afterwards for information about their families, people that they had been unable to locate after the war. Of course, I knew very few. Yet I put one family in touch with their mother and brother, whom I happened to know very well. Bernie was there with me and witnessed the way some were thirsting for news about families and friends.

To my great astonishment, my own family never asked for details about our life during the awful years. Whether they did not want to hear about our privations, to spare their own feelings or did not want to bring up memories, in order to spare us reliving them or whether they felt guilty, in their own minds, about not having cared to think about it during those elapsed years or whether they had come to term with the thought that millions were destroyed in Europe and their family, too. I never reached a conclusion about that matter.

My sister Sali once said to me that no experience whatever can rival the experience of giving birth to children, the way she had. Of course, it was naive to have expressed oneself that way, especially since she was a very bright woman. She could not accept the fact that I had gone through any more powerful experiences that she had. In time, I myself had two children - but who, in his right mind, would compare a human function, like childbirth, to the horror gone through by my parents and myself. So they thought it preferable not to discuss it, so as not to make us feel as martyrs or that we deserved extra consideration. Even the great attention lavished on us initially by my uncles was somehow resented.

Related to the way my brothers and sisters communicated with each other, there was a difference in approach from the way I was used. During the several years, previous to my arrival in the States, when somebody needed something, one just asked. If the other person could do it for you, she would and vice versa. People were more direct and they helped one another. There was not much time for indirection, for formalities. In New York, where I found myself, people were saying: How are you? and the other person invariably answered: Fine. After having observed this for a few days, I asked aunt Syd why people always said: fine. Don't they sometimes feel sick or low or upset? She answered categorically that people don't want to hear about other people's troubles. They have enough troubles of their own. If you call somebody and he or she is going to tell you lots of bad news, then you won't call again. So I realized that people present a façade and you don't penetrate that façade easily.

Coming back to the evolving home life. Bernie and Connie were preparing to move to Florida; Eli was making preparations to buy a house in Brooklyn, for himself and for us. All three sisters were residing there and it was natural to be moving to that borough. Eli got a low mortgage as a veteran of World War II and some help from Mother's brother Morris. Thus, Bernie spent a few weeks with us, before leaving New York, in the fall of 1947. He took Father to the doctors, helped me register in Queens College, for the remainder of the semester, since I had missed the start of the term at Columbia.

What were other first impressions? Bernie warned me to avoid answering, if cousin Ben would ask me: How do you say "fire" in Romanian? In English, it is a four letter word, that starts with the letter 'f'. I would feel embarrassed if I answered and others would laugh. This way I learned my first four letter word, from my own brother.

My Mother was amazed about the availability and abundance of all that food; about chickens without feathers; about borscht in a jar. I was astounded about the variety of foods in a super market, about the packaging, about the great array of fruits and vegetables available so readily in autumn. There were many kinds that I had never seen before. To my surprise, I was told that everything could be had all year round. I was struck by the idea of washing machines. It had not occurred to me that human hands could be replaced even to that extent. The highways and the bridges astonished my Father greatly, especially the bridges.

My sisters seemed so different from the way I remembered them. Sali, the one closest in age, mother of two children. Her tone of voice had changed; she spoke German or Yiddish with an English accent. The brothers-in-law, all so different from people that I used to know: Betty's husband Nat - distant; Sali's husband Willie - friendly and enthusiastic; Gertie's Jacques - a real character, a devout Communist, who told me that I didn't understand what I saw when I criticized the Soviet system.

My cousins, close in age to me: Jack Stadler, one year older than myself, had just got engaged the week when I arrived and Albert, a few years younger - none of them could talk to the newly arrived uncle and aunt, since they spoke only English. My aunts were elegant American women, dressed in silk and fur, with diamond rings and charm bracelets and other bracelets as heavy as chains. Their moving hands were jangling, they were playing a symphony in gold. The style of these people was so different from mine. They were as strange to me as I must have looked to them.

That fall of 1947, women's fashions had changed entirely. While I left Bucharest, went through Europe for a month, a new 'look' was launched in Paris by Christian Dior. Skirts were long, coats big and long, a sloppy style, a 'new look', the Dior style.

My Mother's brothers, Max and Morris Stadler, treated me with love and admiration. They loved me also for the fact that I seemed to have saved their only sister, to whom they were very devoted, as long as they lived. Max was going to pay my tuition, Morris offered to furnish the house, that Eli bought under the G.I. bill. They were as good as their word and more. They were proud of this girl who came straight from the boat to the Graduate School for a master's degree at Columbia University, where it used to be almost impossible for Jewish students to be admitted.

However, I had missed the start of the fall semester and had to register at Queens College, for English courses. The Immigration authorities had decreed that a person, on a student visa, had to be enrolled in an academic institution if he or she came late to a specific school. Thus, foreign students, from all over the New York area, came to the English Department at Queens, for that particular purpose. It was not easy to commute from the Bronx to Queens and one month later, from Brooklyn to Queens. I had to change three or four trains and finally a bus. I learned, first hand, what commuting at rush hour meant, right from the start.

My two aunts - Syd and Marge - felt that I needed some clothes in my new co-ed life. They took me to Lerner's for some blouses, new style long skirts, a dressy dress and a double-breasted camel's hair coat, college style.

It may have been the first time that my aunts set foot in Lerner's; after all, I was only an immigrant.

Queens College proved to be an experience, rather interesting, often amusing and all very new. Since it was a recently founded college, there was only one four story building, the rest were temporary structures, more like army barracks. The area of the campus was large, but barren and desolate looking. Here and there were some quonset huts - one served as a bookstore. In the vicinity was one Greek diner. Of course, I could not imagine then that, many years later, I'd be living in this area, bring up my children here. In time, this college became an educational center for tens of thousands of students. That one building, that I mentioned, is the oldest now on a very large campus. But, of course, that was almost 40 years ago.

We had three instructors for the foreigners: Gries, Kurz and Makris. We were grouped in three sections, according to knowledge of the language and proficiency in speaking. I was in the most advanced group. Since there was no real program, we had mostly conversation. The teachers were curious about the customs of the different countries, the foods, the cultural backgrounds of the students. Most came from wealthy, influential families. The teacher once told about a student, in the previous semester, an Arab prince, who when asked what he missed most since coming to the Stats, said he was used to move around on horseback. He missed his horse.

Soon after the war, travel for studies from one part of the world to another was still rare. Only the very rich could offer that to their children. Among the students was a very lovely Swiss girl, daughter of a watch manufacturer; there was a daughter of a Swedish shipping magnate; the young Turkish wife of a doctor from Afghanistan, who came to specialize in America. He was the son of the prime minister of his country; the daughter of the Turkish representative to the United Nations. There were Iranians, Greeks and a Venezuelan. I was the only Romanian. After the war most people in Europe remained impoverished. To send a daughter or son to study overseas was the epitome of luxury. I happened to fall into this group by my unusual circumstances.

At the onset of the Christmas vacation, the Turkish diplomatic family invited the entire group to a party in their home on Long Island. That was the most elegant reception that I had ever been at. Musicians played on the upper balcony, while the guests were talking, eating a sumptuous Turkish buffet, dancing afterwards. I had a small golden pin attached to my blouse. Evi's cousin had sold it to me in Bucharest as scrap, cheap. At the party, a Turkish diplomat approached me and spoke to me in Turkish. It turned out that my pin was the emblem of the sultans of Turkey, before the country became a republic under Attaturk. He thought that it was an heirloom in my family. The only time I was mistaken for a Turk.

When I told him that I came from Romania, he enjoyed that fact even more, since he had been a Turkish consul in Romania, before his assignment to the United Nations. There were many interesting incidents during that short time, about three months, at Queens College, from October 1947 till mid January 1948.

One of the teachers invited us to his house, where we played bingo with him, his wife and young son. He wanted us to see a typical American family, in a typical Queens home, very modest even for 1947. These sophisticated people, sons and daughters of magnates and diplomats and bankers thought the environment so provincial, kind of Archie Bunker like.

One of the young men called me up one day and said that he would like to visit me. "Of course, come to-morrow" I said and gave him my address in Brooklyn. Before he arrived, he sent me a magnificent arrangement of flowers. We had moved to Brooklyn in November and had the essentially necessary furniture, but no flower vase. When the flowers arrived, I used two borscht jars to put them in.

Carlos Bendayan arrived and we talked and talked. He was the son of a wealthy Sephardic family from Venezuela. Carlos was a young man, about 21, on his first trip abroad alone. He was telling me that he realized that I must be Jewish and it became clear to me that I knew very little about Sepharadim. His name was Hebrew, it meant: son of the judge. He was going to spend the Christmas vacation with his parents and younger brother in Spain. Actually, he was being groomed to enter his father's business.

Of course, I lost touch with the students from the Queens College course. The only things that remained are two pictures with them and very fond memories. There were two Iranian brothers, Jewish. One confided in me by saying: "Wouldn't it be heaven if we could marry whomever we wanted? But I have to look for an American girl, in order to remain here; you probably have to find an American man." I lost touch with all of them.

In November, about one month after our arrival, we moved to 611 Remsen Avenue, Brooklyn. It was small, new two-family house, within walking distance to Betty and Gertie. The proximity of a synagogue and a kosher butcher store were a conditio sine qua non. We had two bedrooms: one for the parents, the other for Eli, while I slept on a convertible sofa in the living room.

Father was getting weaker and weaker and eventually bed-ridden and we knew that it could only worsen. The sisters had young children and thus busy home lives. They would visit whenever they could. Father, being so sick could hardly stand the noise that youngsters make or the running around in the apartment. That was the saddest part of his life's end: what he expected most fervently, the joys of grandfatherhood - all this never happened. He suffered in stoic silence, he never complained about his fate, he accepted God's will. Once, he mentioned to me that he probably has the same sickness as his rabbi. His rabbi had died of cancer.

Eli had been used to living alone or very early on, with Gertie. Here, he lived with the 'Europeans', whose ways were a little different. When I came, he first called me 'the child'. I was the youngest in the family and really a child of five, when he had seen me last. However, twenty two years had elapsed since and the child grew into a mature person of 27. For him the transition was hard to breach. Somehow, Sali could not accept that easily either. She was the older sister, who always knew better, when we were at home. She left at age 21 and I was seventeen. Yet ten years in between were a rough school for survival. She could also not readily accept that I had grown up and had been steeled by a hard life.

Coming back to life in Brooklyn, with the parents and Eli. Whenever he doubted whether something was right, he consulted with Gertie, whose judgment he always accepted as decisive. He often questioned Mother's opinions or decisions as well as mine. That made Mother unsure of whatever she did, even in small, daily matters. He was very soft-spoken, kindly and well intentioned, yet he could quietly say something to the effect that you don't know what you are talking about or you don't know what you are doing. Father was too sick to listen or to care and Mother was too proud to show how much some observations hurt. I understood it well, for he did not spare me with his observations, although he would call me 'honeychild'. As much as I disliked this treatment, I never argued with him, but I hoped that it would not be for long.

Gertie had been helpful in getting me information and application forms for New York University as well as Columbia. I am certain that she felt happy about our coming to the States. Yet, soon after coming here, we realized that there were tensions between her and the others, except for Eli. He was very much under her influence and he asked for her advice about every detail of daily life. Later on, when he married Charlotte in 1956, she took over and dominated him completely. Strange enough, after her death in 1973, her reverted back to Gertie and stayed under her sway until the day he died. (1978)

Thus, we suffered first and most because of Father and besides, because we had become dependent, where before, we had been people in our own right, allowed our own minds. My uncles understood how difficult life was for the newcomers.

They would visit very often, trying to keep my parents company and cheer us up.

Mother's medical problem recurred, again a growth on the lip. While in Bucharest it caused months of medical treatment, here it was taken care of with one small surgical intervention by a skin specialist. There were the usual problems of daily life, a routine was supposed to set in. Mother had to get used to shop for food, but things were different - everything in the supermarket came in boxes, with names incomprehensible to her. Being a woman with a certain pride, she felt like an illiterate, apprehensive about the fact that people may make fun of her, may snicker behind her back. Eli was at work and I was in school and she had to try to get used to the new circumstances. Betty tried to be of help, but she had three small children, Frances was five and the twins just over two years old. Mother, a woman in her sixties, found it hard to adapt to new and fundamental changes around her. Her children supported the household, yet everything else weighted heavily, especially her gravely ill husband.

All of us were intensely caught up in the activities of the United Nations, in Lake Success. The fall of 1947 proved to be the decisive period in the creation of the State of Israel. I listened to the radio and read avidly about the deliberations that led to the hoped for vote of November 29, 1947. That was the day when the United Nations voted for the partition plan of Palestine with a Jewish State and an Arab State. I was corresponding with Yuda frequently as well as with my friends in Bucharest. Later on, friends in Israel told me that my detailed reports about the U.N. deliberations and the decision in November, 1947, were read with great interest in Bucharest and were passed from hand to hand - an eye-witness report. All my friends started to make preparations for emigration to Israel; all of them left within the next few years.

At that time T.V. was in its infancy; we did not have one at the time, but radio and the press kept people well informed. To me, the birth of Israel was the beginning of the solution for all the survivors in Europe, eventually including myself. At that time, the Jewish survivors, most of them homeless, were trying legally or illegally to reach the shores of Palestine and were sometimes interned in camps in Cyprus or one boatload was even returned to Hamburg, Germany. The creation of Israel proved as important to me as to all the homeless in Europe, since I did not feel that I had a home, for good. Within two years I myself left the United States to settle in Israel.

Coming back to my situation, at the time. To study for a Master's degree in Modern American Literature and Comparative Word Literature seemed like preparation for a profession without a future. Since I was greatly interested in world affairs and politics, I inquired about such studies but was told that they accepted only American citizens. Thus I embarked on the study of literature in February, 1948 and commuted daily from Brooklyn to Columbia University.

In the first semester, I had to take two extra courses in the School of General Studies, besides the regular load of credits in the Graduate School, Department of Philosophy. The extra were a speech course, including phonetics. The other requirement for a foreign student was Composition, taught by William Kunstler, the now well-known lawyer, dedicated to the defense of radical defendants. He was then a literary critic, before going off to law school.

The studies at the graduate school were demanding, since I really had no knowledge of American literature. Here and there, I had read a book by Upton Sinclair or Jack London or Sinclair Lewis. Here I was among all top American students, the only foreigner. I had to catch up so much, that by the time the written exam approached, I read a book daily. I completed the master's in three semesters, from February 1948 to June 1949. During the summer months of 1949, I wrote the thesis, which was accepted in October of that year.

Imagine, in such a short time to read all of Henry James, Willa Cather, all of Thomas Wolfe, Hemingway, Steinbeck and more and more. Of course, lots of poetry: T.S. Eliot, Walt Whitman, Robert Frost and many more. Well, once I started, I just went ahead non-stop.

The first semester was tough; my Father was nearing his end. Immigration did not give me a respite either. By May 1948, I had to renew the Romanian passport in order to extend the student visa. That matter was complicated. If I applied for an extension and was refused - I would have no more passport and would be stateless. Through friends in Bucharest, I got a recommendation to the Romanian cultural attaché in Washington. He was

Jewish and somebody that I knew was acquainted with him. The connection was established. Uncle Max and his wife Marge drove me to Washington on a Friday morning, the fourth of May. We were supposed to remain there over the week-end and return Monday.

I would visit the cultural attaché on Friday afternoon, at his home and on Monday, with a bit of luck, the Consul would extend my passport.

I said good bye to my parents on Thursday evening, kissed my Father and wished him a good night. We slept over in Max's house and left Friday morning, as planned. I was received with great friendliness by the attaché and his family and left with some assurance of success. Saturday morning Eli called Max at the Mayflower Hotel, where we were residing, and told him that Father had died in the morning hours. Of course, we returned home on Saturday and on Sunday, May 6, 1948 was Father's funeral. He had been so interested in the deliberations at the U.N., before the Declaration of Independence of the State of Israel, which occurred on May 15, 1948, about nine days after his death. Father was buried on the Stadler family plot, on Mount Hebron Cemetery in Queens, where my Mother's parents (my grandparents) and her brothers rest in peace. Mother survived Father by 23 years; she was laid to rest, next to him, in 1971.

Although we had been aware of his hopeless condition, yet we lived with it day by day and still got some moments of pleasure and joy from his presence and he from ours. I used to come home from school, go into his room and he would invariably ask me, the way he did during the war years in Czernovitz: "What's new in the little town?" (This is a rough translation of a Yiddish expression; one could also say: What are the rumors in the shtetl?) The idea was always - to bring some reassuring news, some ray of light or hope.

The parents would read the Jewish newspaper daily and listen to the Yiddish news programs on the radio, yet the question remained as before - to bring some joyful news from the 'little town', now New York. I tried to cheer him up and would usually tell about new developments connected with the creation of the State of Israel.

Really, the three of us had come out from bondage and we had that in common. Those years had somehow glued us together. Although I could more easily adapt to the New World than my parents, I was the strong link between the two worlds - of the then yesterday and the now, the present. We had some little expressions, hints, that were the common bond, that were just ours. They were made up of our common experiences of antisemitism, endured in Romania, of sudden Russian oppression, the dread of the Germans

- the twin dictatorships of Stalin and Hitler. We had felt squeezed from all sides and lived through it together, forging a strong bond.

I knew that the unavoidable would happen soon and would free him from his travail. The last few weeks, a nurse had taken care of Father because Mother was exhausted. The end was no surprise, but when it happened, I felt especially hurt not to have been at home.

When I came to the U.S., I did not fully realize how wounded I was, how much I hurt. Life went on day by day with a lot of activity and no time to stop and reflect. Nobody asked me essentially how I felt and I gave no expression to my feelings. Perhaps, it may have made a difference if anybody would have 'de-briefed' me. Father's sickness, my studies and everybody's busy life with families and children - in this situation, everything from before was unacknowledged, unresolved. These are facts and nobody is blamed for them.

I had to see a doctor, for during the previous years my female functions were completely irregular. They stopped for over one year, at a time. This happened to many women during those times of great distress.

Later, when I met a group of students in the seminar on American Literature, I could not relate to them as well as I would have liked to. The girls talked a lot about fashion, about clothes, which to me seemed unimportant. Whenever we ate lunch in the cafeteria, they made disparaging remarks about food, like: "What is that junk?" or "This sandwich tastes like garbage". I could physically not tolerate people throwing away food or talking that way about a meal. In my mind, starvation and want were still there. Although people did not discuss with me anything about it, I did not tell them how I felt about their remarks. I was still hurt deeply. To this day, I can not throw out any food.

After sitting shiva for a week, I went alone to Washington and received a renewal of the passport, but only for three months. I had missed two sessions of the writing course, where we had weekly assignments. When I came again, Kunstler was very solicitous. He understood what had happened, he knew me as a newcomer from Europe after the Holocaust. I once wrote a description of a city: Prague. He read it to the class and gave me an A plus. He knew that it was one of the stops on my way to America. He was greatly interested in the events in Europe and I conveyed to him, first hand information and some of my thoughts about the war years.

Well, the first term was over. All during that time, I used to have the writing course in the evening and another course next morning. Morris and

Syd proposed to me to stay overnight, in order to spare me going home to Brooklyn late at night and travelling again next morning. Theirs was a very pleasant, comfortable home on West 86th Street; very close to Columbia. During that time I had occasion to get better acquainted with Jack, his wife Rae Lynn and with Albert. We had many animated discussions about all kinds of subjects. I really liked Albert very much; he was interested in literature, he talked well about art since he was studying it and slowly evolving into a painter. I probably told him some things about Europe and about earlier years. During the war Jack served in the Pacific and Albert in Europe.

The School of General Studies conferred grades, while in graduate school there were no exams at all. When one had taken 30 credits and had gone through a seminar in Modern American Lit., where one chose the topic for the master thesis, then there were two days of written exams: a four hour written exam in the major and next day a four hour written test in the minor. If one passed both, then one had to complete the thesis, the topic of which had been chosen and the work already started in the seminar course.

Since the amount of work for Modern American Literature was so overwhelming, I did not prepare at all for the Comparative Lit. I hoped that my previous knowledge sufficed - and it did. In June 1949 I passed the exams and wrote the thesis during the summer: "European Criticism of the Works of John Steinbeck." It was accepted in October, 1949. That was the end of my studies - three semesters at Columbia University, proud possessor of a degree from an American university. The diploma was signed by the president of the university, Dwight D. Eisenhower, later to become president of the United States.

Of course, many interesting incidents happened during these studies; some of the teachers were outstanding; I learned a lot about the literary establishment around Columbia, about new authors, about the theater. I read more than ever before - out of necessity. Before the two days of exams, I slept just a few hours nightly, for the number of books to be read was insane and I made a maximum effort. After all, how could I dare disappoint my family? How could I disappoint Max, who paid my tuition? Yet, I don't know how I accomplished it. I was like caught in a whirlpool and kept going, going. I remember, one night, my Mother woke up at 4 a.m. and asked me why I was up so early, yet I had not gone to sleep yet. I had to finish a novel every day, no matter how long it took.

Some impressions about Columbia. The dean, who advised me what courses to take, was none other than Prof. Oscar Hamilton, a famous Shake-spearean scholar. He took time to talk to me about my interests and my former studies. I told him about my abiding interest in the theater and thus he recommended me to take the Drama course taught by Joseph Wood Krutch. He was, by that time, an influential drama critic and a most admired professor. At the first lecture I realized what a gold mine I had struck. A big lecture hall was completely filled, half were probably not his students. People just flocked to hear him.

The man had a fairly plain appearance, with a walrus-type, sandy colored moustache. When he came in, with a broad brimmed, shapeless hat and coat, he looked like a pauper. His voice was that of an asthmatic, wheezing and short of breath. Yet when he spoke, you heard a brilliant, witty, charming, inventive speaker, a man of enormous literary knowledge and sharp judgment. His reading list was long and one was expected to read the plays before he lectured about them. Whenever there had been an opening night a day or two before, it was expected of him to express his opinion of the play and the performance, before writing his critique in the "Nation".

Following such expert guidance and advice, I saw a number of outstanding plays on Broadway, like: "A Streetcar Named Desire" with Marlon Brando; "Washington Square" with Basil Rathbone and Wendy Hiller; "Man and Su-perman" with Maurice Evans and few more of unusual caliber; comedies like: "Born Yesterday" and "Bells are Ringing," the latter with the unforgettable comedienne Judy Holiday.

By the time Professor Krutch retired from Columbia, he moved to Ari-zona and embarked on a new profession: biologist. He studied the ecology of the desert. In his autobiography, he asserts that the ideal would be to change professions every seven years. He started out originally to become a mathematician, was a biographer, writer, critic, professor and, later in life, a biologist. He appeared several times on national T.V. in 1958-9, discussing the fauna and flora of Arizona and of Baja California. It was my privilege to be his student. On T.V. I relished the sight of him and the sound of his voice. His autobiography "More Lives than One" gives the whole pic-ture of this universal man, the life of this extraordinary intellectual, of his unbounded curiosity and depth of observation.

At that time there was one real cult figure at Columbia - Lionel Trilling, who was teaching Modern American Literature. At the time, I was not aware of the New York group of intellectuals and critics, many of them left-wing. I did not know about the different currents just below the surface, about the shades of red or pink in the literary establishment. To me, at the time, Trilling was the name of a professor, whose course I had to take.

His admirers were there basking in his sun. They savored every word he uttered; they listened to the special tone of his voice. When asked about a writer or a book, his answer or just a motion of his hand, made or destroyed that author in the student's minds. He was great at debunking. I came with no preconceptions and I really did not care for him or his lectures too much. I found him affected, bathing in the adoration by which he was surrounded.

After all that I have read about him since, I may have looked at him differently, perhaps interpreted his opinions more carefully. His name comes up in works by Alfred Kazin, Mary McCarthy and many others. Some considered that he was the 'token Jew' at Columbia, at the time.

Some of the professors were great scholars, but dry as bone. I had no personal contact with any of them, except for the woman teacher, who led our seminar and was my thesis adviser. Since I had no exams, the contact with the teachers was non-existent. All were lecture classes, with great numbers of students - candidates for masters and ph.d. degrees.

The seminar group had some cohesion, as we were all preparing for the same final exam and also presented topics for class discussion. Of the dozen participants in the seminar, about half were Jewish. After the Second World War, all those returned from the service were entitled to free education, under a new G.I. bill of rights. The soldiers of yesterday became the students of most colleges and universities, including the Ivy League schools. That law opened widely the doors of academic institutions to students of all social and religious backgrounds.

One episode in the seminar remained vividly in my mind, especially since I was painfully sensitive to antisemitism. Each of us chose a topic for presentation in the framework of our studies, to the group and the professor. There followed a discussion. I chose to deliver a kind of lecture on American Catholic Writers. As an introduction, I underlined the differences between Catholic, Protestant and Greek-Orthodox Christian dogma and on what levels Catholics see life and relations among people in a different way. Then I talked about some of the Catholic writers. There followed a lively discussion and the whole session was animated and interesting.

One of the students, whom I did not know well, approached me afterwards and complimented me on the exposé. He knew little about the Greek-Orthodox branch of Christianity and he thought that life in Romania gave me that background. He then invited me to his house, he and his wife, a young actress, lived close to Columbia. I enjoyed my lunch with them, on that spring day in April, 1948.

The two of them invited me to visit them during the Easter vacation, at a prestigious university in New Hampshire, where his father was a professor. They thought that I would enjoy to see a smaller school in New England. I loved the idea and accepted the invitation, but had to check the date at home.

A few days later, I received a charming note from his mother, with directions to the town; my fellow student and his wife would pick me up at the bus stop.

When I figured out the dates, Passover coincided with Easter. This happened about one month before my Father's death. I did not want to leave home on Passover, the last seder we spent together. I answered immediately, thanked for the invitation but explained that Passover happened to be at the same time and that I had to celebrate it with my parents. My fellow student had not been aware that I was Jewish for I had spoken with such knowledge about the Christian religion. It must have come as a shock, a surprise. However, after the Easter vacation, he hardly said 'hallo' to me, he absolutely ignored me. I thought how odd I would have felt, had they found out about my Jewishness while I was their house guest. This incident happened during my first semester at Columbia.

When we all graduated, we all exchanged addresses, telephone numbers except for him. He kept aloof, away from the Jewish colleagues. Not that the others kept in touch, but, at least, there was a semblance of closeness. Once in a while I see a volume of poetry published by him and the fly page announces that he is a professor of English at a university in the State of New York.

It hurt enough at the time, because I never forgot it after almost four decades. I felt deeply disappointed then because I had hoped that the U.S., a democratic country, instilled revulsion at the inhumanity with which we had been treated. When a simple Joe hated Jews, I thought that he was just ignorant; when a sophisticated young poet, son of intellectuals from New England felt that way - that hurt worse.

I thought that the only real solution would be a life in Israel. That thought ripened as the years 1948, 49 progressed and finally, I considered it my solution by going to Israel, as soon as my studies were accomplished.

At Christmas time, 1948, my uncles offered me a special treat. They visited Mother, while I was in Queens to see visiting friends from Bucharest.

Max and Morris thought it would be a good idea for me to visit Bernie and his family in Miami. Morris called me at the Teitelbaums and asked whether I was afraid of flying. Of course, I had never flown - but, of course, I was not afraid.

They reserved a ticket for me; I came home in a hurry and by 11 p.m. that night I was on my way to Florida, from Newark. (Kennedy Airport had not been in existence yet).

Bernie did not even know about my arrival. It was a glorious morning when I landed. I took a taxi and reached his house around five in the morning. Not wanting to wake them up, I sat in front of the house and watched the lovely, sunny surroundings - palm trees and flowering bushes, a delight to the eye. When somebody stirred inside, I rang the bell.

Florida was the first sub-tropical area that I had ever seen: colorful bougainvillaea and oleander, palm trees - they looked so exotic to me. Bernie and Connie took me to see different worth while sights and to the beaches with coconut trees. What a delight to see a real coconut. Neighbors called the Miami Herald, to tell them about the European visitor. They came to interview me and next day I was photographed at the Herald headquarters. They published an article with my picture next day. Those were exciting 8 days.

I still remember a dinner at the Miami restaurant: "Fran and Bill's," where my Uncle Max was a part owner. I wondered why a serving for a person could feed three. The same applied for the main dish as well as the dessert. Bernie explained that at a good restaurant, where they charge steep prices, it was the accepted way to serve much more than one could consume. I wondered at the awful waste.

Wherever I looked, I saw waste. Yet people thought nothing of throwing out food that could feed thousands upon thousands. They took me to see dog races, which are the most nonsensical type of sports. When the mechanical dog fell over, every racing dog stopped and went its own way. That visit to Florida was a lovely change and a pleasant time, away from books, the subway and the real problems, which did not go away; they were just disregarded for a little while, put on the back burner. Although I had no real clashes with Eli, yet little incidents, of trivial importance, soured our relationship.

My sisters had young children and were often confined to the house, tied down with family responsibilities. Although my situation was completely unsettled, yet I could move freely, go places unfettered, unhindered by family ties.

While I was a student at Columbia, Bard College, at Hastings-on-Hudson, upstate New York, organized a symposium on world affairs. It was convened for a three day spring week-end, in April, 1949, all expenses paid by Bard. I was approached to participate as a representative of Romania and I accepted. I still remember, when I came home and told about it, one of my sisters asked incredulously: "Are you going to go?" with an undertone: of course, not. However, I had gladly accepted the invitation. I still remember fondly the very interesting people that I met and the discussions we had. Bard College was in the proximity of Hyde Park, the ancestral home of the Roosevelts. Mrs. Roosevelt was one of the hostesses. On the third day, on Sunday, we were her guests at Hyde Park.

Adolph Berle, Jr., former Undersecretary of State conducted the symposium, which consisted of three panels. I was on the military panel. After I had expressed my views, he asked me whether I would hand him in an exposé, in writing, which I did. On the same panel was a student, originally from Yaffa, in Israel. After talking about world problems and whether there were military solutions for international grievances, he said to me: If I were in Yaffa and you were there, too, we would be deadly enemies. Yet, as we are sitting here, discussing the problem, we can be good friends. - Thinking about the same problem to-day, the situation has not changed one bit, after 37 years. In 1949, war was raging in Israel. To-day, the situation has still no solution, the enmity remained the same.

Mrs. Roosevelt talked about the difficulties of formulating the Bill of Rights for the United Nations, where she was head of that committee. When she addressed the International Student Conference, we were all full of expectation. Her voice was shrill, high-pitched and not too pleasant at first. Within a few minutes, you were enthralled by her warmth, her humanity, her genuine concern for the people of this world. We had a most enjoyable evening, with food and drink and a chance to meet her as well as all the professors from Bard College.

On the third day, Sunday, we were guests of Mrs. Roosevelt, in Hyde Park. She gave us a conducted tour through the house, the Museum, which houses all the presents that the president had received, while in office, and to the garden and we stopped at the grave of F.D.R. That remained a very special week-end, a memorable highlight during my two years as a student. I still possess a snapshot, which a Greek student took of me in front of the Roosevelt Estate in Hyde Park, New York.

During those eventful years in New York, besides studying intensely, I also went to museums, shows, lectures; I even joined a Zionist group, with whom I sometimes went on hikes, on Sunday. One woman from this group settled in Israel soon after me and we remained in touch for a while. I stayed in touch with a girl, who was a ph.d. candidate. I helped her with her Latin, which used to be a requirement as a classical language. By that time, I still knew it well but have mostly forgotten since.

In 1949, while the War of Independence was raging in Israel, I had written to Yuda that I was about to decide to come to settle there. He served in the engineering corps from May, 1948 till the end of May, 1949 and had one more year of studies at the Technion. At that time I knew that by October 49 I would be getting my master degree.

Two months later, on December 21, 1949 I embarked on the liner La-Guardia, destination Haifa and landed there on January 3, 1950.

Chapter 11

The Decision

My parents were hoping and dreaming for years to finally be reunited with the family in the States. Their expectations for a life among their sons and daughters was like the proverbial 'to see the light at the end of the tunnel,' to arrive at this almost illusory goal. All the striving was directed toward that end, toward that day, when they would finally set foot on American soil. They would not consider any plan without me. Plans were therefore made for all three of us.

The parents could receive a preferential visa, I would have to wait for my turn on the quota, as an immigrant, which could take many years of wait. My family suggested my coming as a graduate student. The plan worked, as a temporary solution. In the long run nothing led to a logical, practical conclusion: what would happen by the time my studies were over? My passport would expire and I was unwilling to return to Eastern Europe. I had no right to work, since I was not an immigrant. Nobody in my family would consider my working illegally as an option.

After the end of the war, thousands of Jewish survivors, from different concentration camps started roaming all over Europe, in search of a place to call home. Most of these homeless people desired to settle in Israel, some waited to reach the U.S.A. The Western countries were debating how to handle the problem of the 'displaced persons' or D.P.s, a termed coined at the time.

As for myself, I qualified under that category. We consulted a lawyer about my status and he advised waiting, since a law concerning D.P.s and what number to be admitted to the States, was supposed to be taken up in a newly proposed bill in the Congress. Actually, I was among the earliest

D.P.s, already in this country.

Yet I looked at my own situation differently. Since coming to New York, at the end of 1947, I became deeply involved with the political activities at the U.N. concerning the creation of Israel. My political outlook had veered toward Zionism for years, especially since I became aware of the impossibility of a Jewish life in the Socialist countries. As the Soviet Union was so flagrantly against Zionism, even against Labor Zionism and Jews were for ever hunted and accused of 'cosmopolitanism' and of being unreliable - it became clear to me that the salvation for the survivors of the Holocaust was settling in Israel, rebuilding the shattered lives of the handful that had remained and building up the state in the process.

Thus, while trying to get acquainted with my family, whom I really had not known before and getting to see and assimilate knowledge about the U.S., finishing a course of studies and enriching my intellectual life, yet my yearning and striving turned toward Israel.

Yuda and myself exchanged very detailed, open letters about our lives and our plans for the future. He had volunteered to the Haganah (the forerunner of the Israel Defense Forces), worked sporadically as a construction worker, in order to support himself as an engineering student at the Technion, the Israel Institute of Technology. He had no immediate family, just uncles and cousins and his newly-arrived from Europe, beloved octogenarian grandmother. As Yuda had come to Israel on an illegal refugee boat, with just the clothes on his back, he could offer me nothing except love and devotion. I, myself was looking for a life of fulfillment, of shared responsibilities and surrounded by people, like ourselves, survivors. I thought that I would be happier living among people who had gone through similar life experiences to my own. I felt that I really needed to have a home of my own, built by myself and Yuda. I was not afraid of life in a new country, struggling and poor. I supposed that I could feel at home there, find a place in that society, not a displaced person any longer.

At this point, I am reminded of an English movie, titled: "I Know Where I'm Going," which presented a fictional, but similar situation to mine. The heroine in the film embarks, with great assurance, on a trip to the remote Hebrides Islands. What follows shows that she did not know really what she was going to face. Yet, the trip once started, is pursued with the greatest effort. It proves way harder than anticipated, but is not given up. The analogy to my own plan applies as the reality of life in Israel in 1950 was harsh, much harder than expected. I thought of my day of departure from the U.S. as my declaration of independence, as my Fourth of July.

The decision was not taken lightly and did not ripen overnight. I was nearing an age when I knew that I had to create my own home, my own family. In New York, a few months after my arrival, I met a gentlemen from Venezuela, who was anxious to marry me. He came every few months to New York and tried hard to influence me, to consider a life with him in Caracas. As a person, he possessed many qualities: he was honest and considerate, good-natured and generous, a business man of great acumen and a most patient man. He hoped that, eventually, I was going to get used to the idea of living in South America and travel to see my family as often as I wished. Yet, I could not see myself, sharing my life with a poorly educated man. At that time, even more than to-day, literature and art and music were of paramount importance to me. As much as money has always been an attraction to people, in my frame of thought, it did not tip the scales in his favor.

When I first shared my decision with the family, there was an element of surprise, bafflement, incredulity. Nobody had previously discussed with me what my options were or, later on, questioned the wisdom of my decision, yet, at the time most people thought it was pure folly to leave America - period.

Mother understood me better than anybody else, since she, herself was not very happy in her new environment. She did not try to stop me from acting on what I deemed right for me. Among my immediate circle, some understood better than others why I had taken such a drastic decision: leaving the U.S., going to Israel, where the fighting had barely stopped. My sense of independence and of self, acquired in my beginning twenties was slowly being eroded during my stay in the States. Everybody had an opinion concerning my person: soft and tough; hard-working and fun loving; refusing to follow stereotypes, not impressed by wealth. The advice. "It is preferable to marry the rich man rather than the poor man" did not carry weight. The fact of the matter remained - Yuda and I had decided that we were going to get married and brave a new life together. We had our education, but no worldly goods, we had the willingness to make a go of it, that constituted our foundation - shaky but idealistic.

In order to leave out any doubt, I let my passport expire, without trying to extend it. I applied for an Affidavit in lieu of passport, valid for a trip out of the U.S. to Israel, dated November 30, 1949.

Just as two years previously my family came to say 'hello,' now they visited to say 'goodbye.' Some were puzzled by my decision yet they found it interesting and idealistic, since I was going to labor in the vineyards of the newly established Jewish State. Maybe, some thought, they would have treated or approached me differently, had they known that it was only a temporary stay, a two-year visit. Of course, it made no difference any more. That stint was an interlude between life in Europe and my settling in Israel, where I remained for over seven years.

Chapter 12

To Israel

Preparations for another dislocation proved, this time, more complicated than, let's say, leaving Bucharest. While in Romania it was unclear whether any last moment hitch might not retain me, leaving America was easy from a legal point of view. However, there was a large family, whom I barely managed to acquaint myself with, sisters and brothers and a very large, extended family. There were lovely nieces and nephews, a generation of sweet youngsters and I was about to leave them all.

Frances was five years old when I came and seven when I left. A slight, dark- haired girl, with large brown eyes, a quiet yet intense, sensitive, bright child, whom I befriended through tales from mythology. Once I babysat with her and offered to tell a story. She just hungered for more and more. Our link strengthened through the Greek and Roman legends and became deep affection. Before my leaving, she would come with my sister Betty, her mother, and watch me from a corner of the room, when there were people around, as if to imprint my face in her memory. She wept softly when I left and we promised to exchange letters from then on. We did for a while; I still have some of them. She had younger twin brothers, Irving and Martin, sweet little four year old boys.

My nephew Allan was a skinny, freckled, blond boy, bright and lively - six years old when I left. He was adoringly describing his kindergarten teacher and hard put when asked whether she was prettier than his mother, my sister Sali. Darling little Susan, six months old when I came, was almost three when I left. Her blond curls and round face, so doll-like, made me long to have a girl just like her. Of course, I have two sons, no daughter.

How could I leave without saying good-bye to my brother Bernie and his family in Miami? He offered me a wedding gift: a rail ticket to Miami and back. The beginning of December, I spent a week with them, enjoying the new baby Marcia, almost one year old and big daughter Judy, aged four. We had a grand time together; the tiny tots gladdened my heart but at the same time made me realize how much that I loved is being left behind. The leave taking was painful but I had to start my own life some time and my conviction was strong enough so as not to waver, not to doubt my decision.

Back home, in Brooklyn, the day of departure neared: some shopping, receipt of some gifts, getting my ticket as a gift from Max and a refrigerator, gift from Morris. Funny, when I think of it to-day, thirty six years later. One sister gave me dishes, another a set of silver and cousins brought me several table cloths. It took me a few years before I had a regular table. I had a refrigerator but no kitchen; table clothes but no table; wide sheets and no bed - just army cots.

By the time I was leaving, Mother became visibly more upset. I promised her that as soon as my life would get organized, normalized, she would come to me, be my guest for as long as she wished or perhaps, for good. This thought appealed to her and gave her reassurance that it was not forever, that we'll see each other soon.

Brothers and sisters, uncles and aunts came to see me off at the boat and I was on my way to a new life, chosen freely and anticipated as a fateful new chapter in a - so far - no run of the mill existence. I said "goodbye, I'll write to you all about my wedding." Off I went on a wintry two-week crossing: one week on the Atlantic and another on the Mediterranean.

A group of young chalutzim, from a Zionist youth movement as well as a newly- wed American couple were going to settle in Israel. One middle aged Israeli man, who was returning from a business trip to the States, spent most of his time with us.

Dov Landmann became an interesting companion on the trip. He was full of humorous stories, yet a bright, serious man, who had gone through battles in the War of Independence and was looking forward to organizing a group of veterans into a business association, opening movie houses in Tel Aviv. His attitude was positive, encouraging.

We formed a lively group, especially the youngsters, who were carefree, the first time away from home, on their own and yet - all had families to return to, in case their plans did not work out. I, on the other hand, had to make a go of it, no matter what. This was a very sobering thought all along. I was asking myself: did I get used to the fleshpots of America? Had I grown a little soft by living two years surrounded by the amenities of American life? Did I get spoiled? Did I take for granted that the house was always lit and warm? food plentiful? that I was conversant in the language? that I saw plays, heard concerts, took trips? The two weeks gave me a chance to think of the many changes I was going to confront.

Of course, the reality of life in Israel during the first years of statehood proved to be much harder than anticipated. Additionally, I had not seen Yuda since 1944, almost six years. What if what we wrote to each other did not translate well into the reality of life?

On that trip I had all the time to think of the new society, where people from all over the world were supposed to form a new, cohesive fabric. How will all this mesh? As for myself, I confronted a transition between a world that I knew and a world that I could not exactly fathom, yet a world that I had slightly idealized in my mind.

Interestingly, we had a New Year's party on the ship. Some of the youngsters tried to ignore it, as it was not the Jewish New Year. We all partook of a festive meal in the tourist class, where we were travelling. In first class was an Israeli gentleman, a man in his late forties, travelling alone, returning from a trip to the States. On New Year's eve, dressed in tuxedo, he came down to us and invited us to come up to the first class dining room, where they had music and dancing until after midnight, perhaps even into the morning. This man, a textile merchant from Haifa, Dov and myself sat down at a table, first talking jokingly about the winding up of our voyage, two more days until we reach Erez Israel. Dov, who was a veteran of the War of Independence, talked about the challenges of life in Israel and was positive about the future. He made me feel that everything good and exciting lay ahead of us, a solid future to work for, the settlement and absorption of newcomers from all over the world - a challenge for a generation. The other man, the elegant one in the tuxedo, started to reveal that he felt life, in Israel, at this point, was unbearable. Whatever Dov and myself countered with made no difference, he was despondent. Every now and then he walked over to the bar for a drink, asked me to dance and soon returned to the bar. Our positive thoughts were falling on deaf ears and we decided to return to our tourist class and let the neurotic rich find solace at the bar. Little did we realize how despondent the man was, because by the time the boat arrived, he had disappeared, probably ended in the Mediterranean.

On the first and second day of January we were all getting impatient, full of expectation and apprehension, eagerness mixed with some fear of a new reality.

A day before, our stop at Piraeus was a wash-out. Nobody went ashore as it was raining heavily. We could not even catch a glimpse of Greece. A few days previously, we had stopped in Naples for the day, visited Pompeii and enjoyed our few hours on solid ground. Now, approaching the end of the journey, we were chomping at the bit.

On January 3, 1950, everybody got up early and came on deck to see the Land, as we approached. The day was cool and clear and soon the mountains were visible - Mount Carmel, of the Bible and of song was clear to see. The Bay of Haifa, instead of an expanse of blue water, was filled with boats of all descriptions. The variety of vessels with immigrants was staggering the imagination. We thought that our big ship would have to wait for ever for an opening at the pier. Everybody was impatient but could do nothing about it. The newly appointed American ambassador to Israel, who was a passenger on the ship, was picked up in a small boat, but the regular passengers had to wait for hours.

As we were standing and watching the commotion, a small row boat neared us, came straight toward us and, lo and behold, Yuda was on it. He was waving, as the row boat neared us and I realized it was my own Yuda, impatiently approaching the liner LaGuardia. The people with me, all noticed the same thing: his hair is thinning on the top. He came close to the liner, we saw each other, yet he was not permitted to come up.

Well, we disembarked toward late afternoon and I finally set foot on Israel's soil, in Haifa.

Chapter 13

Impressions of Israel

In the first days of 1950 Israel was a brand new country, in an agitated state, all in motion. Daily, all sorts of boats arrived to its shores bringing immigrants from Europe. The survivors had first gathered in towns in Austria, Germany, France, Romania, Hungary and under the guidance of "shlichim," young men and women organizers, sent from Israel. The homeless proceeded to port cities in Southern Europe, mostly Italy and France, and eventually reached Israel. Whatever boat could keep afloat was leased to transport those desirous to reach the shores of the Land.

Immigrants from the Arab countries arrived simultaneously - from Algeria, Morocco and Tunisia in North Africa and from Yemen as well as from the Middle East, namely Iraq, Iran and Syria. The Yemenis were brought in by plane, in an undertaking called the "flying carpet." Later would arrive the Jews from India, called "Bnei Israel." The newcomers needed everything that sustains life: food, shelter, work and the knowledge of the new language, a means of communication.

However, from the day of arrival, they needed shelter, unavailable in a small country that had just achieved its statehood, after having fought and won a harsh war against all its neighbors. The task, at the time, was Herculean. What struck me, a newcomer like all the others, was the diversity of people's looks, the diversity of their dress and the diversity of the languages spoken by the new immigrants. The Tower of Babel could hardly hold a candle to Israel in 1950. The diversity of cultures having to co-exist, having to mesh, eventually, need extreme optimism to appear possible. What united us all was the fact that we were all Jewish, had a common past, a common ancestry. Yet, we could not be more different if we had made up that scenario in our minds, if we had tried to imagine possible differences. The cultural differences between the European Jews and the Yemenis, who were small, swarthy, lived in a society where brides were bought from their fathers at the age of 10 or 11; where men could have 4 wives and an extended family of children from all the wives and all living together. They spoke Arabic and some archaic, biblical Hebrew. The North African newcomers spoke Arabic and French and their traditions, their culture was different, too, from the Israelis, who were mostly of European descent. It looked like a country badly in need of a melting of gigantic proportions, of a way to absorb the variety of groups and give them some coherence.

Yuda and I tried to figure out how we would create a life together. We enjoyed each other's company, we knew that we wanted to get married, we had not changed too much in those six years, when we were apart. Yet we had no apartment, Yuda still had half a year of studies before graduation from the Technion. Both of us possessed no funds, no close family. He had three uncles and aunts, a sweet old grandmother and some cousins.

We had no real "connections," which was as bad as having no money. Protecţia or pull or connections, by whatever name one would call it, made an enormous difference. Everybody was looking for a job and the one who knew somebody in charge had better chances than a person, like myself, who had come with a diploma from a top university in the U.S., but no friends in high positions. As an example, there was an opening for an English teacher in a high school in Haifa. The principal was ready to hire me but needed the consent of the inspector general for English instruction in Israeli schools. He came once a week to Haifa. He was an elderly gentleman, who had been living in Palestine for years, a graduate of Teacher's College at Columbia. He may have resented the fact that I was a graduate of the Graduate Department of Literature, a school of higher standing than the Teacher's College. He advised me to come back in a year, when my knowledge of Hebrew will have improved and soon gave that job to a person, who had arrived with a diploma from Bucharest, which I had achieved beforehand. That applicant knew less Hebrew than I did, but he probably had an in.

Life for new arrivals, who had to live in temporary shelters, in quonset huts or tents on the outskirts of towns, was just one step up from camps in Europe.

Of course, they were "at home" and waiting for times to improve. The government looked at them with benevolence and provided all the immediate necessities. I had very little to start with but never asked nor received any help. I was well dressed and did not look like a poor newcomer. In fact, I never considered myself "poor," I just thought of it as a temporary situation.

We happened to be short of money, but that was a passing state of affairs, we hoped.

We rented a furnished room in the center of town, in an old house. The landlady had furniture that she had brought from Russia before the Revolution (1917); she boasted about the fact that she had studied medicine in Switzerland and had met Lenin and Weitzman, who were temporarily living there, too. Looking at antiques is one thing, but using 30 to 40 year old, rickety furniture was a different story.

Soon, I found people who wanted to take English lessons and that tided us over the first few months. In June, when Yuda graduated, he started working and I found a position in an evening language school. Yuda came home around five and I went to work before six. In each of my classes were about 20 students and they spoke 15 different tongues. The only language we all had in common was the new one, which I was teaching them. Of course, I understood a few of theirs. We had weathered the toughest months valiantly, in fact we decided to go to a movie once a week, just to keep up the morale.

Haifa, a small town with a picturesque location, became a congenial pleasant place. I met some of his friends from the Technion as well as some, with whom he had spent months together in the military, during the War of Independence. On Saturdays, we took long walks on Mount Carmel; we strolled through the old Arab section, mostly vacated by the original population and inhabited by many new immigrants. The notion of "old" sunk in here, as some roads, villages were ancient, not quaint, filthy and dilapidated.

We visited old friends in the "maabarot," the make-shift, temporary colonies, on the outskirts of Haifa. My only aunt from Czernovitz, my Father's sister and her family were there for a short time. Of course, in time, people moved into permanent housing provided by the government.

Our beginnings as a married couple were unusual and cemented our relationship strongly. The hard work and meager means did not weaken our morale, for we felt confident of a better future for ourselves and the larger community around us. Had we not gone through the years of the war and the grave hardships - we, probably, would have felt despondent. After all, we were both thirty years old and rich in experiences, rough times behind us, completely devoid of any means and still looking ahead at rough times faced by an entire nation.

The fact that the majority of the population were newcomers and none of us had a decent place to live in - made the situation easier to accept. "The trouble of many is half consolation" as the Hebrew saying goes. We weathered that hard time with fortitude and expectations of better days to come.

At the time, food was in critically short supply. The influx of population and shortage of production resulted in poor availability of food. Although meat, eggs and fats - oil and margarine - were rationed, the monthly allotments were minimal. A person would receive, at official price, about one pound of meat and eight eggs monthly. Shortages brought about a relatively minor black market. Even unrationed fruits and vegetables were not readily available.

Yuda and myself did not dwell much on the matter, but it brought about discussions about food constantly. As an example, in the first 4 to 5 years of my life in Israel, I never ate an apple. I enjoyed the plentiful citrus fruits and never made an issue that apples, pears and peaches were beyond my means and expectations. The first few years, known as years of "Tsena," austerity, shortages, remained in my mind as trying times because other areas of daily life were also hard to cope with: housing, high rates for electricity, no telephone, shortages of textiles - a tough life. Yet, we had gone through similar times before and much worse, and had learned how to cope, how to do without. The spirit of unity and pride in achievement of the State compensated for the daily hardships. In those times, hope was our constant companion; old friendships and new kept us going. We were open and helpful and trusting. On Friday nights or on Saturdays or holidays - people got together, drank tea, ate cookies and talked, talked, discussed endlessly. We had finally arrived, we were finally at home, we had finally survived and most were on the point to finally start a family. Interestingly, men and women, who had lost their mates, their children, during the war, in the preceding years in Europe, re-married and created new families.

The first years after the creation of the State of Israel were a time of promise of a better future, of a national life in one's own home. Little did we foresee that the future would not exactly bear out the expectations. The "shalom ve shalvah," the peace and contentment were supposed to set in but remained illusory, indefinitely.

Chapter 14

Our Wedding - January 18, 1950

Since we decided to get married, we had to take a few practical steps in that direction. First, we rented a furnished room in the center of town, close to the Technion, where Yuda was in his last year of studies, six months to graduation.

Yuda approached the chief rabbi of Haifa, Rav Kaniel, to marry us. They decided on the date, a week from their meeting. Talking matters over with Aunt Sonia, Uncle Nachman and with his nonagenarian grandmother, who was living at her daughter's, it was decided to have a midday meal there, right after the ceremony.

Of course, what can one prepare in times like those, at the height of "tsena," when most food items were strictly rationed? On the strength of a letter from the rabbi, notifying of the date of the marriage ceremony, Yuda received an extra "wedding ration," namely about 4 pounds of sugar, 2 pounds of margarine, about 5 pounds of meat and ten eggs. Aunt Sonia was delighted with the wealth of ingredients and she prepared a meal and two cakes.

How about the guests to be invited to the wedding? Yuda had his Father's two brothers and their wives, all living in Tel Aviv, two cousins and their wives, Zaka, Sonia's daughter and an elderly couple, friends of the family, who had known Yuda from his early childhood. As for myself, I had a cousin in Nahalal, my own Father's age, whom I had never met and another cousin, Max Rosenkranz, whom I first met after my arrival in Israel. The Rosenkranzes were formerly living in Poland.

Interestingly enough, at a religious wedding ceremony, there had to be a quorum of ten men present. At ours, there were ten men, the rabbi and the groom included. The ceremony had to be performed out of doors, according to ultra religious custom. The climate is sub-tropical and winters, as a rule, are mild. Not on our wedding day. Every ten or fifteen years it happens to be cold and snowy for a day or two. Of course, it was snowing on our wedding day and I was sloshing through the snow, in the rabbi's yard, in my white shoes.

After the ceremony, all of us walked over, about one block, to Sonia's and Nachman's apartment, where Grandmother, who was bed-ridden was anxiously waiting for the young marrieds and the wedding guests.

We ate a well-prepared, festive meal and talked and joked. I met Yuda's Tel Aviv family for the first time and we all became acquainted with my two cousins. Mr. Schleien, the cousin from Nahalal, a veteran settler, a farmer, brought as a wedding gift ten eggs. There was no symbolism intended, it was a practical present of a rare and precious food for city dwellers. We received two sets of silver plated tea spoons, a few ash trays, a few egg-cups. As we had no furniture, the uncles' gift of fifty Israeli pounds was intended for the purchase of a piece of furniture, a clothes wardrobe.

After the meal, after receiving all their good wishes and blessings, the guests all went home. The out-of-towners left on a bus and the newly weds? We walked about five minutes to our furnished room and started our new life together. The wedding was simple, a short ceremony in a new town, among a few people, whom I hardly knew, far away from my entire family, no friends present, nobody giving away the bride, no honeymoon, no real home to go to. Yuda was in familiar surroundings, yet he had no parents, he did not know whether his brother Michael was alive. He didn't invite any of his friends because the aunt's apartment was much too small to accommodate more than the group assembled.

Two days after the wedding, we went to a photographer and had a picture taken of the two of us, so as to send my family a wedding picture, to let them see what my husband looked like. I think we made a good, loving, devoted couple. We created a family, we had two fine sons within the following four years.

In March 1980, on the day before our older son Mark's wedding, we travelled by plane to Detroit, where it took place. We reminisced about our own wedding day when we were two fairly lonesome individuals, survivors of the greatest tragedy that ever befell our people and we stood almost alone facing the world. On that March day, we were full of expectation for the coming wedding next day. Our Mark and Ruth were surrounded by loving families and friends, who showered them with gifts and saw them leave for their honeymoon.

How much better life looked thirty years later! Could our sons understand what was on our minds as we approached our older son's wedding? When I shed tears of joy that I lived to see that day, my memories were so manifold, such a kaleidoscope of images passing through my mind. It was more than I had expected of life, for we had stood on the brink so often and remained to tell the tale. Le chaim, to life, to a good life.

Chapter 15

Random Thoughts

Did I learn anything that I can impart to people of the generations after me? Did the behavior of the world around me in the horrible years between 1933- 1945 lead me to any conclusions about human nature? Did any discernible pattern emerge? Did I see any reason or justification why millions were put to death and some survived?

How could those who killed, do it?
How could those who watched, keep silent?
How could some survive and bear it?

The hatred of the anti-semites, especially in Germany, Austria and Poland, was so intense, that they thought to appease all the apprehensions of their nations by physically eliminating the Jews. The cold-hearted complicity of the rest of the populations, in those European countries, exhibited the inherent inhumanity of masses. The Western powers showed no willingness to rescue the threatened Jews in Europe. That proved to the murderers that the rest of the world refused to take a stand, which was almost complicity.

The population, who was not part of the destruction process, kept silent, closed their eyes, raised no questions, expected no explanation. Few and far between were some compassionate individuals, who hid a Jew here and there. Those were the exceptions that proved the rule.

The ones who survived lived in places where one had a chance to slip through the cracks. In some areas of Europe, for example, the Old Kingdom of Romania (Moldavia, Oltenia, Muntenia), most of the Jewish population survived. In Bulgaria and in Italy, the majority of their small Jewish communities survived, lived to see the end of the Second World War. There happened to be a few, too few, areas where our brothers and sisters survived.

The destruction was so random, the evil struck so indiscriminately. The saintly were not spared; no divine intervention anywhere. Evil people destroyed them all, at random. The prayers of the pious were not heard, the weeping of the mothers and children were not heard. Evil was lording over the lands. I learned no lesson, I found no pattern.

The murderers did not crawl and hide after the war. They may not have felt guilt or remorse. The survivors did not hunt to kill them, when the slaughter was over, when it had run its course.

I presume that since we were not murderers at heart, the experiences during those years did not turn us into human hunters, even after all that. It did not brutalize decent people, but it saddened them, it branded them, it wounded them - it had inflicted wounds that no medicine can ever heal.

Some think that survivors may suffer from guilt. Looking back at people who survived and whose close relatives did not - there may be a feeling that "had I done this or that, at the time, my father or mother or wife or husband or child may have made it, too. I did not do the right thing at that particular time." This may torture some and, in hindsight, my trouble them as having failed their beloved ones. Remorse, remorse. However, at the time, that was not possible or feasible and yet, the remorse and the doubts and the self-reproach may overcome and destroy the survivor, consumed by guilt feelings.

Some survivors torture themselves for these reasons, yet the perpetrators of "the crime of the millennium" may sleep well and block out that entire part of their lives.

Those years have made me feel more strongly part of the Jewish community, part of a group with whom I suffered together, lived and labored together, they gave me a feeling of belonging, of trust and warmth. If some may have thought of leaving the fold and find shelter in the larger group of non-Jews, where they would never by persecuted, I, on the contrary, could not see myself joining that world, that could inflict such pain and destruction, that brought back barbarity in the 20th century in Europe.

Chapter 16

What's in a Name

During the years of my early childhood, the older sisters and brothers used to joke and kid each other, using the names Stadler, Herzog, while I knew for sure that my name was Spiegel. Of course, they, being older, enjoyed the privilege of knowing many things that I was unaware of and yet, these funny, amusing ways of joshing were intriguing to me, the youngest in the family. I may have asked for an explanation and may have been told that I was too young to understand. As years went by and I could sort out bits and pieces of our family's life and history, an unusual background, an unusual bit of cultural history revealed itself.

When my Mother was 16 or 17 years old, her parents sent her from the small town Zablotow to the nearby larger town of Kolomija, where one of her mother's sisters lived. A girl her age, having grown up on an estate, was sent to a bigger place to acquire some of the skills needed for a marriageable girl. In her youth, she got her schooling from a tutor, who was teaching the landowner's children as well as those of the administrator, my grandfather. Of course, a girl had to learn to sew, to knit, to run a household, to become, eventually, an efficient wife and mother. At home she had no chances of meeting any people, as she lived in a quiet, isolated place. She was surrounded by five brothers and the landowner's children, who also left for the city to accomplish their education.

In the aunt's house she became acculturated to life in town and realized how much she would prefer leaving the provincial life. Shortly after, her aunt became her matchmaker. A teacher she knew had a son of marriageable age and thus - enter my Father on the scene. He was the son of a Hebrew teacher, a learned man who had encouraged his sons to engage in business activities, although they were steeped in religious learning from the age of three or four. My Father was a handsome, thoughtful, contemplative man, intent on making a life of his own in a big city. As a travelling salesman he saw places that appealed to him. My Mother had a sharp mind, was handy and capable at whatever she endeavored to accomplish. However, she felt self-conscious because of her appearance. A red birthmark on her chin and left side of her face made her feel "marked," she felt that children would pull on their mother's dress pointing towards her. She resented the cruelty of her appearance as opposed to her five brothers who had unblemished faces. She mentioned to me once that when her mother was expecting her, a fire broke out in a hay loft and her mother clutched at her own face in a gesture of fright and that was the fire-red set of fingers and hand on her own face. Whether this interpretation had any validity or not - I don't know - but she believed that to have been the origin of her "red mark."

Needless to say, Mother was happy to marry a man as gentle and good-looking as my Father. They were 23 and 20 years old at their wedding. When the question of settling down arose, they decided on living in Czernovitz, a three-hour train ride from Kolomija. Father was a commercial salesman and on his trips through Galizia and Bukovina he was impressed by the beauty and cleanliness of the big cities Lemberg (Lvov) and Czernovitz. He saw the cultural and societal life as much more satisfying and desirable, life greatly enhanced by an environment of beautiful streets, fine public parks with orchestras playing on summer evenings, extensive school systems and theaters, a fine life compared to the dullness of the small towns, the shtetls without running water or electricity. To paraphrase the song of later years: How can you bring them back to Kolomija once they have seen Czernovitz?

There may have been another strong personal reason for my Father to want to start married life in a different town. He had lost his mother as a very young boy, around the age of eight and did not get along well with his step- mother. She had borne several children and favored her own sons and daughters over the older children of her husband. Father was the youngest of the orphaned ones and suffered most acutely after the loss of his mother.

The wedding ceremony of my parents was performed by a rabbi according to the "laws of Moses and Israel": a glass was shattered by the groom, a "Ketubah" or marriage contract was signed and the rabbi pronounced them husband and wife and they were expected to live happily and be fruitful. At that time, all observant Jewish couples were married in religious ceremonies.

The young couple moved to Czernovitz right away, in the year 1904. In fact, they settled on Mehlplatz and lived there until 1935 - except for the years as refugees in Vienna, during the First World War. Father opened a store and stayed in business until 1939.

Coming back to the start of their union, they were fruitful, indeed. After one year of married life Eli was born, in 1905. When Father came to register the birth of his son at City Hall, they requested the marriage certificate of the parents. Since the Austrian authorities did not recognize the religious marriage as officially valid, they insisted on naming the baby by the mother's maiden name. Thus, he was Elias Stadler, his mother's son, father not being acknowledged.

Not much attention was paid to that fact and life went on. About a year and a half later Bertha (Betty) was born. Upon registration of this baby, the clerk accepted the fact that my parents were married and she was granted the name of the father - Spiegel. The same procedure worked in Gertie's case - her name was Gusta Spiegel and life went on more or less merrily.

However, in 1910 another son was born, Bernhard. In vain did my Father plead with the clerk in charge of registration. That one started out with endless questions - whether my parents were officially married at City Hall; whether my Father's parents had been officially married, etc. He reached the following decision: this child's name should be Herzog, my Father's mother's maiden name. Home he went, puzzled and upset since both his sons did not carry his name; only his daughters did.

I guess, life had to go on and times were hard, what with four small children and Father struggling to make a living and Mother, forever busy with a growing family and rumors of war gnawing at people's nerves constantly. Before the onset of the First World War there were constant rumblings of discontent within the Austro-Hungarian Empire and in the Balkans. The problem of the children being named Stadler, Spiegel and Herzog were not of paramount importance at the moment; they were too young for school yet.

However, time passed and the war started and eventually my parents fled before the Russian invasion, going West through Hungary toward Vienna. The older children went to elementary school and Eli and Betty were placed in the same grade, despite the difference in age. Girls sat on one side of the classroom and boys on the other. Elias Stadler and Bertha Spiegel were just two refugee children and even the teacher was not aware that they were brother and sister.

The others went to first grade and kindergarten. All four did their best half a day in school and stood in line for food the other half.

When the war was finally over, the family returned to Czernovitz. The store had been looted, the apartment ransacked but life had to be resumed in an unusual situation. The Romanian authorities took over the province of the defeated Austro-Hungarian Empire and people were supposed to register and apply for citizenship in the Kingdom of Romania. At that juncture, my Father decided to consult a lawyer about the tangled, nonsensical family situation. Of course, our family was not unique; most Jewish families were in the same predicament. The Romanians, just like the Austrians, did not acknowledge a religious marriage as valid in civil matters. The legal advice given went as follows: "Go to the civil authorities and get married officially and then - adopt all your children legally."

Thus, my parents got married in 1919 in front of a judge, after 15 years of married life an after the birth of six children. The children were all legally adopted shortly after because, according to civil laws they were all illegitimate.

There was joy and merriment on Mehlplatz 3, for everybody was finally and officially named Spiegel and Father was legally the proud parent of two sons, who were previously named Stadler and Herzog. When I, the youngest, was born, all those entanglements had already been solved. The parents were married inside and outside of religion. The parents had been blessed by a rabbi and fifteen years later, by a judge; my name of Spiegel did not have to be argued about; I was a genuine Romanian citizen, no cross-over from Austria. Seemingly all official hurdles had been removed after the First World War. Nobody could have surmised, at the time, that my legal wranglings would be even more complicated as I grew up. At age 18, my Romanian citizenship was denied to me and also to my parents by the incoming Fascist regime of Goga-Cuza.

Coming back to where I started: "Wasn't it confusing to hear the older siblings joke? You, you are a Stadler; no, I am a Herzog, said Bernie, and that is more than you'll ever be." Herzog, in German means "duke," a title of nobility, highly prized in the Austro-Hungarian empire. It took me a long time to understand those jokes and puns, but they were only partially a laughing matter. They were complications of Jewish life. We often preferred to joke and poke fun at situations which were tough to bear, but "if you wouldn't laugh, you'd have to hang yourself" as the Ukrainian proverb says.

Chapter 17

Carmen

At the age of fourteen, towards the end of eighth grade, my friend Lola and myself engaged a math teacher, to help us with algebra for six weeks before the end of the school year and to make sure we were well prepared for the "Kleine Matura." This was a comprehensive exam in Romanian, French and Algebra. Success in that exam made it possible to continue high school.

We were both good students and the tutor had a very easy time with us. Being used to try hard to make a student understand the subject, we were "a piece of cake." The tutor was a graduate of mathematics of the University of Czernovitz, a top mathematician. However, his appearance put him at a great disadvantage. He was short, thin, prematurely graying and - he had a voice - no broken record could outdo his harsh, screeching tones. Being so short, he wore a higher heeled type of shoe. A fine tutor with a miserable appearance.

We passed the exam well. I almost forgot him until the second half of the following school year. Being sick and missing a lot of my classes, I had to make up everything on my own. My older sister Sali suggested calling Mr. Kugler again. She contacted him. He pleaded to be too busy to teach me but offered to send his younger brother, a math student at the university.

Well, the brother came. A shock. He was good-looking, with a dandy-like appearance: blond, wavy-haired, smooth, slightly oily-voiced, wearing well tailored clothes and a pinky ring. This type of bourgeois get-up looked ridiculous to me. The lessons went well. He, too, enjoyed teaching somebody who grasped the concepts with ease. By the end of the school year, he let me understand that he liked me.

The following school year, in the fall, he came one day to our house and told me that he had been called up for two months of military service. He had to divide up his students among other teachers for the duration of his absence.

So what? Well, he thought that I could tutor one of his students, Carmen, for those two months. She was an eighth grader. I was a tenth grader at the time. I could hardly believe his suggestion. Was I good enough in math to teach the girl, to prepare her three times weekly for school? Well, he thought so. Besides, she lived close by and, besides, they paid very well. He had dragged it out and told me all about the good pay and the proximity of the location and just waited for me to accept it. Finally, I accepted the two months fill-in and asked who the girl was and where exactly did she live.

Carmen was the youngest daughter of the chief commissar of the secret police, Commissar Grossariu. He didn't have to tell me where she lived because it was near, about five minutes walk from me and I was always afraid to pass by that corner villa. He was the one, who had arrested my best friend for political activities, the year before.

I was dumbfounded. He assured me that whenever I would come there, the father would never be home. The mother was a fine woman and would be very friendly to her little Carmen's teacher. To me, it felt like stepping into the lion's den.

The Grossarius lived beautifully, elegantly, in a spacious home with a garden.

When I came to instruct her, do with her the assignment for the next day (she had math three times a week), we sat in a pleasant, well-heated room and her mother would invariably treat me with cookies or cake and coffee.

The girl was good-looking, slim, with dark eyes and olive skin, a pert, up turned nose, charming, but slow to comprehend math. She was willing and attentive and we got along fine. She respected me as she did all her teachers, yet I was just two years older than herself. She was a student at the Christian-Orthodox High School for Girls. It was the first time that I ever came into a Christian, Romanian home. I may have been the first Jewish girl that she had ever met.

There were two older daughters at home, both much older than Carmen or myself:

one was the head librarian of the City Library, the other, a high official at the police. The librarian, seeing me in the school uniform, told me that I could get any book in the Iorga library; the other, I hoped, never to meet in her professional activity.

Early in December, that house became a beehive of activity. In the yard, they had a pig slaughtered for the holidays. The butcher and a helper were smoking meats, making sausages and everything smelled of pork. To me, that smell felt unpleasant, but I came there to do a job. Mrs. Grossariu became friendlier as Carmen continued to receive passing grades and could keep going, even with a young girl teacher. They were trimming the tree, the piano teacher came after me to teach Carmen to play carols. Everything switched into high gear, approaching a crescendo. The oldest daughter was going to get engaged at Christmas time. Carmen was impatient for the coming holidays. I came out of their house smelling of brandy and candy and of all the goodies that were being cooked and baked before Noel. A few days before Christmas vacation, Carmen received her report card, with a good grade in math. When I came, everybody was friendly. Mr. Grossariu was at home and his wife introduced me to him, saying: "This is the lovely young girl I told you about. She taught Carmen so well in Mr. Kugler's absence." My knees almost buckled.

Mrs. Grossariu brought in a nicely packaged, big sausage, home-made and offered it to me as a Christmas present. I thanked her but refused to take it - because we eat only "kosher." "Oh, yes" she said "How could I forget? I liked you so much, I thought you were one of our own."

In my mind's eye, I can see Carmen to-day. She must be a mother and grandmother, in her sixties, living in Romania. In that country, food is scarce, meat a rarity. She may be telling the story of her one-time Jewish algebra teacher, just a little older than herself. It was in the good, old times, in her parent's house, in Czernovitz. She won't mention her father's profession to her grandchildren, in communist Romania. Yet, she will tell them that times were so good, that food was so plentiful that, in her parents' house, they used to slaughter a pig for Christmas. There was so much meat and sausage and ham that they even offered the tutor a sausage as a Christmas present and, imagine, the tutor refused to accept it - she ate only kosher.

Chapter 18

A Slight Romance

During the high school years, as we were reading more and more Romanian literature, from the earliest chronicles to contemporary poetry and fiction, I developed a certain liking and appreciation of some poets, like Mihail Eminescu, as well as of some writers. Among the living novelists, Ionel Teordoreanu became a favorite of mine and of a whole generation of readers. He possessed the intensity of feeling as well as the facility of description of Thomas Wolfe. Of course, in the years 1936-38, I was not aware of the existence of Thomas Wolfe. Every new novel of Teodoreanu was read and discussed and usually admired, especially by young people.

In my senior year in high school, the writer came to Czernovitz to deliver a lecture at the National Theater. Anxiously awaiting this afternoon lecture, scheduled for three o'clock, I arrived earlier, in order to secure a good seat. Sure enough, I sat in the center, first row mezzanine.

The time approached, yet at three o'clock it was announced that the novelist would be delayed by about half an hour. Next to me sat a young man alone, awaiting the same literary experience as myself. We started talking casually about the delay, then about the writer. To me it was clear that the man was a Romanian, a few years older than myself. He was charming and we were exchanging ideas about Teodoreanu as well as about other writers. As I was in uniform, he could tell even what high school I attended - I could not tell whether he was a university student or a professional man.

As the public became impatient about the delay and started clapping and expressing their restlessness, the young man and myself were enjoying our conversation and almost forgot about Teodoreanu. We just enjoyed each other's company; we joked, exchanged ideas, seemed to be impressed by

178

the same qualities of the writer, who had brought us together that wintry afternoon. It was near five when the writer showed up. The lecture was fascinating, the lecturer even more. He was handsome, full of wit, enthusiasm, charming and romantic-looking. The public practically forgot the two hour delay.

The lecture over, everybody streamed out of the theater. A quiet, snowy evening, with lights around the theater square, made the whole area a softly romantic winter scene. We continued to discuss the lecture. When I said that I was going down that particular street, he said that he was going in the same direction, too. Near the Temple, I said that I was going down 11 November Street. He was also heading in the same direction. When we reached another intersection, I pointed to the house across the street, where I lived, he stopped. He was going to go down a different street, but he did not take me to my house. He must have thought that I would not want to be seen with a Romanian, taking me home. He realized that I was Jewish. It was just like: East is East and West is West and never the twain shall meet. This same rule seemed to apply to Romanians and Jews.

Then he introduced himself and said: "My name is Mihalache. I am a student of theology." I told him my name, too. He kissed my hand and said: "Good night. The pleasure was all mine."

I crossed the street and before entering the house, I turned around. He was standing in the corner and mentally, probably, saw me to my house. He waved and I entered the house.

Once in a while I'd see him in the street, in my neighborhood. He would smile, doff his hat - but that was all. If not for the unbridgeable chasm that separated a Romanian clergyman from a Jewish girl, we could have had a great relationship. That way, we only had a fleeting moment of romance, a brief encounter, a memory that has lasted almost fifty years, a lifetime.

Chapter 19

Erich

In the second year English course, under the Soviets (1940-41), we were eight students - four young men and an equal number of women. Nelly and Erica were friends from childhood and Martha and I were close since her arrival in Czernovitz, at the age of fifteen.

Erich was a local student, close friend of Paul Antschel (Celan), who was in the French section. The other three male students had come from Bessarabia. None of us had known them previously. Erich became a close colleague and friend of mine. We spent half a day in class, six days a week, enduring classes of history of the Communist party, according to the latest revision by the politbureau, Ukrainian and Russian grammar and "Preparedness for War," a military course, taught by a colonel and using regular guns and ammunition and English courses, too. In the afternoon, we did some of the assignments together, at my house.

He was not politically oriented at all. The only son of a successful lawyer, Erich was highly educated and widely read - he had not made up his mind what to do professionally. He definitely had a strong literary bent. We became very good friends and had a true understanding of each other's ideas, even if they were not fully translated into words. A look sufficed. We had a kind of shorthand, an unspoken understanding.

Erich was tall, dark blond, blue-eyed, athletic looking. He looked the picture of health and well-being. Actually, he could be mistaken for a typical Northerner, German or Swede.

That school year differed from others because of the great difficulties that we, the local students, confronted. We had to learn, in record time, two new languages: Ukrainian and Russian. Dictionaries were non-existent and the textbooks were of poor quality. We grinned and bore it, with good humor and sarcasm. Looking around us, at our mediocre teachers and at the low level of the Soviet students, we really had so much knowledge and now, we needed to acquire knowledge of something completely different and this in a hurry, in record time, immediately, now.

He was honest and reliable, as a friend. I knew that I could trust him implicitly. We knew what to expect of each other, how much to rely on one another and what to expect from the strangers, from the others. In a time when friends could become informers, I knew I could trust him. If I expressed an unorthodox idea, according to the concepts of Stalinism, I knew it could go no further, it would never be used against me. That was no mean feat.

We prepared together for exams; some subjects were too boring to do alone. He was quick and highly intelligent. When I was sick, he or Martha would bring me the necessary notes from school.

When June 41 came and the war, the majority of the students went into evacuation into the interior of the Soviet Union - Erich left, too. Paul and myself were left without our dear Erich. In 1944, Erich returned to Czernovitz in uniform. He was in the military service and spent a few weeks back home. Again, I enjoyed immensely his lively company, but his easy going manner had been dampened. He had been touched by tragedy. His girl friend Erica, whom I had known well, had perished somewhere in the Caucasus.

In my house, he met Tamara, a girl with whom I was working at the Railroad telephone office. The two hit it off well. Soon he was transferred to a unit of people, who were fluent in foreign languages. It was a unit of translators, going West with the advancing troops. I hated to see him go, yet that was the pattern of the war years.

Tamara was anxious to see him off at the railroad station. I went with her to say "good bye." We knew that towards evening, there were purse snatchers everywhere. Yet, we dared go down to the station and kissed a dear friend good bye. As we walked toward the exit, somebody grabbed Tamara's purse. She carried the obligatory "passport" and thus had to report the loss of the document to the railroad militia. I have never forgotten the contemptuous look and tone of that militiaman. Answering why she was there, he said: "Who goes to see off soldiers? Only prostitutes." Such despicable words. After all, the soldiers were their praised heroes.

Well, half a year later, I left Czernovitz; soon after Tamara left, too. We never saw Erich again. Erich became a translator at international peace conferences, first in Vienna then in Berlin. Somebody spotted him in the street in Vienna, but he made a sign, a finger on his lips, which meant: "Don't talk to me." He was afraid to be seen with a foreigner.

Erich settled in Moscow after the war and wrote for a German publication in the Soviet Union. He married a Russian woman. Whenever a former friend would visit him, at his basement apartment, his wife made him feel unwelcome. He felt cut off from all his previous friends and family. He died of a heart attack in 1974, at the age of 54. Shortly before his end, a childhood friend, Gustav Chomed exchanged a few letters with him. The tone of his letters was "lyrical, tinged with sorrow and regret," said Chomed.

I don't know, it is a moot question, whether Erich or Paul would have been happy, had they remained at home. But home, as it used to be, did not exist any longer. Paul went to the West and felt "déraciné," uprooted; the other to Moscow and felt "deracine" and we, the others who survived? We are all uprooted, just a matter of degree, depending on the individual sensibilities. We all remained D.P.s, displaced persons - yet the place, the home, the anchor, it itself had disappeared.

In 1987, my friend Rosl, who resides in Germany, visited me for a few days. She read my reminiscences and filled me in on some facts about Erich. In the 70s Rosl's daughter was studying in Moscow. On a visit there, Rosl visited Erich, who was suffering from a severe heart condition and could not climb the stairs, was confined to the apartment.

When she saw him, he was alone and deeply despondent. He told her about his only daughter, who had reached the age when a teenager had to apply for her own "passport," the identification card carried on one's person at all times. She had filled out her date of birth and other personal information, but when it came to "nationality," she asked her father what to fill in. She knew that he had come from Czernovitz, which is in the Ukraine.

In the Soviet Union, a person born in Uzbekistan writes Uzbek or if born in Armenia writes nationality Armenian and this applies to all the republics, but if he is a Jew, no matter where he was born, he has to write Jewish. This has never been a great asset.

When she inquired about his nationality, he answered her "Jewish." She thought that he was joking and repeated her question and got the same answer, whereupon she burst out in shrieks: "You are telling me that you are a Jew? You are telling me that I am Jewish?" The scream was of anger, disappointment, distress, fury and hatred. "That, he said, happened this week."

A few days later Erich died of a heart attack or of a broken heart.

Chapter 20

The Absent Minded Professor

Mister B. was the personification of the absent-minded professor. His daughter Martha became my friend by the time she moved with her family to Czernovitz and registered in our high school. We were about fifteen years old at the time. Both of us exhibited similar interests in a number of areas: literature, languages, politics. Discussions among friends centered around new books that we had read and, of course, a "Weltanschauung," a view of world affairs. In lighter moments, we were often ridiculing our teachers, yet she would top all of our stories with examples of her father's foibles, habits and his absentmindedness.

She once told about the parade on the 10th of May, the most important holiday of Romania. The schools were marching in the parade and all the teachers were heading their assigned groups. As the hour approached and her father was getting ready and was almost late in leaving the house, he grabbed a hat and ran. As he hastened through the street toward school, all dressed in black suit and tie, people turned their heads and giggled, yet he never noticed a thing. However, when he reached the school yard, students burst out laughing. Somebody asked: " Herr Professor, what's with your hat?" He removed it from his head and noticed, to his horror, that it was his wife's hat with a long ostrich feather.

Martha enlivened our chats with many more incidents of this kind. There were good-natured ribbings from his family, which he took in that spirit, for his was a highly developed sense of humor. Yet he was formal and straight-laced and well aware of his social standing. A high-school "professor" was a well-respected member of society and he kept youngsters at a distance, expecting due deference.

In the provincial town, where he had spent his professional working life, many people knew him and respected him. When walking along the street, people would greet him and they would often engage him in conversation and showed respect for his opinions. He was somebody, he was well known, a well-regarded intellectual in that society, a professor, a family man with friends. When he retired and moved with his wife and youngest daughter to Czernovitz, all that was lost – he was a newcomer, a stranger. he moved for the sake of his youngest, who could finish school and go to the university. The older daughters had established themselves in Bucharest and the parents had hoped to remain with one daughter, at home. In the new town, when he would walk along the street, nobody knew him; he had lost his status, he was just a pensioner, an elderly man.

About one year after settling in Czernovitz, his wife became ill and died of cancer within a year. Thus Martha remained alone with her father. Both had a hard time running a household. Poor Mister B., a former teacher of religion, a highly learned man, a person who knew Goethe and Schiller and Heine and other German classics by heart, a lover of Latin and Greek, a scholar of Hebrew texts, a walking literary encyclopedia – a very absent-minded man, impractical, forgetful, always distracted, he missed the gentle but firm leading partner of his life, his wife. In fact, he once remarked that in India, they used to burn the wife on the funeral pyre of her deceased husband. According to him, it should be done the other way around. However, this was not our custom and he missed his wife desperately.

He shared small living quarters with his youngest daughter, my friend. As he was advancing in age, he became progressively more forgetful, more distracted and disorganized. For instance, he would search for hours for certain notes, copied from texts or observations on comparative alphabets. I still remember when he would expound on the similarity of the Hebrew aleph, bet, gimel, dalet to the Greek alpha, beta, gamma, delta and would go on to the end of the letters, – omega, the last letter of the Greek alphabet and say: etcetera, etcetera. To us it sounded terribly funny to say etcetera after the last letter, but who would have dared to smile and insult the elderly professor?

In the back of my mind I admired him for his literary scholarship, but in daily encounters, he struck as tragicomic and pathetic and painfully lonesome.

In the first days of July, 1941, soon after the German attack on the Soviet Union, our town was occupied by the Nazis. Thousands of our townspeople fled with the Soviets, among them also my friend. Mr. B. remained behind, all alone. A few days after the initial shock, he came by to find out whether I had remained or not. To his surprise, he found me and my parents at home. Thus, some of his anxieties had been relieved, there was a friendly family close by whom he could visit and, of course, I was a kind of replacement or reminder of his daughter. he once expressed his satisfaction in coming to us, by saying: "I come to smell Martha smell. "

Times could not be worse. Practical people could improvise, could make do with very little, somehow. Food was in extremely short supply. This elderly intellectual was incapable of performing practical daily activities: he could not cook or sew or launder, at least, not well. The man suffered daily in his helplessness and lonesomeness. Lucky for him, his landlady, who admired him for his intellectual capabilities, tried to alleviate his plight by making sure his room was heated, his bed was made, his clothes were washed. All these were not easy to accomplish at the time for it was a problem getting a piece of bread or a cake of soap.

As Jews were permitted to leave their houses for only two hours, from ten until noon, he would often come to us during that short interval. My Mother was an understanding, compassionate woman, who helped in her own fashion. Between my Father and the Professor there was little that they could agree on.

Father as a strictly observant, pious Jew who admired certain rabbis, who was a personal friend of some of them; Father kept all the religious observances meticulously, while the Professor was a Zionist, once a delegate from Bukovina at a Zionist Congress in Switzerland. He was proud to have met Nordau and other luminaries of Zionism before the First World Was. He declared himself as "enlightened," a modern Jew, a rationalist, who denounced the belief in rabbis as primitive, keeping some of the traditions as irrational, old-fashioned. He stopped short at declaring chasidim as ridiculous, stupid. Luckily, the two men did not argue much, they tolerated each other, they let each other continue with his own convictions; they did not try to influence one another; it seemed unimportant to argue about differences in outlook on religion, at a time when nobody was sure of living another day, whether chasid, traditional or enlightened; the world around us killed us, without difference, anyway.

Mr. B. did not come to us as my Father's friend but as a lonely person, who was glad to be welcomed by us; he came to see a surrogate daughter. He used to smoke a lot. Whenever he would sit down in our kitchen, for we kept only the kitchen heated, Mother would offer him bread and jam, tea or coffee. By the time he had finished the hot drink, he lit a cigarette, and warm and satisfied, he would slowly doze off. As the fingers held the cigarette, the ashes would drop on his trousers and, Mother or myself would gently remove the cigarette, for it would reach his fingers and singe them. As time approached to get home at the curfew hour, he would wake up slowly or we would nudge him to get ready to go home.

Once, when he did not come for a week, I walked over to find out what had happened to our old friend. I found him in his room pale and shaken and he told me about his accident. He had fallen asleep in bed and had still been smoking the last cigarette of the day, when he dozed off and put the bedding on fire. His landlady smelled the smoke, walked in and saved him. His moustache, his eyelashes, his eyebrows were singed, his bed and bedding doused in water and his demeanor shaken. Well, he could not give up smoking, but he decided never to smoke in bed again.

Times did not improve; the winter of 1942 to 43 was bitter in every respect. Food was scarce; the deportations of June 42 thinned even more the ranks of our co-religionist and those who had remained in town did not even dare hope to see the end of the war. Just as before, Jews were not permitted to leave their apartments for more than two hours a day and we mostly used the time to sell our last possessions in order to buy some food.

Professor B. never missed saying Kaddish – the prayer for the dead – for his wife on the date of her death. He would go to a synagogue to recite the prayers with a group of ten men, a minyan, a quorum. In the winter of 1943, when it was forbidden for a Jew to be walking the street at any hour other than ten to noon, he left his house before sundown and walked to a place where he knew they had a minyan. No sooner had he walked out of the house, with the yellow star sewn on his coat, when he was spotted by a policeman and arrested.

For about ten days his landlady did not know where he had vanished. Neither did we. There was no way of finding out where a Jew had disappeared. However, ten days later, he came home: thin, dirty, disheveled, a shadow of an old man. The story came to light: arrest, internment in a temporary camp in Sadagura, a small town near Czernovitz. Since the Romanians did not deport at that time, they placed every person caught trespassing the law – according to them – in a temporary camp. They threw all kinds of shady characters: thieves, prostitutes and our Professor into one big hangar. A minimum of food and drink was offered them by their captors; since their crimes were undefined, one day, they sent one or another, home, back to Czernovitz, where they had been apprehended.

Again our old Professor was slowly coming back to his old routines, but he was frightened. He watched the curfew hours meticulously; he made sure to spend more time reviewing his Greek grammar or reading over a Latin text by Cicero or Virgil or practicing English according to the Langenscheidt Method, all in the privacy of his room, alone.

However, he continued to come to us, a place where we felt concerned about his precarious health: an asthmatic cough, forgetfulness and a weakening of his resolve. All the trouble seemed to be going on endlessly and the day he was waiting for – to see his daughter again – loomed far away. The mood was getting grimmer as the weeks went by in that bitter winter, in January and February of 1943.

One day the Professor came up, climbing the hundred stairs to our fifth floor apartment and smiled broadly, a smile from ear to ear, a blissful joy spread over his usually grim looking face. As he stepped in, we asked: "Has peace broken out? Has the Messiah come? Has Hitler died?" "No, no," he replied "but something nice has happened to me. As I was walking along the street, a woman stopped me and asked: 'Herr Professor, don't you remember me?'" He looked at her somehow bewildered, unable to place her, but she continued: "I am Molly, your Kriminalskollegin[1]." "It was nice to see her" he added softly, smiling with a joyful glint in his eyes. I asked him who Molly was and he gently replied: "a prostitute."

At last, walking along the street, somebody knew who he was – Herr Professor.

---

[1]Prison colleague

Chapter 21

Homecoming

At the end of June 1941, during the first days of the war. after Germany had attacked the Soviet Union. the Soviets acted as if the most powerful earthquake had hit them. I am talking about my home town. Czernowitz. and the events I witnessed there.

The authorities panicked so utterly - they started following two courses simultaneously: trying to send their families into the interior of the country. Eastward. and at the same time putting the maximum number of men in uniform: grabbing men in the streets and loading them on military trucks. None of these young men had a chance to say good-bye to their families and off they were sent to war.

Hella, a young woman. about four years my senior, had got married a few months before the onset of the war. Theirs was a love match like no other - she thought. She adored Herbert, and thought there was no luckier woman alive. Nobody could measure up to him - she had just married the man of her dreams and desires. However, in that first week of the war and panic, Herbert did not come home. Somebody saw that he had been grabbed in the street and put on a military truck. Suddenly she felt lost, abandoned, incredulous. hurt, bereft - for her it seemed the end of the world.

Soon the Germans occupied our town and there followed the ghetto, the deportations and after years of incredible suffering and longing and praying for Herbert's safe return - the Russians were defeating the Germans and finally the Soviets occupied our province and our town again.

Hella was roaming the streets trying to find out from people who returned, whether anybody had seen Herbert or heard from him. She started to work in the railroad section where I worked and thus - I saw her daily. The woman avowed that she had kept striving to survive - just to be there when he returns.

In the meantime. during those three years, we had all become impoverished. We could not earn a living and we slowly sold everything that anybody would buy - to keep body and soul together.

About two months after the "liberation," Hella received the longed for letter from Herbert. He was alive and had recovered from a war injury incurred at the beginning of the war, was demobilized and lived in Uzbekistan, one of the Soviet republics in Central Asia.

He was anxious to find out whether she, her parents and his parents were alive.

Delirious with joy Hella answered and asked whether he could come home or whether she should come to join him. Luckily his parents had also survived and they all expected him back. Another few weeks passed without any news from him, but finally a missive came. Here he gave some details about his situation. When he was discharged from military service. he was run-down, didn't know the language, had no place to stay and became despondent. An Uzbek woman took him into her home, nursed him, fed him, gave him shelter and comfort. He did not know whether his family, back home in Czernowitz, was alive, while she saved him from starvation or death. He married her. Then he added. "I married her because she had a cow. She fed me milk. She gave me my life back."

Thus he found himself in a dilemma, that he deemed hard to solve. Hella and his parents faced a situation which nobody should ever be forced to confront.

The fact was - he was a bigamist and that fact in itself did not seem to bother him because there were thousand of similar cases during the war.

In the Soviet Union they said that most of the people under German occupation had been killed - especially the Jews. Thus, a man, coming out from a hospital, after having been wounded - a war veteran - alone in a strange land, a complete stranger wherever he went - he was looking for help, for food, for shelter, for a clean bed and a clean shirt. There were women, whose husbands had been taken to the front and they never knew whether their husbands would return. These situations became conducive to those kinds of new set-ups. A helpless man and a giving woman - lover, mother, who knows?

Here was the existing situation - Herbert had an Uzbek wife and was quasi settled in Central Asia. Two years before he didn't even know of the existence of Uzbekistan - and 1944 - this was his situation and his new home.

Hella and his parents beseeched him to come back, to come for a visit - just, to come. The mail service being especially bad during the was, it took weeks or months for a letter to reach its destination.

After another few weeks, he wrote that he was coming for a visit, but did not commit himself to anything; he had made no decision; he did not even allude to the fact that he had to make a choice.

Hella told me with joy and trepidation about his coming visit. She was older than myself and I refrained from asking any details - everything was fraught with embarrassment and suffering in this unique situation. She did not know whether he had told his present wife about her.

One morning, coming to work, she came by the office where I worked and asked me to see her during our lunch break. At midday I saw her. She burst out telling me what preparations she was making for his homecoming. She asked me whether I had a beautiful, alluring nightgown and if so, whether I would lend it to her. She really intended to almost seduce him, to present herself in such an attractive way that he should not doubt any more and choose her rather than the faraway - to her - stranger. She figured on making her room, her bed, herself so attractive that he should forget the other one.

To me she sounded so pathetic, so desperate, so sad, that I can not forget to this day the outpourings of this woman, she was just about drowning in sorrow. Needless to say, I could not give her any advice or offer her any attractive day or night wear. I was just hoping that her man was not so changed - that she might feel estranged from him. After ali, she remembered him as he was before these war experiences - battle. injuries, hospitals and life with a different type of woman, in a very unusual place - Uzbekistan.

He returned for a two week stay in his hometown, to see his family after a four year absence.

At that same time. I left for Romania. Whether Herbert remained with his wife Hella or whether he rejoined his Uzbek wife - I'll never know.

Chapter 22

New Year's Eve - December 31, 1945

The end of December, with Christmas and New Year's Eve, is a time of celebration and merry making. As long as I can remember, New Year's eve was always eagerly anticipated with joy and expectation of a lively party, with dear friends, with good food and drink, with singing and dancing and noisy, silly ways of blowing whistles, clapping hands, just carefree merrymaking. Some people attended masquerade balls or parties and played tricks on unknown revellers.

Sylvester, as the New Year's party was called - for Saint Sylvester day, which is December 31 - meant a grand time. If any partygoer were to get tipsy, it did not matter, for that was a time before the prevalence of cars. Thus, if one was not too steady on one's feet. One could still stagger home, singing and laughing on the way.

At the age of 14, Lola made a grand party at home. It was a beautiful dinner served to the 10 or more young people. In fact, we made it very fancy, the way we saw it in Viennese operettas. There were name cards - boy, girl, boy, girl. Lola and I made sure to sit with the young men we chose to have as dinner partners. Dinner was served at about nine or ten and by the time we were done, midnight neared. At 12 all the church bells in town rang, all the clocks chimed the hour and we drank "Prosit Neujahr" (Happy New Year). The dancing went on till early morning, to the music of records.

The following years, we still celebrated Sylvester, in the house of one or another of our friends. I remember that in 1938, when I was already a student at the university, we had a Sylvester party in my house. In 1940, as a student under the Soviets, the university organized a huge masquerade ball. I was dressed up as a Japanese, with a lovely authentic kimono, a big horn hair pin, the hair pinned up to the top of the head, real Japanese. That was to remain a memorable evening, because there followed years of a very grim existence; parties were just memories.

Since 1940 I had no place to celebrate and no reason to, unless surviving through another year merited to be seen as a monumental achievement. Every day was about the same, with more or less trepidation and little reason to cheer. The old year and the new year were the same: drab and dangerous.

However, at the end of 1945, there were reasons to celebrate, indeed: the war had finally come to an end, the side we favored had achieved victory, our deadly oppressors had been defeated and I, additionally, had also escaped from the Russians. More reason than ever to make merry. I was living at the time in Bucharest, sharing a room and bed with my friend Dorzia. That was my first year of freedom, but living under very precarious conditions.

A friend from earlier years invited me to a party, at her place. She was living with a well-to-do uncle and aunt and they were splurging on a real celebration, the first New Year's Eve in peace. I knew about the get-together but could not decide whether or not to attend. Why the uncertainty? I had no party dress, no dressy shoes, no good-looking coat. Thus, I felt, that it might be preferable to stay home, in the room that I shared with my girl friend.

When I visited an older cousin of a friend of mine and told her about the "Sylvester party," she insisted that I take a dress of hers: a navy dress with a white collar and white piping around the sleeves. I tried it on and it looked fine, except a trifle too big in the waist. She, a dressmaker, adjusted it for me and insisted that I wear it.

Wearing her dress, I went to my friend Blanka. When she heard the story about the party, she insisted that I try on her black coat with a silver fox collar.

Well, I looked stunning, she said. Everything seemed perfect, except for the shoes. Her pumps fitted perfectly, too. I was all dolled up. We were laughing so - she, her husband and myself; we were so amused. I sure had a sense of humor that propelled me to find amusement in such lean times. I also had no family, just friends - good and devoted ones.

Well, they thought I looked great, a knock-out. Jancu came to inquire whether I had decided to go and celebrate. What a new look, what a different person, he exclaimed in amazement and amusement.

We went to the party. Everybody was dancing and drinking to the success of all of us - all survivors, so far. We were all considering life in Bucharest as an interim, a way station, a platform from where to launch our futures - be it in Palestine (as it was called before the creation of the state of Israel) America or Western Europe.

The dancing and singing and celebrating went on till three in the morning. At that time Cinderella was supposed to go back to her little room, take off all the finery, the borrowed clothes and return to the usual. When I reached the house, where I lived, all the lights were on in the entire house. I was sure that the landlord and his wife were staying up because it was New Year's night.

When I knocked on the outside door, the landlord opened and hardly recognized me. Soon enough he gathered his composure and exclaimed: "You were celebrating! Bravo! We were celebrating right here! Our two daughters returned to-night! Happy New Year!"

If nothing else brought me back to reality, the return of the daughters did. We had rented the room with the condition that if the two daughters, deported by the Russians, came back, we would vacate the room within two or three days.

Thus, he said "Happy New Year" and I knew that I had lost the roof over my head. Cinderella had feasted, feted, danced and forgot about reality for just a few hours.

January 1, 1946 was a cold, snowy day and ushered in a cold, uncertain new year. Homeless again. Happy New Year.

Chapter 23

Whose Son Is He?

Rita, by trade a dressmaker, was the cousin of a girl friend of mine from high school. Older and less educated that we were, she had come to acquire a trade in Czernovitz a few years before I met her. In 1937, at about twenty-one years of age, she decided to start her working life in Bucharest, where she supposed her chances were more promising. At that time, the capital was expanding rapidly and work was more readily available for skilled workers.

While at home, in a small provincial town, politics played no role in daily life, the bigger town Czernovitz opened her eyes to a different type of awareness. All around her, people were drawn into politics, more than she had ever expected. It affected her, of course. She started sympathizing with the socialist ideology as did a great number of workers, at that time. In Bucharest, she joined a Socialist Club, which sponsored a gymnastics group and social activities like hikes and lectures and all kinds of courses. Within the new circle, she met Dinu, one of the lecturers, a few years older than herself, from a well-to-do Romanian-Jewish family. He was a rather quiet, shy, well educated, intellectual man, socialist by conviction. They became a couple.

In June 1940, when the Soviet Union took over Northern Bucovina, Rita and Dinu chose to come to her former home; they came to Czernovitz with great expectations, they both chose to live under Communism. She returned to a familiar town, while he started a completely different life, not only politically, but also away from his familiar surroundings and from his family.

He missed especially his older brother, whom he adored. The family had never looked with favor at their younger son's political orientation, however, the older brother, although a business man like their father, accepted Dinu as he was. Marrying a poor girl, a dressmaker, thrust Dinu out of the family mold.

Once settled in Czernovitz, they decided to start a family. Before the year was out she gave birth to a son, whom they named Arthur. Life seemed to settle down, but the expectations for the happy life were soon dashed. Life under the Soviet regime turned out to be grim, full of fear, forever uncertain whether anybody might point an accusing finger at you or could submit a damaging report about you or doubt whether your family background was trustworthy. After all, there were house administrators, most of them informers to the secret police, who could cast doubt on your reliability; or colleagues at work, neighbors, anybody with a grudge - life in Stalinist Russia became a grave disappointment a shattered expectation, a tarnished ideal. Just the fact that Dinu stemmed from a wealthy family, notwithstanding his own political convictions, could have landed him in the frozen Far East, in Siberia. Yet, he tried to adjust to the new situation; they struggled to make a go of their new life, in spite of all the disappointments and the difficulties with the new language, the tiny apartment and the loss of close family.

In June 1941, Germany attacked the Soviet Union and one week later our town was occupied by the conquering Germans and Romanians. Rita and Dinu did not flee with the retreating Russians toward the interior of the Soviet Union, but stayed in town, partly because they had a small child and partly because Communism had proved such a let-down. The couple and their baby son survived the first few months unharmed, while her parents, in the small town had been wiped out. However, the uncertainties and the approach of the ghetto and the deportations threatened daily.

Dinu's brother sent word through a Romanian, an acquaintance from Bucharest, that he would be willing to help, in whatever way Rita and Dinu would suggest.

I do not know whether the plan to shield the child originated from the parents or from the brother and sister-in-law in Bucharest. The brother and his wife sent a woman to pick up the baby boy and had him brought to them, to Bucharest. Thus, at least, the child would be kept safely by a loving uncle and aunt. The situation of the Jews in the capital stayed calm to the end of the war, except for a few bombardments towards the very end of the conflict. Thus the war years went on and finally, Rita and Dinu survived. In the spring of 1945, when the Soviets permitted former Romanian citizens to apply for ""repatriation" to Romania, they left with the greatest of joy and expectation.

Finally, after almost four years of separation, they would be reunited with their son, about four and half years old by then. Dinu would also see his beloved brother as well as the entire family.

They returned as penniless refugees to the place that used to be their home. The thought of the reunion with their child, of completing their small family, all this was reason for exhilaration. However, when they arrived in Bucharest, the brother and his wife told them that they had adopted the boy and insisted he was their son; they may as well accept the reality. The child did not know his real parents, he had seen them as a baby six months old. Rita and Dinu could not convince them to return the child. All their arguments that the war was over, that the child should return to his own parents, all this, to no avail. The disappointment with his own brother, the tension within the family - nothing helped. The reality turned to desperation. When the talks became more heated, the sister-in-law left town with the child. Rita and Dinu did not know of her whereabouts.

Now, besides themselves with pain, they seemed unable to cope with the nightmarish situation. At that point they turned to the Ministry of Justice. The new interim regime, before it turned completely Communist in 1947, was amenable to the plight of the parents. There may have been a number of similar cases as a result of the years of horror and racial laws. Other parents may have left children in care of orphanages or with some Christian families, in an effort to save a child's life. The Minister of Justice at the time was Gheorghe Maurer, a Romanian lawyer, a just and decent man, a known anti-fascist. They approached him in their desperate plight and were assured that some legislation would right the wrong inflicted on them.

A law was enacted, by which legal procedures that had been passed through the courts during the time of Nazi persecution, because of the desperation of parents, would be declared null and void. Adoptions of children because of fear of death would become invalid. That law was caused by the case of Rita and Dinu's son Arthur and was applicable to an entire category of similar cases.

In the mean time about two years passed. Both families fought for the child intensely, no matter what the law proclaimed. The real parents yearned for their son; the other couple, Dinu's once beloved brother and sister-in-law clung to the boy, whom they had raised since he was six months old and refused to give him up, no matter what the law proclaimed. They could not have children of their own and had grown so deeply attached to him. It needed the wisdom of Solomon to find a satisfactory solution or, perhaps, even Solomon would not have been able to find a good way out of this tragedy.

Rita bore another child, a girl, in 1946.

By the time I left Bucharest in 1947, the legal wrangle had not come to an end. By that time Arthur was six years old.

In 1983, on a visit in Israel, I saw my old school mate, Rita's cousin, again.

On inquiring about Rita and her family, I was told the result of the fights in the courts and the bitterness of the relationship between the two brothers and their wives. Legally, the son was supposed to be returned to his real parents, yet he was emotionally more attached to his second set of parents. The tug of war never ended; he was torn between them and ended up in a precarious mental state. Both couples never left Bucharest because both had one disturbed son.

Officially, World War Two ended in May 1945, but for some it never did. For them, it will end on the last days of their lives.

Chapter 24

Selma and Her Friends

Among my earliest recollections of sunny afternoons and childhood joys, of climbing rocks and running along steep hills, in the late 1920s, they all happened in the large park known as Habsburgshohe (Hapsburg Heights), in my native town Czernovitz, in the province Bucovina, Northern Romania, formerly Austria. Mother used to take my older sister Sali and myself on that long walk to the park, from early spring, around the middle of April, till the end of autumn, until the snows set in. As I grew older, I spent just as much time there in the company of my friends.

That park was a heavily wooded area, from which the Austrians had fashioned a recreation section called the Plateau, with flat surfaces for sandboxes and playgrounds and for vendors of pretzels, sunflower seeds, sodas and ice cream. The park area spread very wide; people would decide to meet in different sections. There were locations like "Kaiserfelsen," a wide, high rock named "Emperor Rock." At the age of six or seven, I felt proud to be able to climb to its top. Many baby nurses would bring their charges to spend a few hours in the fresh air of the woods. As you went down the steep hills, there were benches along the lanes, along the quiet, shady walks. One could have as much playground as one desired and as much quiet and privacy, as one felt like.

This was a favorite meeting place of poets, of lovers, of people who would get together and just talk or discuss books or politics and of thinkers and brooders, who spend undisturbed hours communing with nature. It was also favored by groups of young Zionists, who would discuss, sing, socialize there. The other two parks in town: Volksgarten (People's Garden), which was in a different part of Czernovitz, with a skating rink and soccer fields and a carefully tended flower garden and Schiller Park, a hilly but small park - these two had none of the natural attractions of our beloved Habsburgshohe, with its atmosphere of calm forest. In my life and that of my friends, nothing compared and ever will with that place. The chestnuts, the beeches, the fir trees and pine trees exuded an aroma rarely matched anywhere. Whenever I happen to take a vacation in high mountains, that aroma returns as a smell of delight from years long gone...

I got to know, at least by sight, many other faithful lovers of that place. Some people sat at a certain bench daily. Their muse met them at that particular spot. I remember going to the park with Paul Celan (Antschel) and he carried a volume of Rilke poetry. He stood up on a bench and started reading a poem, while I was standing and enjoying the poetry as well as the lyrical sound of his voice. Something romantic as well as intellectual was permeating our activities. We talked of matters of feeling and of the intellect; nobody paid attention to making money or considering jobs; we were teenagers then; we lived frugally, left the making of a living to our parents. If we did some tutoring, it was not worthy of discussion.

Many romances started there and many ended there, too. What out-pouring of ideas, of political convictions - Socialist or Zionist; what poems where written there; what declarations of immortal love were offered; what deceptions, what quarrels followed; we poured our hearts out in this forest.

Among the younger people that I often saw in the years 1938-39-40 spend-ing time in the park were my cousin's friends, a group of boys and girls who belonged to a Zionist Youth Organization named "Shomer Hatzair," Hebrew for "The Young Watchman." They used to meet in town, in the Zionist Center, but in the summertime, they preferred the park. All were four years younger than myself and made up a group called in Hebrew "Kwootza."

The original organizer of this Shomer group, the one who brought these boys and girls together was Abrasha (nickname for Abraham) Gimpelman, a high school student, my own age. He was a dedicated activist, who instructed the young members of the group in Zionist-socialist ideology and how to prepare for life in Palestine. In fact, he had left high school two years prior to graduation in order to take agricultural training, to be ready for life in kibbutz, a collective settlement in Palestine. Besides his capabilities as an inspired organizer, he happened to have been unusually handsome, a very attractive personality, a rare human being, trusted and admired by all who knew him.

Selma Meerbaum-Eisinger, who lived not far from me, just a little closer to the park, was one of the girls in the group. I often saw her with Renée, Abrasha's girlfriend. Among the young men in the group was Leiser Fichman, my husband's younger cousin. I remember Selma as a lively girl, short, with long, curly, dark brown hair, often in the company of girl friends. Her appearance was striking, a little sloppy, rather careless about her looks, as her brown hair was windblown. When walking alone, she looked preoccupied, oblivious of the world around her. Leiser, or Leisiu, as she would call him, was a quiet, serious, introverted youngster, very handsome, somehow in the shadow of his older brother Arye and older cousin Yuda. When Selma and Leiser would walk together, they struck as contrasting types: he was tall, impeccably neat, all in control, while Selma seemed rather lost in thoughts and impervious of appearance. They looked like different types of individuals, yet, she absolutely adored him.

Selma, a highly gifted poet, started to write at the age of fifteen. Whether by coincidence or as a family trait, Selma was a cousin of Paul Celan. The themes that permeated her poetry were nature, in all its shades, shapes, moods; she wrote about the rain, the wind, the night, flowers, dreams, fall, summer, storms and the deep, all consuming love for Leiser, who seemingly did not reciprocate her ardor. From the age of fifteen to the day she was deported to Transnistria, in June, 1942, she wrote of her joy and suffering because of unrequited love.

When the Soviet Union occupied Czernovitz in June, 1940, all political organizations were banned from existence, except Communist activities. The group led by Abrasha continued to meet, unofficially, in the park, as a couple of friends who just got together, with no agenda. However, people became aware that anything connected with Zionism was suspect in the eyes of the Soviet authorities. Somebody drew Abrasha's attention that it may be dangerous to get together, even as a small group, for not all former members participated any longer. Renée and Selma came regularly and, perhaps, another two or three.

One of the young men in the group, sure that Labor Zionism would be acceptable to the Soviet regime, wrote a long letter to Stalin, in which he explained that Shomer Hatzair believes in Socialism and communal living in kibbutzim, where there is no private property and thus no exploitation of workers, for they are all agricultural workers all equal members of a kibbutz. The only difference between a Soviet kolkhoz and a kibbutz would be that Shomer would encompass Jewish people in Palestine. This naive young Zionist wrote that he was sure that the leaders in the Kremlin were not aware that his ideology corresponded with that of the Soviets.

Little did he suspect the viciousness of the authorities. That letter, I am certain, never reached Stalin. The post office, probably, handed it to the N.K.V.D. (to-day K.G.B.) and the writer of the letter was arrested. He implicated Abrasha and another member of the group. All three were swiftly put on trial, found guilty and deported to Siberia. Abrasha was never heard of again, he perished somewhere in the frozen Far East.

Needless to say, after the arrests, they never met again as a Zionist group. Some remained friends, some were classmates in high school. Selma finished tenth grade in June 1941, a few days before the German attack on the Soviet Union. The airport of our town was bombed on the dawn of the first day, as we were living at the border and within days, the area was occupied by the Germans.

The Romanians and the Germans herded us into the Ghetto (October, November, 1941) and the majority of the Jewish population was deported to the Ukraine, yet not all. Leiser and his parents came back to town on the basis of a permit signed by the governor of the province Bucovina; Selma and her parents received a permit issued by the mayor of our town, Trajan Popovici. Half a year later, in June 1942, the Jews who resided on the strength of a Popovici permit were deported to Transnistria, the name, coined by the Romanians, for the territory East of the river Nistru - in Russian Dniesrt, the western part of the Ukraine, today called Moldavia. The territory between the rivers Nistru and Bug were newly named Transnistria and became the dumping ground for the Jews from our province. They were deposited there and abandoned to die there of starvation and sickness - no shelter, no food, no medical facilities.

In June 1942, the Romanians handed over the new deportees to the Germans at the Stone Quarry, called in Romanian Cariera de Piatra, near the river Bug; some were sent to the village Mihailovka. Of the thousands from our town, deported that summer, just a few individuals survived. Before the Germans retreated in defeat, in March and April of 1944, they shot the ones, who were still alive and, in some instances, set dogs upon stragglers in the forests.

Before the deportation, Selma handed to her girl friend Else a notebook, in which she had neatly copied her poems and asked her to give them to Leiser Fichman, who was, at the time, in a labor camp in Romania. The title page bears the name of the collection: Blutenlese (Anthology). The Romanian motto stems from "Lorelei," a novel by the Romanian writer Ionel

Teodoreanu and reads as follows: "I sing hoarsely below the windows of your house as the Italian children sing, in the streets of our towns, in the misery of their beauty, with Mediterranean eyes..." On the next page was the dedication of the poems:

> To Leiser Fichman, in remembrance and thankfulness
> for a lot of unforgettable beauty, dedicated with love

Upon his return to Czernovitz, after a few months in labor camp, the notebook with its fifty seven poems were given to him. Selma had fifty two original poems, two translations from Yiddish, two from French and one from Romanian. All were handwritten and were dated between the years 1939 to December 23, 1941. Whether any other poems existed but had not be transcribed into the notebook, will never be known. She was deported half a year after the date of her last poem.

The poetry showed an unusually sensitive person, who experienced nature in its most delicate changes and moods. She experienced great joy in living and laughing and loving. The love she felt so deeply so overwhelmingly was expressed with tenderness in *Lullaby for You*:

> I'll braid a cradle out of my hair
> here a cradle, see.
> You sleep in it without despair,
> dream in it painlessly.
>
> My eyes I will give to you
> as a twinkling toy.
> My lips I will give to you,
> drink from them with joy.
> (page 66)

Although so young, Selma expressed the whole range of feelings that people experience in a lifetime. Her joys, her happiness, her moods, her doubts, her despair - all blend in with the moods of nature - the winds, the rain, the rustling of the leaves, the softness of the sand, the opening of a blossom, the crackling of the snow underfoot, the clouds, the withered leaves like brown gold, the trees, the changes of the seasons - all of nature around her was part of her. A burst of color, the sight of yellow daffodils, brings forth this exuberant verse:

A Song for Yellow Daffodils

They're looking at me brightly through the rain
so bright that they replace for me the sun.
And surely nothing of the mourning rainfall
can mar the shining yellow joy at all.
Bursting with laughter, they bend amid the green,
which cleanly fresh accompanies their laughter.
I place my song at their feet to-day.
To-day they're bringing joy my way.

(June 30, 1941) p. 6

The more remarkable about it, this poem was written just about the time when the German troops were about to invade our territory and nobody knew whether we would be alive next day. This was composed a week after the outbreak of the war and yet, the sight of flowers could fill her with such uninhibited delight.

In the poem *Chestnuts*, she muses about nature and the melancholy passing of summer, the end of the life cycle:

On the smooth, bright path
scattered and weary they lie around,
brown and smiling, like a soft mouth;
full and shiny, dearly charming;
I hear them like a bubbling piano sound.

As I pick one up and put it in my hand,
softly caressing it like a small infant,
I think of the tree and of the wind
which sang softly through the leaves, alone.

and that the chestnuts must have taken this soft song
as the summer, which left unnoticed, sped along,
and as its last farewell has left his tone.

She hears the song of the wind through the leaves of the tree and the loss of vitality, the loss of color and tightness of the chestnut, as fall approaches.

> And the one here in my hand
> isn't brown and shiny like the rest.
> It is flat and sleepy like the sand,
> which through my fingers I set rolling.
> Slowly, step by step, as if unwilling
> I let my feet wander on, ahead.
> (September 24, 1939) p. 7

A later autumn scene comes alive with a word painting of all the colors of the leaves, trees, an eagle flying high above, and, down below, a half-frozen patch of grass.

> *Crystal*
>
> All's calm. And many withered leaves here lie
> like brown gold dipped in sunshine.
> The sky is very blue
> white clouds are rocking by.
> Hoar-frost blows brightness on the pine.
>
> Firs are standing fresh and green
> lofty tops rising into the height.
> The red beeches, slender and keen,
> listen to the eagle calling in his flight
> and dare go ever higher as heaven were.
> Lonely benches standing here and there
> and here a patch of grass, now half-frozen,
> the sun as its own darling had is chosen.

(December 8, 1940) p. 5

The scenes describe perfectly Habsburgshone in all the seasons. The music of steps on frozen snow flakes, nightfall in the icy landscape, nightfall and the darklooking fir trees. All these are depicted in the short poem *Colors*, written on December 18, 1939, at age fifteen.

The blue hovers over the snow-white snow
and so black are the green fir trees
that the quietly fleeting-by doe
is as gray as the endless sorrow,
which I so gladly would ban.

Steps crackle in the snow's music
and winds dust all the flakes back
over the white veiled trees;
and benches stand like dreams.

Lights fall and play with the shadows
like unending ring-a-rosies.
The far-away lanterns twinkle a faint glimmer
a light lent from the snow's shimmer.

(page 4)

However, at times, sadness and sorrow overtake this unusually sensitive poet, who expresses her despair, her fright and inability to cope with the utter hopelessness of life at the time. *I am the Rain* was written on August 8, 1941. I still remember that summer, when we, the Jewish population, were forced to stay in our houses, except for two hours a day, forced to wear a yellow star on our clothing and we did not know whether we would live another day. At night, one heard shooting and could not tell whether the Germans or the Romanians were killing people in our street or a block away. That was the summer when they burnt the Temple, when the flames lit the night with a fire that was to extinguish the Jewish life in our town, our own lives. This was the atmosphere in which the poem, which follows, was written.

I am the Rain

I am the rain and I am walking
barefoot along, from land to land.
In my hair gently plays the wind
with his slender, brownish hand.

My sheer dress is made of cobwebs,
it is grayer than gray sorrow.
I am alone, though here and there
I fitfully play with an ailing doe.

After these two stanzas, she brings forth her feelings of a young girl, who weeps lonely in the night. Besides the sorrows of everybody around her, the loneliness and longings and her awakening as a girl in love burst out in deeply sad tones.

> I hold these ropes tight in my hand,
> and on them there are strung and kept
> all the tears, which pale girls
> lonely eyes have ever wept. I've snatched them all
>
> from slender girls, who late at night
> trod hand in hand with longing,
> on lonely roads, with fright.

The last stanza of the poem is a repetition of the first and frames within it the grayness, the sense of poverty and deprivation: "I am walking barefoot from land to land" and the horror of homelessness. She gave expression to a time and place, when all the grown-ups were too petrified, too numbed, to put into words what the world around was inflicting on them. She never mentioned the words: guns, army, war, Nazis, ghetto, deportation - all the horrors which afflicted her and the world around her were never actually named, yet they loomed threateningly in her metaphors.

Selma's unusual talent, blossoming at so young an age, had no chance to fully ripen, to mature. Her poems were the creations of a girl from the age of fifteen to seventeen. When one considers that she was educated in Romanian public schools and, in tenth grade, in a Yiddish school (1940-41), where Ukrainian and Russian were taught, too - yet all her poems were written in perfect, rich, literary German, the language spoken at home and among her friends. One can not draw any conclusion whether her focus in poetic creation would have taken a different turn, away from the trend in which she had started. Like Anne Frank, who expressed herself in prose, Selma poured out her feelings in poetry, at that same time, under similar conditions, in a different part of Europe.

Her awakening feelings of love, of loss and a mood of resignation and quasi acceptance show in *Lullaby for Myself*

I sing and I sing and I sing me a song
a song of hope and good fortune,
I sing like the one who walks, failing to see
that he can never more return.
⋮
I play and I play and I play me a tune
of days that are no more
and free myself of that truth
and make as if I were blind.

(January 1941)
page 1, first and last stanza

From the start, it seems that her deep feelings of love for Leiser were not reciprocated and caused deep pain. Whether this experience made her express her feelings in poetry may be just conjecture on my part, yet I am inclined to think so. Among her first poems, entitled *Song*, dated December 25, 1939, at age fifteen, she started out with the statement:

To-day you hurt me so
Around us there was only silence
Only silence, only snow.

To-day you told me - leave.
And I left.

Her eroticism in the love poems reveals not a youngster but the feelings of a woman: they are fullblown, deeply felt and painful. In the poem *Red Clouds*, which was not dated in the collection, the depth of her passion as well as the poetic images just overflow, like a torrent of emotions and sights, too full, too rich to be contained in words. The full gamut of love, fear of loss of the beloved, implorations and fervor gush forth overwhelmingly. Here are some of the lines:

I am afraid. I am oppressed by the darkness of every sultry night.
It is so quiet and I am smothered by the heavy splendor of the
    silence.
Why? Why are you not here? I have trifled, I know - forgive.

> I trifled with my luck - it broke asunder - forgive.
> It is so painful being alone.
> We will laugh us into new happiness, believe me and return, there
>   is
> so much laughter yet.
> Look at me. Is my image still in your far-off glance?
> I want you as the grape wants, when ripe, to be plucked.
> My hair is waiting. My mouth wants you to play with it again.
> See, my hands beg you to envelop them in yours.
> They long for your hair and they long for your skin
> Just like a child yearns for the dream that she only sighted once.
> Look, it is spring. Yet it is blind, it weeps for evermore
> As long as we are not together, and weeps as long as the wind
>   weeps
> when its dearest forest has withered.
> See, everything waits for us: all the lanes, all the benches
> All the flowers are just waiting to be plucked by me and offered
>   to you.

She feels stronger in his arms, feels sheltered by his height and strength, she longs for every facet of his being, of his appearance and sorrowfully begs for his return:

> It's true, you'll come? I won't weep any longer. Oh, no, I won't
> feel empty any more.
> Doubting again that the reality would change, she continues:
> I am still here. The dream is over. I am alone -
> like red wine, my hot blood is seething.
> You are not here and we were so near and we were such sweet
>   wild fire.
> Spring is weeping. It weeps for us. Will you let it weep for ever?

In the *Song of Longing*, she attempts to bring forth, to compose a song, yet no melody arises, no tone comes out and she sadly tells herself

> You will always long for that unplayed sound
> long for the happiness, which had only slightly touched you
> in the quiet nights, when the moon rocks you
> and the silence does not understand your tears.

> (January 9, 1941)

The last two short poems, both dated December 23, 1941, show Selma so devastated by the unresponsiveness of Leiser, whom she so deeply loved, that she invokes no metaphor from nature, no element that could soothe or temper her heartbreak, alleviate her pain. They are terse and devastating. One has no titles, just *X X X*.

> Don't you sense when I cry for you
> are you really so far?
> And you are for me the beauty of life, the only one,
> for whom I endure loneliness

and dated the same day, another four lines entitled *Tragedy*

> This is the hardest: to give oneself
> and know that one is unneeded
> to give oneself fully and to think
> that one disappears like smoke into void.

While all the turmoil of love and desire was filling her own world, the large world around her was in just as much turmoil. The political events were tearing the world apart and were tearing the remaining Jewish population into shreds. Thus, in June 1942, Selma and her parents and thousands more were cruelly chased to their doom, the last bloodletting from among the small number that had remained in Czernovitz. In that last transport were also her relatives, Paul Celan's parents. Nobody knew exactly where they were taken or what their fate would be. Needless to say, the expectations were dismal, yet the reality turned out worse than ever imaginable.

Since the deportees had no way of communicating with anybody anywhere, the known data are sparse. After a short stop at the Stone Quarry, called in Romanian Cariera de Piatră, the Eisingers were sent to Michailovka, a village near the river Bug. Selma managed to find a person, who would take along a letter to her friend Renée[1], who was in another locality in Transnistria, a village called Obadovka. This letter reached Renée and has been preserved, the last anybody heard of her, her last piece of writing, last communication.

Rena, Tatanca, it is so hot here that I am too lazy to close my eyes, that I am not able to hold the pencil, and I find it hard to toss a thought through

---

[1]Renée was deported from Czernovitz in October, 1941

my head. Nevertheless, I want to write to you. Actually, I don't even know whether I will have a chance to send you this scrap of paper - never mind. Now I have at least the impression that you are sitting next to me, that I can talk to you after almost a year.* What do I say: almost a year. Actually, the last year in Czernovitz was as if we were far from each other. Actually, it is over two years since the time when we spent long afternoons together, without talking; afternoons when you were playing (the piano) and I was listening and both of us knew how the other felt[2]

Perhaps it is no good bringing back these memories. But never mind. I don't know how you feel, but I, sometimes, long for the unspeakably sweet pain of such memories. There are moments when I try to conjure up a specially hot, live picture and don't succeed. At most, once a fleeting touch of a face or a word, but without really grasping or absorbing it. I sometimes think: Berta. Or - Leisiu. Or - a kiss. I don't grasp the meaning of these notions. Let's leave it. I have a poem here, the author of which I don't know. It is beautiful.

The title of the poem is: *Heimweh* (Homesick). The pervasive feeling expressed is of utter desolation, of wrenching pain felt by a person, who longs for every stone, bench, house - everything that was home. She felt that this poem put into words her own extreme longing for what used to be home. Then the letter continues:

> Nettchen, how long will this go on? How do you bear it? I have been here less than three months and I imagine that I will surely go out of my mind. Especially, in these unspeakably bright and white nights that overflow with longing. Sing sometimes, late at night, when you are alone: Poljushka[3]. Perhaps you will understand my frame of mind.
>
> Do you remember the fifth chapter of "Home and the World?" [4] I'll copy a few sentences: Why can't I sing? The faraway river glitters in the light; the leaves glisten; the morning light spills over the earth like the love of the blue heavens and in this autumn symphony I alone remain silent. The sunshine of the world hits my heart with its rays, but it does not hurl them back: August is here. The sky sobs wildly. And streams of tears crash on the

---

[2]Selma may have alluded to the time after Abrasha's arrest and deportation to Siberia.
[3]Poljushka is a romantic Russian song of longing.
[4]"Home and the World" by Indian writer Rabindranath Tagore (1919)

earth and, oh, my house is empty."[5]

I feel as if all my coming days are freezing together into one solid mass and will lie forever on my breast. Rena, Rena, if only you were with me. I don't know, maybe, if we were together, it would be too much. Maybe not. Anyway, we could still endure it for a month, if we were together. Of course, one bears it anyway. One endures, although one thinks again and again: Now, now it is too much. I can't bear it any more, now I am breaking down. Just now, Tunia brought me a note from Rochzie. I am using this chance to send you this incomplete outpouring.

Kisses, Chazak Selma

This letter reached Renée (Selma addressed her by her Hebrew name Rena) and has been preserved intact. Chazak was the greeting of the members of Shomer Hatzair and means: be strong.

The letter, written in August 1942, speaks for itself, her own words say it all - the brutality of tearing people out of their homes, just to let them perish of hunger, of sickness, of exhaustion, of despair. Yet, in the letter there was still a slight expression of hope.

One of the few survivors of this camp, Arnold Daghani, kept a diary, which he published on his return to Romania. In it he wrote on Wednesday, December 16, 1942: "Toward evening, Selma breathed her last." On December 17, 1942, he wrote: "Professor Doctor Gottlieb died of malnutrition. He and Selma were buried at the same time." As an explanation, he added that: "her real name was Meerbaum; the name Eisinger is that of her stepfather, I learned. She died of typhus, in her teens." On that page, he drew a picture of her body, wrapped in a shroud and mourned by people around. The original of that drawing is kept in Yad Vashem, the Holocaust Memorial in Jerusalem. It is entitled: "Pieta." Mr. Daghani wrote that her parents died soon after of typhus, too.

When Leiser returned from the labor camp, he received the notebook with the poems. Since he was forced to return to the camp, he was not in a position to take along anything besides his clothes; again he left the poems in the hands of their common friend Else. Yuda and his cousin Leiser spent months in the same location, during compulsory work: digging trenches. Leiser never found out about Selma's death.

---

[5]In his diary, Mr. Daghani mentioned that Selma had promised to lend him this book, but it had been used as cigarette paper.

In 1944, when the Russians approached Romania, while the German armies were retreating westward, toward their final defeat, Leiser escaped from camp and reached Bucharest. After contacting the Zionist Organization, he was granted first priority to board a small boat of illegal immigrants of their way to Palestine, from the Romanian port Constantza. The ill-fated boat Mefkure, on which he was travelling, was torpedoed and sunk in the Mediterranean Sea and none of the passengers survived. A few weeks later, when Yuda reached Bucharest, the fate of the boat was already known.

Thus the three young people about whom I wrote initially - Selma, Leiser, Abrasha - were all gone by 1944. A the age of twenty-one, Abrasha was lost in the frozen wastes of Siberia; Selma, at eighteen, perished in the steppes of the Ukraine and Leiser, at twenty, in the waters of the Eastern Mediterranean. All three young Zionists, idealists, never saw the land that they were yearning for, never lived to reach Palestine. Abrasha's father remarked in great sorrow that his son, like Moses tried to lead his people to the Promised Land, however, he did not live to see it.

There is no grave, no marker for any of them, yet they live in the memory of those who loved them. Selma left her poems, the spark of her vital personality, the fullness of her lively mind and the memory of Leiser, whom she adored.

In the poem *The Storm* (March, 1941) Selma dwelled on the gentleness, the fragility of a rosebud and the expectation to see it open and bloom and about the precariousness of all life. The verse is her own epitaph:

> If now a frost comes - it dies,
> dies and has never lived its life.

When we write nowadays that six million perished during the Holocaust, the number is awesome, abstract; it is hard for the mind to comprehend that number, yet each one was a world. Can we fathom what we lost, what the world lost?

NOTE:

For years only her small group of friends knew about the existence of the poems. Her two close friends, who kept the manuscripts, and her former mathematics teacher from tenth grade, Hersh Segal, got together and published the Anthology - Blütenlese in Rechovot, Israel, in 1976. This privately financed publication reached a larger public and her name and fame spread, but very slowly. A second edition was published by the Diaspora Research Institute, Tel Aviv University, in 1979.

The translations in this article are all my own, from the original text: Selma Meerbaum-Eisinger (1924-1942) Blütenlese

Postscript March 2005:
Selma oder Die Reise um den Tisch.
Eine szenische Recherche mit Musik

In the year 2000, to my great surprise I received a call from Fürth, Germany, with news of an intriguing project. The caller explained that his wife, an actress, had read the poetry of Selma Meerbaum – a small volume of her writings published in Germany.

The actress, Jutta Czurda, and a group of friends – a composer, a writer, and his actress wife–decided to create a play about Selma and put some of her poems to music. However, they knew very little about her, other than that she had died of typhoid fever n Ukraine in December, 1941. Mr. Minasian, the husband of the actress, decided to turn to the Internet for information. As soon as he entered Selma's name, there appeared the chapter from my memoirs, *Before Memories Fade.* He found my address and telephone number and the connection was established.

Mr. Minasian informed me of the group's plan and asked whether I would cooperate in the creation of the play. I enthusiastically agreed. I wanted Selma to be famous, if only posthumously. For a year we spoke almost every week, about the town, the community, the war, Selma's lover for Leiser (my husband's cousin). I answered their questions, in German, and some of my statements were incorporated into the play.

In march of 2001, I was told the the premiere would take place on April 21, in the Stadttheater Fürth, Studio auf dem Theater. The theater invited my husband and me to attend the premiere, all expenses paid! We were of course moved and were excited to have the opportunity to be there. We took along our older grandson, Michael, who was seventeen at the time. We arrived on April 19, 2001, and were met by Mr. Minasian at the railroad station in Nuremberg. We had talked for a year, for hours at a time, and now we met in person.

On the morning of the day before the premiere we were received at the theater. There was a crowd: actors, musicians, the press, radio and TV reporters. That was the only time in my life that I was interviewed in German. Fortunately it worked out well. On the following day, the day of the premiere (which was only open to invited guests and the press), a long article, with photographs, appeared in the Fürth newspaper. It was a wonderful performance, on an open stage with musicians all around and the composer at the piano. The writer's wife, Katharina Teuffert, played Selma.

The play was performed often in Fürth, then at a film festival in Munich, and in 2002 in Zurich. And then in Czernowitz. On the anniversary of the world premiere the cast travelled to Selma's hometown, where it was put on in a theater very similar to the one in Fürth. As Jutta Czurda reported in a letter to me, both performances were almost sold out and the audiences were very enthusiastic: "Almost 1,000 people saw *Selma* . . . After the play we all signed countless programs and answered questions. And so for us, you, too, returned symbolically to Czernowitz with your voice, and built a direct bridge to Selma for the audience." She is right. Although German is not spoken in Czernowitz today, Selma and I came home somehow.

Chapter 25

The Visit

In October, 1947, I took the train from London to Southampton and embarked on my voyage to the United States. The night before, the one night in a London hotel, sleep just wouldn't come and no wonder. Next day, I was going to leave Europe, perhaps forever. I was going to New York, perhaps for the rest of my life. Everything would be different from that day on. I will cross the Atlantic on the Queen Elizabeth, cross the Atlantic - when before, I had never spent a day on anything afloat. Yet nothing brought joy to my heart, when my brain was working feverishly, overtime. I would arrive and be with my hopelessly sick Father; my legal situation unclear, my bridges burnt behind me, unclear what my home would be, no more home to go back to, a person in limbo, yet finally going to the U.S.A.

The woman, who was travelling with me from Paris to New York, a matron in her fifties, was going to be reunited with her young son and was expecting to marry a rabbi. I didn't know her well, she was appended to me, just to help her. The woman spoke only Polish and Yiddish and could not talk to anybody, except me. She would share my cabin on that stormy autumn passage to America.

Next morning, we arrived early at the railroad station and seated ourselves in a compartment, which had three or four seats and the same number of seats opposite us. In the center was a door that opened from the platform. Thus there would be a maximum of six or eight passengers. It was an empty compartment and the two of us looked out on the platform.

Soon a middle aged gentleman arrived, put his suitcase on the opposite side and walked out. He had arrived with a lady and the two of them talked, held hands, kissed and looked at each other. We may have had half an hour before the departure. My travelling companion and myself had nothing to talk about, just plenty to think of.

The man and the woman, an elegantly dressed matron, with a fur boa and a stylish hat, were holding hands, as before, looking at one another and every now and then, kissing. As the time of departure neared, they looked more anxiously at one another and as the train was about to leave, they kissed and hugged and held on to one another, as if it were their last day on earth.

The gentleman got into the train, they waved good bye and we departed. The train ride to Southampton took a few hours. As we settled down, the two of us on one side, the gentleman opposite us, he introduced himself as Mr. Sharf, from Brooklyn. We told him that we came from Poland and Romania respectively, on our way to the U.S. Mr. Sharf was on his first visit home, in Leeds, England, after decades in America. He returned after so many years as he could not afford to do so sooner. When we asked who the lady was from whom he parted with such reluctance, he told us his story.

He was a poor boy from a large family. When he was in school, he started to court a tailor's daughter, from a family even poorer than his own. They adored each other but could not figure out how to start a life together. They decided that he would go to America and try to make a living. By the time he could afford it, he would send her a ticket to join him. Based on that understanding, the two poor lovers parted.

Ben was not successful for a long time; he struggled for years and could not make a go of it. Thus time went by and later, he found out that Regina, the tailor's daughter had married a rich man in Leeds. Ben, eventually married, too, had children and settled into a family and ordinary, everyday existence, like millions of others. The young lover, who had left to make his fortune, grew into a middle-aged, sedate family man in Brooklyn.

In the summer of 1947, after his sons had returned from military service, he decided to return to Leeds, to see his family, his home town. The homecoming was full of joy and emotion, yet he was not prepared for the events to follow. By the way, his brother told him that Regina, his childhood sweetheart, still lived in the neighborhood. She found out about his visit. Ben called her up.

They met. She was more beautiful than he had remembered her from so long ago. She had married and lived an affluent life; by this time she was a widow, a beautiful, wealthy widow. When they met again, he said, he loved her like on the day he had left. Her feelings for him were just as intense.

He said that he felt like a youngster again, his heart beat to bursting at the sight of her.

His family realized that their love had been rekindled, their emotions could not be hidden. With every passing day, the day of his return to America was nearing. She proposed to him to offer all her wealth to his wife, if she would consent to a divorce. He told us, in a pleading tone that he could not possibly consider her offer, for his wife had gone with him through good times and bad and they had built a family together. How could he do this to his wife and to his children? His wife would be a victim, badly hurt. His children would hardly understand what their father was inflicting on them and their mother. He repeated several times: My wife is innocent. How can I do it to her? and yet, this new-found old love possessed him with a burning passion.

The two of us had watched the farewell - such a display of emotion, such a desperate way of holding on but yielding to the reality of a departing train. They were torn apart and we were witnesses. That was rekindled love and that was the woman who saw him off at the London railroad station. Those kisses will remain a memory for the rest of his life: we shared his most intimate secret.

The two of us just sat and listened. He could unburden himself to us, strangers, for we would never see him again, we were only witnesses to a most private affair. That experience made my train ride from London to Southampton memorable. It also made me think about myself . . .

Chapter 26

Student Activities

At the age of eighteen, when I started my studies at the University of Czernovitz, nobody talked or thought of student activities. The ones who were needy and there were plenty of them, sought out a meager living by tutoring young children or teaching high school students in their special field: math, physics, languages. They had no time to think of anything but survival - food, shelter - and passing the exams. Others, who were luckier and did not have to make a living, devoted most of their time to studies and to friends, lovers and often politics.

The university environment in itself did not offer great chances of involvement, socially or politically. Of course, political activities went on outside the parameters of the university: Fascists, Communists, Socialists, Social-Democrats - the range encompassed from the extreme right to the extreme left.

During my year as a student under the Soviets in 1940-41, the university regressed to the level of high school: daily attendance from 9 to 2 p.m., a fixed program without any choices, daily homework, exams. However, the intention of the regime was clearly put into practice: teach and enforce the Communist ideology. Students were encouraged to join clubs: chorus, instrumental groups and, above all, the Comsomol, the Young Communist League. Not much initiative was fostered, yet strict ideology was inculcated.

The irony of life is hard to put into words. While before any inclination toward Communism was punishable by heavy prison sentences, suddenly, overnight, we had to become Communists or else be candidates for Siberia. Of course, life was stranger than fiction as a year later we were again supposed to abhor Communism and three years later turn back left again. But people do not change just because governments decree it overnight. That was a chameleon-like existence, one was supposed to change color according to the occupying power.

Coming back to the situation under the Soviets. In order to join the Comsomol, one had to have the acceptable background: to have been a sympathizer of the ideology was not enough. The family background had to be proletarian, farmer or peasant not landowner or left inclined intelligentsia. How could anybody create a background to fit acceptance? Most local students were middle class, rarely were they children of workers. The Romanian students had all fled to Romania and, what was left were mostly Jews and a small number of Ukrainians and Poles.

Whoever applied for admission had to tell or read his or her autobiography in public. The rest of the student body could then ask questions, interrogate the applicant in front of several hundred students. Most of the local students knew the applicant and his family. Trying to join could prove to be a trap if any eager young climber chose to put tricky questions. Half of the student body were sons and daughters of the occupiers: Ukrainian and Russian.

Student activities, in this atmosphere, could become a tragic entanglement. It came to light that someone had had a business or a house or that somebody in the family was a Zionist or a Socialist - all these could pave the road to Siberia in Stalin's times. That was dirty linen washed in public, that could cost lives, that could destroy families.

The only enjoyable activity in that year, organized by the university, was the masked ball on New Year's eve. There was music and dancing and food, a great party. The celebration of the October Revolution, celebrated in November, finished off the day with a grand dance. On these two evenings we enjoyed the revels, the dancing. One just had to make sure not to get drunk, for then one might say things that one would later regret. The honest thoughts were dangerous, had to be kept inside, for "in vino veritas" applies at all times; there were eager ears all around.

When I studied in Bucharest, after the war, no student had any social connection with the institution. You registered, you attended the lectures sometimes, you made sure to study for the exams - from the reading list and from the lectures, which you could buy in stencil form.

In 1947, when I came to the United States, I heard people talk about student life and I did not understand what that entailed. Yet I was a person always ready to learn and become aware of the ways in which an American university differed from what I had known beforehand. In January, 1948, I enrolled at Columbia and found out that I was a co-ed, a woman student. At first, the big lecture classes were not conducive to any personal contacts with fellow students. Eventually, when joining the seminar in Modern American Literature, I became a member of a small group - about 12 students in all. Here we established some personal contacts with one another: we exchanged notes, lent each other books, information on where to look up essays or summaries, etc.

Soon enough I found out about the foreign students' club, where one could drop in any time. I saw people from all over the world, yet I was the only graduate student in English. Because of my intense course of studies and my situation at home, I could not foster that interest. I just knew that the club existed. The Hillel club, a Jewish student organization, had mostly undergraduate activities, catering to the interests of the very youthful crowd, while I was much older.

Before Christmas the foreign students were offered the opportunity to speak in their own languages over Radio Free Europe to their relatives and friends and address good wishes on the occasion of Christmas and New Year. My friends in Bucharest were thrilled to hear me address them by name and talk to them in Romanian.

Another foreign student activity brought me for a weekend to Bard College as a participant in a symposium on World Affairs. The contact with great personalities in American life like Eleanor Roosevelt and Adolph Berle Jr. and the real honest discussions on the relations among the great nations and the rifts that were developing, these remained very meaningful experiences in my life.

The months before the Declaration of the State of Israel on May 15, 1948 were filled with drives and calls for aid to the needy newcomers there as well as for establishment of the institutions of a state, for the defense of its existence. I read the newspapers, heard radio reports and they all mentioned tremendous sums of money, millions and millions donated for this purpose. I was awed by the generosity of our people. What had not been done for the millions who died was done for the survivors.

One day, at Columbia, I saw an announcement from the Club of Graduate Women Alumnae, who were convening a meeting and were inviting all women graduate students to come, meet and participate in a joint endeavor, namely, raising funds for a scholarship for a female graduate student from the Philippines, to study at Columbia. In our seminar were just three, two girls from Brooklyn and myself, who was also residing in Brooklyn at the time. The three of us decided to attend that meeting, see the establishment ladies, who were active in university affairs, catch a glimpse of the kind of women we may perhaps become in another 20 or 30 years. We went to that meeting on the campus at about four in the afternoon. Needless to say, we did not know anybody there. The organizers greeted us in a friendly manner. About sixty to seventy people gathered - some old, some young - all former or present graduate students.

When the meeting was opened, the chairlady mentioned that we would all try our best to give a woman, from an underdeveloped country a chance at the kind of education that we were so privileged to enjoy. They favored to train somebody in the field of social work or health care so that, at her return, she would offer that society a needed service. It sounded like a very worthy undertaking. The organizers had a big surprise in store: the alumnae had approached the president of Columbia, Dwight D. Eisenhower, to lend his support and he had promised to attend and be of assistance.

Soon after the door opened and Eisenhower, the hero, the supreme commander of the Allied Forces in Europe, the organizer of D-Day, the future president of the United States, came in. As one, the entire group of women stood up as he walked in trim, erect, elegant in a light grey suit, but he blushed so, his face and bald head - all flushed. We all applauded and he stood there, blushing and embarrassed. As we sat down, he said that he was used to men standing at attention, but it was the first time that a group of women greeted him thus. He really looked embarrassed and short of words, taken by surprise.

That was a very special moment; I think that everybody who was present at that meeting will never forget it.

We sat down at his invitation and he addressed us in his succinct and cadenced manner, praising us for our concern toward educating women from underprivileged countries. As a gesture of generosity, wanting to help in our drive for funds, he offered a photo of himself and autographed it right in front of us. Handing it to the chairlady of the club, he offered it to her as a fund raising donation. Soon after, he left and the photo was auctioned off to the highest bidder. Starting out with one dollar, the price soon soared to 10, 11, 12 dollars, then the going got rougher. Finally it was sold to the highest bidder for 17 dollars. Right after the auction, all of us partook of tea and cookies, some small talk ensued and soon after the women alumnae closed the meeting.

When I left, I felt kind of struck by this experience, by this typically

American institution. I was amazed that in a group of women of that caliber, a photo and autograph of Ike, the genuine American hero at the end of World War II, the person who each party wanted to attract as a candidate for the presidency, for he would have carried Democrats or Republicans to win the election, a picture, given almost personally in that club environment, that afternoon at Columbia, and all in a good cause, that picture fetched 17 dollars. At that rate, I wonder whether a Filipino woman really received a scholarship from the Columbia alumnae?

Chapter 27

Arye Fichman

A few days after my arrival in Israel, Yuda's cousin Arye came from Kibbutz Beit Oren to Haifa in order to meet me. After having been told all about him, I was full of anticipation before being faced with a genuine hero, a brave young man, who at age 23 chose to confront the enemy world face to face in Europe, fully aware that his chances of survival were minimal; yet he voluntarily braved that world, in order to try to bring comfort and encouragement to fellow Jews.

When he came, I saw a thoughtful, peaceful, quiet individual, modest in his dress and his demeanor, a soft-spoken kibbutznik, plainly clad in khaki pants and a cotton Eisenhower jacket, unassuming.

Yuda and Arye were the same age and had grown up together from early childhood till age 18. Their fathers owned jointly a house in Czernovitz and they lived next door to each other. Arye's father Hersh was the financially more successful of the brothers. He hoped that his older son Arye would fulfill all his expectations, for he could afford whatever his son would choose to do.

Arye was showered by nature with a variety of gifts - mental and physical. He was handsome, with wavy chestnut hair, regular features and a winning smile, as striking as a movie idol. In school, few could rival his achievements, a boy of outstanding intelligence as well as sensitivity. While the father was a practical, hard-nosed businessman, his older son had a tendency towards intellectual pursuits, a heart full of compassion and a strong feel for his own people. Early on he became a Zionist and held the conviction that the Land of Israel had to be reclaimed through Jewish labor.

He joined a Zionist youth organization at the age of 14 or 15. As his ideological bent turned toward educating the poor, he switched from Noar Zioni (Zionist Youth), a student youth organization, made up of middle class youths, to Dror, which consisted of the poorest element in our town, the least educated youngsters, sons and daughters of almost indigent people. He became not only an ideological guide, but also a teacher, a role model for "the poor of his people." While at home, he had been tutored in Hebrew, he started teaching the group, bringing them to Hebrew literacy.

In 1938, when he finished high school in Czernovitz, a conflict between father and son came sharply to the surface. His father longed to have him study medicine, while Arye's conscience impelled him toward a future in Palestine. Refusing to go abroad to Paris or London, for studies, he insisted on going to his chosen country. The father hoped that he would register at the Hebrew University in Jerusalem, but Arye first joined a group of laborers, who were building a road to Atlit. In spite of his lack of experience at hard labor and braving the rigors of the hot climate, he persevered. Actually, road work and construction are the most gruelling types of labor in that geographical region. The heat and the dry conditions during the windy spells of "chamsin" - the desert winds, demand unusual physical stamina. But chamsin or not, Arye did not waver, he felt it a badge of honor to be a member of the road builders, to put his muscle to achieve visible results. The foreman said about him: "He is a worker," the highest accolade one could bestow on an idealistic 18 year old, with soft hands and lacking the muscle to lift sacks of gravel or push a fully loaded wheelbarrow. He persevered, the will won out.

Soon after, he joined a group of young people who founded Kibbutz Beit Oren, on the crest of Mount Carmel. He started working in the fields after having cleared the brush and stones of that rocky virgin land. By tilling the soil he became knowledgeable about agriculture and worked toward the attainment of the dream, toward the creation of the Jewish State. Shortly after settling in Palestine, he met and married Yaffa, a native born, a sabra, daughter of a rabbi from Safed, who had turned to kibbutz life, just as different from the orthodox background of her family as Arye's was from his middle class European life. Sheer idealism brought these two people together, two youngsters of completely different backgrounds.

His talents as an organizer became apparent soon. The kibbutz had a breath- taking geographic location, but nobody could live just on the beauty of the sight. The development of its economic base became of paramount importance. Yaffa, who had studied at the Higher School for Agriculture in

Nahalal, developed the chicken and egg production; he became the moving force of the slowly growing settlement. They built a recreational facility, a kind of summer resort for paying guests. The location on the heights made it into a "Little Switzerland," a cool retreat in the summer, with soft breezes toward evening. That proved to become about the best income generating asset of Beit Oren.

He taught himself economics and administration, as he went along and realized the needs of a newly founded, poorly endowed young community, without much grazing land.

This happened shortly before the outbreak of the Second World War in Europe. As the tragedy of European Jewry was unfolding, the Jewish community in Palestine decided to form a Jewish Brigade, made up of volunteers. The Brigade was attached to the British Forces, as Palestine was then a British Mandate, under British Administration. The Jewish Brigade was trained in Egypt, where England had stationed sizable forces. The scope of this fighting outfit was, first of all, to contribute to the defeat of the Nazi powers and, secondly, to give the community in Palestine a better bargaining position after the war, in their striving to attain an independent Jewish State and to rescue the survivors in Europe. That was the long range political objective of the Yishuv, the Jews of Palestine, under the leadership of the Jewish Agency.

In 1942, Arye volunteered to join the Jewish Brigade, although he was the most peace-loving person, the last one to feel comfortable in an army setting and at army training. His friend Ljova Gukovsky, a volunteer in the Brigade, like him, approached Arye and told him that they had news from the Dror organization in Romania. This man, unlike Arye, was very outgoing and liked the limelight. Wherever things were going on, he enjoyed being in the midst of the activity.

Ljova asked Arye whether he would be ready to help his former party friends in Romania. Shortly after the Seder, in the spring of 1943, Ljova confided in Arye that he had already been trained as a parachutist, to be dropped behind enemy lines in Romania and whether Arye would volunteer for the same type of mission. The duties of the paratroopers were two-fold: to endeavor to rescue allied prisoners of war, to work out ways of escape from the camps and, simultaneously, to get in touch with the Jewish community. Arye and Ljova's aim would consist in encouraging the Jewish population in some ways, make them realize that they were not abandoned or forgotten by the Jews in Palestine. Arye agreed to volunteer, too, although he said that the solid ground was his element; he had never gone through any training in the water or in the air, but his conscience dictated him to volunteer. He was 23 years old at the time; he had a wife in kibbutz. Nothing was known about the fate of his entire family in Czernovitz since the outbreak of the war in Europe.

He was granted a few days leave, to talk things over with Yaffa, to whom he had been married just a few months. She agreed to this kind of mission after a very emotional and painful exchange of ideas and opinions. In the end, she said: "I understand and I agree that this is something that you have to do." Nobody except Yaffa and Ljova, knew about the assignment, the secret training and the following long absence. Neither the comrades in his unit, nor the members of the Kibbutz had an inkling about the secret mission.

Simultaneously, several parachutists were trained for mission in Hungary, Yugoslavia, Italy and Romania - none knew about the others. For security reasons, in case they were captured, they should not be in a position to name people on similar assignments. Only Ljova and Arye were aware of preparations for Romania. In fact, they met Dov Berger in later months and had not been aware of his mission to Romania, although they were friends in Israel, then Palestine. As we know now, all the others were captured and all were tortured and put to death: Hanna Senesh in Hungary, Aviva Reick in Yugoslavia, Enzio Sereni in Italy.

After 8 days of training in parachute jumping and aspects of spying and survival, they were sent to a British air base in Benghazi, in Northern Libya, North Africa. From the start, it seemed that nothing was going right, the way Arye described it in his book "Ba Kaf" (in the Palm) meaning in the palm of the enemy. The book told all about the mission and was written in Hebrew, never translated into a different language. There were multiple foul-ups. Ljove, a portly, heavy-set man, seven years Arye's senior, was supposed to be Captain Brown and Arye, a slender young man, Lieutenant Smith. They had been measured for uniforms, gold coins sewn into their shoulder pads, the names on the jackets. By the time they arrived in Benghazi, their uniforms had been mixed up. Arye's uniform had the captain's insignia, while Ljova the lieutenant's. The documents were similarly mixed up. Thus Arye, the slight 23 year old, left as the senior officer and Ljova the Lieutenant. They waited for six hours until the pilot, who had been assigned to fly them out on the mission arrived. He asked them where they wanted to be dropped off. Seemingly, the mission was poorly coordinated by the British. Thus, they were flown out after a six hour delay.

They were supposed to be dropped above the town Timisoara, in the Southwestern part of Romania. They had studied detailed maps and were supposed to contact people, who would be helpful for the mission. By mistake, the pilot dropped them over Lugoj, sixty miles East of the supposed landing site and almost on the Hungarian border. They were dropping leaflets over the Romanian territory, encouraging people to resist, for the war would soon be over and would be won by the Western powers. As the two men bailed out over the town, the British had provided white parachutes instead of black ones. Thus, they were dropped at night but were immediately sighted by the police and soon apprehended by the authorities. The white parachutes were like big, white balloons, descending from above. Ljova landed on a roof and broke a leg right then and was immediately removed for interrogation.

Arye, landing with his white parachute, tried to untangle himself and change to civilian clothes, but was apprehended right there. He realized how badly the mission had been handled from the moment he was floating down. He was interrogated at length and jailed. As intensely as the Romanians tried to pressure him to talk, he insisted that they had merely intended to drop leaflets. Although he understood everything the interrogators said among themselves, he kept to his initial declaration that he knew only English and French. He did not know what had happened to Ljova.

After a few weeks the Romanians sent him to Frankfurt am Main, in Germany, where the Germans interrogated him for two seemingly endless weeks of constant questioning, threats of injections with syphilis and kept him awake at night. Since he did not divulge anything, they returned him to Romania, as he had been apprehended over that territory. Although they knew he was a Jew from Palestine, he was treated as an English prisoner of war, an officer and left alive.

In the prisoner of war camp, he tried to organize an escape by digging a tunnel. He and his fellow prisoners were found out, he was dispatched to a more rigorous camp, without any privileges. In the new place, he met Ljova again, just released from the hospital. They suffered through those months together until they were freed on August 18, 1944, when Romania capitulated to the Allies and was partially occupied by the Soviets.

All prisoners of war were released and everyone tried to return to one's own country. Arye came to Bucharest with a grave fear for the life of his family, anxious to find out whether his parents and brother Leiser had survived, how the rest of the relatives had fared.

At that same time, Yuda and Arye's younger brother Leiser were in a labor camp, in Romania. As the German and Romanian troops were in retreat from the advancing Russian troops, the men in the labor camp were left starving, no bread was supplied to them. Yuda walked out of the camp, without permission, and walked to the neighboring village to buy some bread. While he was returning to the camp, carrying two loaves of bread, he was apprehended. In the meantime when they counted the Jews in the camp, they found him missing. On his return, he was kept for a hearing. Leiser could more easily leave than Yuda, who was detained because of the bread. Leiser left and was supposed to head toward Bucharest and Yuda would follow as soon as he could. Both would get in touch with the Jewish Agency. On Yuda's arrival in Bucharest, he found out that Leiser had already left on a small boat with illegal immigrants, the "Mephkure," from the Romanian port Constanţa to Palestine. Leiser had no idea that Arye was any place but in Palestine. Yuda was supposed to leave one week later, on another small boat with illegal immigrants to Eretz (Palestine). By the time Yuda arrived in Bucharest, he found out that Leiser had already left.

In the meantime Arye arrived in Bucharest and Yuda met him through their contact with the Jewish Agency. They actually met there: Arye out of a prisoner of war camp meets Yuda, out of a labor camp. The meeting seemed unreal, as Yuda took it for granted that Arye was in Palestine. After talking and telling about who had survived where, Arye's parents were still in Czernovitz, under the Russians, Yuda's parents never made it through the war years, Yuda's brother Michael was somewhere in Russia. While they were deeply involved in the conversation, trying to make any sense out of the disaster of this war, talking about what had happened to different members of their family, a man walked in and told them: "I have news for both of you, not good news. Arye, the boat on which your brother Leiser travelled to Palestine was torpedoed in the Mediterranean. There are no survivors."

The reunion turned into a session of deep sorrow - for Arye to have lost his only brother, a young man of 21 and for Yuda, to have lost a cousin, with whom he had spent the last two years on and off in labor camps together. Yuda, too, felt like he had lost a younger brother. They sat together and mourned together an irreplaceable loss, a youngster who had had no chance to live and to develop, a youngster of such promise. He had left only a few days ago, feeling so privileged to be able to finally leave Europe, be united with his brother and - now, his brother was mourning his untimely death, by enemy hands, German torpedoes that sunk them in the Black Sea.

Yet life had to go on. Arye returned to Palestine officially, through Italy, while Yuda went on a small boat, manned by the immigrants themselves and arrived in Palestine, via Syria.

The prison warden had returned him the military uniform and freed him as an English officer. The Romanians never realized that there were gold coins sewn into the shoulder pads, to be used as a bribe in case the situation demanded it. At his arrival, after the captivity, Arye returned the gold coins to the authorities. He joined Yaffa in Kibbutz Beit Oren.

On their return, Arye, Ljova and Dov were greeted as heroes, yet the enthusiasm was dampened, others on those missions were gone, their graves not even known.

Arye picked up the threads of his disrupted life in Beit Oren, with his wife. He wrote an account of his experiences, in Hebrew. Although approached by people in the Labor Party to accept a diplomatic post, he preferred to remain in Kibbutz and live there as an active member and as a family man. To their great joy, their son Micha was born and about three years later, daughter Chanah. Arye became an important person in the United Kibbutz Organization: he taught courses in Management of Kibbutzim; he became the head of the Seminar in Kibbutz Ein Charod.

I met him at that point, in January 1950. He struck me as a person completely at peace with himself, at peace with the world, not interested in worldly goods, not trying to achieve any material gain, not corrupted by the world around him, intent on working for the betterment of the communities, for which he labored. He knew no envy. He took delight in his young children, his work for the kibbutz movement and the life of Israel. While times were very tough in the first years of Israel's existence, at the time of the "Ingathering of the Exiles," the influx of an enormous number of newcomers - all poor, all impoverished remnants of European Jewry as well as immigrants from Arab countries - yet his belief in the reality of Israel was strong, immutable and the task of integrating this mass of immigrants was of paramount importance and achievable, possible. His needs were easily satisfied: important work, the simple life, production of sufficient foods for his people.

He often travelled to Haifa and Tel Aviv for the Kibbutz. On those days, the only luxury he indulged in was movies. He loved movies and treated himself to a film any time he came to a town.

When we bought an apartment on Mount Carmel, in Haifa, and he came to visit for the first time, his reaction was unusual. We had practically no furniture, but the flat was lovely, bright, with a beautiful view of Haifa Bay and, on a clear day, the snow-capped mountains of Lebanon were visible from the terrace.

When he saw the apartment, he said: "Now you'll have trouble. You'll have to furnish all this." He had no trouble, his needs were minimal: he dressed simply, ate simply, lived an idealist's life.

On and off we would see Arye: we sometimes visited them in Beit Oren but more often, on his way to Haifa, he would come to us. He was a delightful guest, easy-going and unpretentious, highly knowledgeable in economics and agriculture. His parents had come to Israel a few years after his return from Europe; they had settled in Tel Aviv. They could never understand Arye's deep commitment to the Kibbutz; they never warmed up to Beit Oren but they adored him and his family: Micha was a serious, intelligent boy, who loved to play chess, read voraciously and was a great joy to all. Chanah, a little red- head, was a petite charmer, full of liveliness, quick-silver. The parents slowly came out of their grief from the loss of Leiser.

In the summer of 1954, ten years from the liberation of the three surviving parachutists, the government of Israel decided to organize a celebration in their honor. The special get-together was scheduled for July 29, 1954, ten years of freedom, a good enough reason for celebration. It was to take place at Kibbutz Maagan.

At the time, Arye was teaching at the Seminar for Economic Managers in Ein Charod. The two other survivors came to pick him up and everybody assembled at Maagan. Yaffa came to the festivity straight from Beit Oren. High dignitaries from the government were present, but Prime Minister David Ben Gurion could not attend. He sent a message of congratulations to the festive gathering. Since the three men had parachuted on their daring missions, the prime minister sent the message, which was to be delivered by a small Piper airplane. The pilot was to drop the message by means of a small parachute over the assembled public. The strings of the small parachute got entangled in the rotary of the motor and the Piper plane crashed on top of the three surviving heroes. All three were killed on the spot: Arye, Ljova, Dov. Yaffa, who sat next to him was severely wounded and so were others. Irony of fate ... All of Israel was shocked and in mourning; the pain, the loss were unbearable. His wife recovered from her physical wounds; his parents grieved the tragic loss of their only surviving son, at the age of 34, to the last days of their lives. His father Hersh never recovered from the event in Maagan. They first sat shiva, the week of mourning, and performed the daily kaddish prayer at home, with a quorum of neighbors. After the seven days, Hersh had to go to the synagogue to say kaddish (the prayer for the dead), but he developed a kind of fear and shame. He said that he could not face people, he was afraid of their stares. "What kind of man am I that God chose to punish me so, to take away both my sons at such tender ages? What sins did I commit that I was meted out such punishment?" He became a recluse, he sat at home and said Tehillim (psalms). His wife Poire, as deeply wounded as he, could still muster the courage to live and take care of him and sometimes visit Yaffa, Micha and Channah in Beit Oren. When Yuda and I would visit them in Tel Aviv once in a while, the visit left us shuddering. In a corner of the room, they had a table with all the pictures, they kept them present near them all the time. It looked like an altar. The only time Hersh would leave would be to visit the grave in Beit Oren. He lived many more years, haunted by his loss.

Arye's son Micha grew into a fine, upstanding member of Beit Oren. When he joined the Israeli Army, he volunteered into the elite unit of paratroopers, became a parachutist. He fought valiantly in the 1967 war and soon after formed a group of volunteers, who founded the first kibbutz on the Golan Heights - Merom Hagolan.

At the end of November, 1972, during one of the outbursts of fire from a Syrian battery, everyone ran into the shelter. He rushed everybody in but was the last one to take shelter himself. He was mortally wounded on that autumn day, November 23, 1972, a few months before the birth of his first child. He was 27 years old.

The son was buried next to his father, in Kibbutz Beit Oren, on the height of the Carmel Mountains, overlooking the green valleys of Israel and the blue Mediterranean.

Chapter 28

The Tale of a Pen

Uncle Morris, Mother's youngest brother, visited us in Czernovitz several times during my childhood. When I was at about the age of nine or ten he brought my older sister Sali and me unusual presents, at the time - a fountain pen for each of us. He explained that it had to be filled with ink and that we should carefully use that golden pen, not press too hard, get smooth ink, etc. Fountain pens were definitely a rarity and ours were dainty, lady's pens. Morris himself wrote with a larger, thicker pen, a man's pen, which met with admiring glances all around.

Well, we went to school and were envied and admired and talked about as we did not need to carry any inkwell to school; we never spilled ink on our clothes, never had blue spots on our fingers - we were proud possessors of the latest achievement in writing refinement.

It did not take me long to lose mine. Whether it was stolen or I was careless and lost it, needless to say, I was left without my badge of technical achievement from America, while older sister Sali had hers.

About two years later Uncle Morris came to Europe again, on business, and visited us again. I was too bashful to open my mouth, but Mother told him that I had lost my pen. "Well, my son Jack had his Bar Mitzvah recently and he received a number of pens, one of which I am using now" and he gave me his.

That was the real McCoy! What it lacked in daintiness it made up in size and luxury: a Waterman pen all covered in silver filigree on a black background; the top as well as the bottom parts were just like two pieces of jewelry. I accepted it joyfully and aware that it could be stolen in no time.

Shortly after Morris left, after a family conference, it was decided that there was no sense in possessing a pen and not taking it to school - but how to secure this treasure? Somebody had the bright idea to have a jeweler attach a silver top with a hook and I should wear it attached to a velvet band around my neck. Thus, when writing, the top remains like a pendant and nobody would steal half a pen. Thus I became the proud wearer of a silver filigreed pen the way one wears a jeweled locket or pendant. From the age of twelve on, it was my constant school companion. The girls in school and the teachers knew me with the pen; it was my lucky charm, my talisman. Through high school and university, by that time not on my neck any more, the pen remained a constant.

However, during the years of German-Romanian occupation (1941-44), we were selling practically all our possessions, whatever was left after the ghetto: jewelry, clothes, linens. It never even occurred to me to sell my only luxury item, my pen. Yet there came a time when I went to have our permit for residence signed and lacking that signature meant deportation to Transnistria, to camp. I took along the pen, in case I had to offer somebody a bribe and once again when we were summoned to the police and I did not know what could follow consequently and each time they signed the documents without expecting a pay-off. I may not have had the dexterity how to offer a bribe or I may have felt so reluctant to do it, needless to say, the pen stayed with me.

I survived and went to Romania and finally to the United States and used my pen through my studies in Bucharest and New York and continued to feel that same old attachment for it.

At the end of 1949, after my decision to settle in Israel, Mother looked dejected and sad as the time of departure neared. I told her: "Now you will write letters again. Take my pen and you will have it for a companion now." I would not have parted with it otherwise, but my Mother deserved it, it was part of me. And she wrote letters to me for seven years, until I returned.

Could any of Jack's bar mitzvah pens rival the fate of this one?

Chapter 29

Letter to Sasha

Dear Sasha,

You probably remember that day in the last week of June 1941, it was the 26th or 27th, when turmoil and panic gripped the entire town, when the Germans had just attacked on Sunday at daybreak - June 23. The next few days became a blur in my memory. The Russians evacuated feverishly and the German invasion became imminent.

One afternoon, toward the end of the week, I walked all the way to the hospital where you were working. In front of the building trucks were being loaded, evacuating the personnel. We spoke for a few short minutes and you said: "I am leaving now. Take care of yourself and your parents. Take care of my parents and my sister and her child. I hope I will return to all of you." One last embrace and you boarded the truck. That was our good-bye.

If I cried, I do not recall any more, 48 years and almost a lifetime have gone by. My heart felt like a stone as I walked that long walk home - alone. I was 21 years old. Nobody could foresee what would happen next day, let alone next week or further down the road.

You did not ask me to join you, and, honestly said, I do not know whether I would have accepted it. You never suggested. Everything at that time was done at the spur of the moment. Your younger brother was called up, your younger sister left with the hospital and, somehow, your kid brother joined in the evacuation, too. You were so eager to save your own lives in the first week of the war. Only your parents remained and their eldest daughter.

As I walked home on that sunny afternoon in June, it was the end of the world.

My parents had no consolation for me. At least we were together and the rest was fate.

Our next door neighbor, Mrs. Becker, came in and upon hearing about your departure, told me that you were not really true to me, that she had seen you with other girls. That did not soothe my unhappiness yet it registered deeply. Next day, when the students went into evacuation. I almost left, almost. My parents were crying when they saw that I was about to leave, together with Martha. I dropped my knapsack and decided to stay with them and share their fate. That was the only time I saw my Father crying.

The first days, after the Russians had fled en masse, the Germans and the Romanians settled in for the duration. They shot Jews in the outlying areas of town and everybody stayed indoors - petrified. Your parents and sister and her little daughter came to us and stayed with us for two days. I had never met them before. We got acquainted under these rough circumstances. We were all scared and shocked. The only common thread among us was you. Your Father said: "To have five children and to be left with one. Where are my three sons?" I felt very uneasy facing your family. I myself felt abandoned by all my friends from the university and by you, too.

Two days later, when the shootings seemingly abated, your family returned to their apartment and when saying good-bye, your Mother said: "I hope to see you and my son get married in better days to come."

Why am I telling you this now after 48 years?

I did not see your parents again. We were permitted to leave the house for only two or three hours daily and your family lived at the opposite end of town. We used those few hours to buy food on the market and also sold our belongings, our personal possessions, in order to get the necessary money. We had to wear the yellow star affixed on the outer garment.

We were all herded into a ghetto in the formerly poor Jewish section of town, from October 14 until the beginning of December, 1941. I remained with my parents after receiving the Governor's permit to stay; your family received a permit issued by the mayor of Czernovitz, Popovici. Half a year later, those with the permit issued by the mayor were deported and only a handful returned.

Your family was among the many who never made it.

When the Russians returned in April, 1944, I was awaiting news from you. Among the friends I made during the war years was a girl from Bessarabia, who worked with me as a seamstress in a sewing workshop; all of us were unpaid laborers. She had been employed at the Post Office during the year 1940-41 and intended to do so again as soon as the Soviets returned. She knew about you and promised to bring me any letter as soon as it arrived.

Among the first sacks of mail to reach Czernovitz were three postcards from you, with your military return address. She brought all three. One was addressed to me. All three postcards were written in violet ink by the same Ukrainian hand, a woman's hand. They all contained the same message, that you were alive, well, serving in the Red Army and anxious to hear from me. Were my parents and your family alive? If your parents were, they would need financial help from you. You begged for an immediate answer. The postcards were signed in your name, but not by you.

Who could write for you: a secretary, a nurse, a doctor? Could you not overcome your dislike of letterwriting and write yourself? In case I was not alive, it would make no difference who had written. If I was alive, would it not upset me to get a first sign of life written for you by another person?

You may have thought nobody would receive those cards any more, but let's try, in case ... Or, you may have deemed me naive, but my intuition led me right then into wondering about the writer. These three cards were the turning point in our relationship, they decided your future and mine. I believed that you, like many others, did not wait to find out whether the Germans had obliterated their wives or girlfriends; thus, you found replacements - temporary or permanent.

In those three years, while we lived on almost different planets, the sun rose daily and the sun set daily. Whoever was alive fought to make it from day to day, learned to adjust without: without freedom, without joy, without boyfriend, without much expectation, sometimes without food, mostly without hope - but lived. When the Germans left and the Soviets returned on April 4, 1944, after almost three years of Nazi occupation, I hoped for your return.

I answered you and sent you letters but did not have the heart to say much about your parents. They had not returned and yet, there was still a chance that they might come back. Survivors trickled back: some sick, some crippled, but only very few. In your next letter, in Romanian, you asked: "Why are all the Jews in Czernovitz alive, except for my parents?" Of course, that was not so. More than half the Jewish community had not survived, but that was no consolation for you and I could understand that. You did not ask me whether my parents and I needed any help. Actually, we managed to keep above water all along, but you did not seem to give our situation much thought.

When I received one letter after five of mine, you sent me a picture of yourself in uniform, proudly displaying your medals and also holding your hand in a way that I could see the wrist watch that I had given you on your birthday. You were proud of being a major and chief surgeon and wearer of medals. You wrote that you would return to Czernovitz as soon as the war was over and it appeared that it may take another half a year, a year or more.

You were at the front and must have gone through rough times, as I did. In the summer of 1944, I struggled hard not to be taken to the coal mines in the Donbas and not to be sent by the Rail Road to Murmansk, in the Arctic area. I managed to remain at my job with the Rail Road until the University reopened in September 1944, where I was in my third year of studies.

You asked for pictures from years past, for snapshots we had together; I could not accommodate you. When the Germans and Romanians ruled, we were so afraid to have Russian or Ukrainian books, we burned them all. We also destroyed pictures with people who had fled with the Soviets. I had almost nothing left.

I realized gradually that I had no idea of what you were planning to do, of how you would accept the fact that we were alive and your family had been destroyed. You wrote that your younger brother was killed at the front and I felt very deeply that hurt for I knew him very well and had liked him for his decency and honesty.

The post cards and the writer were on my mind; my intuition told me that this person was more than just somebody who knew Ukrainian well. I knew that you were not good at the two new Slavic languages, you also my have thought that it was safer to write in Ukrainian because of censorship, and yet ...

I hit upon the idea to write to the commander of your unit to ask him whether he could tell me about your status. I wrote explaining that I was your close friend and asked him to tell me what your situation was. I averred that any news that he would forward to me would be accepted by me with strength and equanimity. I would appreciate his answer, whatever the news. The war had steeled my character, I was capable of accepting the truth.

A few weeks later I received a letter from the head of personnel of the unit, who had been given my letter by his commander. He wrote in Russian and gave me details as to your military status, which was very high, and that you kept permanent company with one of the nurses. They are on very good terms, he said, and he was sorry to have to tell me the unpleasant news. He emphasized that I never mention his name or his letter at any time since he was friendly with both of you.

The letter hurt badly, but I was not totally surprised. I knew your weakness for women and I also was aware that women fell for your good looks. You were always aware of being dark and handsome and having a winning smile. I answered the officer thanking him for his reply and promised never to divulge his confidence. He wrote again and offered to become acquainted with me and come to Czernovitz instead of to the Caucasus, his home region, when the war was over. He trusted the major's taste. That letter was not answered by me.

As soon as the opportunity arose to register to leave our town, to be "repatriated" to Romania, my parents and I were among the first to apply. After these years of war, you may have become hardened on the front and I had become self-reliant and determined by a life of unending danger and worry. Neither my parents, nor I had had an easy day from June 1941 until we left in April 1945. They were bitter years with great losses all along, Father's family in Poland had been wiped out, we lived with unending anxiety from all the occupiers: Germans, Romanians, Russians.

I realized that you might come back alone or you might return with your new companion; I felt I could have handled any situation, but I preferred to leave for Romania. We became there homeless refugees. I had already lived without you for four years, I knew I could handle it for good. I chose not to meet you again, I was afraid of your power of persuasion. The Soviet regime had become so oppressive, the secretiveness so pervasive, I could not choose in good conscience to play along with your Communist ideology - I had had enough.

Many years later I was told by a friend that you asked on your return: "Why did she leave?" I never told you of that letter from the Russian in your regiment, I was bound by a promise. It may never have occurred to you that I would leave, since that had never happened previously in the Soviet Union. But when, for the first time in the life of that country, since 1917, the population of Czernovitz was granted the freedom, we opted to leave. Some did not apply for fear of being sent to Siberia. We three took the chance and succeeded in reaching Romania. From there, two years later, we reached the United States. I have never regretted that decision.

In the spring of 1946 I had to go to Suceava, where the records of the University of Czernovitz were available. By chance, I happened to meet your sister Fanny, who lived temporarily in her husband's hometown, before leaving for Israel. Our meeting was like a scene from a sentimental movie.

When she saw me, she burst out crying and repeated again and again: "Why did you leave? Why did you leave? Our lives would have been different had you remained." She told me that you had returned to our town six weeks after my departure. When you realized the fact, you went to all my relatives and friends looking for pictures of me. She said that you were very lonesome and, eventually, went to Kiev to bring Olga. That was the way Fanny put it. Of course, she did not savor the thought that you, with your rabbinical background, married out of the faith and never left the Soviet Union. Fanny, who lives now in Israel, mentioned that you had told Olga of your intention to return home at the end of the war and she had stoically accepted that fact.

I asked her: "Why didn't he write me the plain truth? Did I have to find out from a Russian at the front? Did I have to play Sherlock Holmes? He never imagined that anybody could find out what happened at the front."

Why am I writing this after 45 years?

Yesterday, looking through old pictures, I found a snapshot of myself and your brother Jacob, lost so young on the German front. I thought that you may not have any pictures of him. Thus, I send you this picture and tell you also how I made my decision to leave in April of 1945. I built for myself a good life, with a family of my own, with a loving, trustworthy husband and two fine sons.

The first step was when I said good-bye to my beloved home town. The three post cards decided my fate and perhaps yours, too.

P.S. This reminiscence can not even be addressed to you since I express myself in English, a language which you don't understand. For the last 50 years, you are using Russian or Ukrainian, which I have almost forgotten. Were I to walk by you, I might not even recognize you - you might not know me.

We were 21 and 27 then. I am close to 70 and you are 76. It is just that a seemingly trivial item, a post card, changed the course of our lives. In fact, I can not send you Jacob's picture either, I don't know your address and, I don't even know whether you are alive.

New York, December 2, 1989

Chapter 30

La Rue Du Chat Qui Pêche

My oldest brother Eli was a non-commissioned officer in the U.S. Army during the Second World War. After rigorous and painful training and careful screening, he was sent to England in 1943. At the time he was 38 years old; not part of the combat troops but an interpreter of German and French. This skill put him among the first lines of troops to invade the Continent.

He would have preferred to return to Europe as a tourist in peace time, but he was anxious and patriotic enough to look forward to his duties as part of a victorious Allied army, witnessing the demise of the Reich. The knowledge that his parents, and I, his youngest sister, were in the grips of combatting forces were reason enough for him to be eager to see the defeat of the Germans. The day after D-Day, his regiment landed on a beach in Normandy.

For a time Eli was stationed in Ulm, a town in Southern Germany, on the river Danube. He saw the great destruction, homeless people trying to go back to their homes; he saw horror an distrust all around him. Every German under interrogation swore to being an anti-Nazi; they had done whatever they did under duress, executing orders from above. Eli, a gentle and compassionate man, must have felt relieved only to interpret, not to have to judge the cases in which he was involved.

One day, in his capacity as translator, he was faced by a young French woman about twenty-five years old. The girl was homeless and needed a pass to return home to Paris. At that time, in the summer of 1944, Eli had realized the enormity of the tragedy that had been playing itself out in Germany and in all the European countries involved in the war. Death and destruction all around, Eli felt personally the suffering in the aftermath.

241

Marie-Louise, a small, dark-haired young girl from France, reminded him of me, as he told me later. Her situation touched his heart. As interpreter, he understood that she had been deported by the Germans and she was desperately seeking a way to return home. Eli tried to get her shoes, a coat and most important of all - a travelling permit for repatriation. Thus provided, he sent her on her way to Paris. She left him her home address on La Rue du Chat qui Pêche. By the time Eli returned, after completion of his military service, he continued to exchange letters with Marie-Louise from time to time.

In the fall of 1947, when I was about to leave Romania and go through Paris to New York, Eli asked me to make the effort and meet Marie-Louise. I did not know much about her except that he had written to me that she reminded him of me, that she was a sweet and charming French Catholic. He was anxious to know how she had reintegrated after such a difficult period in her life.

Once in Paris, I made it my business to get in touch with her. She invited me to lunch in her apartment on Rue du Chat qui Pêche. The name of the street intrigued me. In translation, it meant "Street of the Fishing Cat," unusual name, strange.

When I met Marie-Louise, she was not as fragile as I expected her to be. She talked enthusiastically about Eli, who had been so helpful to her but whom I had last seen when I was five years old. Looking at this young woman whom he liked, I tried to find out more about my brother. She knew him better than I did. She related harrowing stories about her involvement in the maquis, the French underground, during the German occupation; about a shoot-out in this same living room, where we are sitting and her deportation to Germany. As proof of the events, there was a hole in the surface of the table, as a result of the shoot-out.

To satisfy my curiosity about the unusual name of her street, she gave me an explanation. The small street, in an old section of Paris, was formerly part of a red-light district. They used to refer to it: La Rue ou Chacun y Pêche.

In translation, it was: The Street Where Everybody Sins. With time, it changed and became: "The Street of the Fishing Cat."

I left with an ambivalent feeling, somehow unsure about Marie-Louise, about whom my brother had written with such tenderness. I promised to convey her feelings of thankfulness to Eli.

The one friend I had in Paris from my Romanian hometown came to take me out for dinner and a ride to see Paris at night. His French wife was anxious to show me the glories of her city, which I had been inclined to admire from way back, in my teen years. As we were talking about what I had done in Paris, I told them about Marie-Louise, as Eli had related and as she had told it to me.

They listened attentively to the story and then gave me an interpretation which shocked me.

They said that no French-Catholic women had been deported to concentration camps in Germany during the occupation. There were some French girls who belonged to Nazi groups, who volunteered to go to Germany during the occupation as supervisors in concentration camps and factories. They smiled bitterly and asserted that my brother, with the best intentions, had probably eased the way for a French collaborator, in service to Germany, to escape scot-free. I felt very awkward and disappointed about how people use other people; about how good and evil can interchange; how good intentions can be used by shrewd people to cover up bad acts or even crimes. I was wondering what to tell my brother when I would eventually see him, talk to him, on my arrival in the States.

I never told him about my friends' intimations.

Chapter 31

September 1, 1939 - September 1, 1989

As the summer of 1939 approached its end, Czernovitz, my hometown in the North-Eastern corner of Romania looked like a peaceful place, a placid university town, where streets, buildings and parks would come alive with the influx of students, who would register for the new school year 1939-40.

However, the end of August brought ominous news, renewed demands from Adolf Hitler, that loud-mouthed history shaper and shaker from Germany. The signing of a nonaggression pact between Nazi Germany and the Soviet Union on August 22 changed the general outlook of the situation. To see pictures of von Ribbentrop and Molotov, the foreign ministers of Germany and the Soviet Union, signing a pact and shaking hands, all this presented Europeans and, probably, the rest of the world, with grotesque images. Do the sheep and the wolf really eat at the same table? Do they drink from the same cup, sleep in the same bed? Nationalism and internationalism - united by deceitful signatures and seemingly friendly handshakes. We had seen deceit by Fascists and Communists before, but what was that a harbinger of? Nobody, at the time, had an intimation of the underhandedness of both giant dictators, of Hitler and Stalin. Each one of them deemed that he had got the upper hand, considered that he had outsmarted the other. Both had decided to divide Europe among themselves; of course Stalin would have an almost free hand in Eastern Europe.

The hell with the West, the hell with the people of Eastern Europe, who had been bargained away between Germany and the Soviet Union.

Thus, in August of 1939, I surely did not know that my life had been planned for me by Hitler and Stalin. Our province had been doomed to become a Southwestern nook in the Soviet Union, a provincial backwater in a giant conglomerate of supposedly friendly Soviet nations.

At the end of August, life went on with its usual rhythms, and the unusual ones would come uninvited. At home, Mother made preparations for the impending fall and winter seasons; she prepared jams and jellies, bought cloth and lining for new winter coats for herself and me; Father made sure to reserve seats in the synagogue for the approaching fall holidays of Rosh Hashanah and Yom Kippur. I had to register for my second year at the university, my friend got ready to leave for Bucharest, where he would complete his sixth and last year in Medical School.

All these activities were overshadowed by the ultimatum tendered by Germany to Poland in the last days of August. The pretext for attacking the Eastern neighbor consisted of a demand to cede Danzig and the Corridor. To-day this port is known to the world by its Polish name Gdansk, with its shipyard and the birth of the labor union Solidarity. Hitler saw his country as a maritime power on the Baltic Sea and coveted this gem of a port and the approaches to it.

All summer, while my friends and myself tried to enjoy a normal vacation - going on hikes, basking in the sun, swimming in the Prut, normalcy was a far cry from reality. The specter of war, a feeling of doom kept creeping into our lives. Yet, we went through the mechanics of living and loving, of growing up and endeavoring not to grow weary, for we still had our youth.

At the age of 13, I became aware of a demonic leader who intruded into everyday life through the medium of radio. From the time Hitler came to power in 1933, all our lives changed. Radio was a more immediate presence in my life than the daily newspaper. When reading, one can keep one's composure much better than when listening to hysterical harangues. Since every radio station in Europe could be heard at any time, Hitler's voice was on almost every evening on German radio stations, to the horror of all listeners. Since we were German speaking, we were not spared any of his boisterous speeches and the response of the German public, which was wildly enthusiastic. History was made on the radio the way it is often made nowadays on television.

On the first of September, 1939, on a sunny, clear, crisp Friday, the world was awaiting Poland's answer to Germany's ultimatum. As much as I was inclined to be optimistic - namely, that war would not break out, no Polish answer could have been a good answer. There was no good alternative.

Had Poland ceded the demanded territory, Hitler could have occupied all of Poland, just as he had previously done in Czechoslovakia and we would have the Germans on the border. No good. If Poland refused, which it did, then Hitler would attack and invade Poland and war would break out. In my own mind there was no good alternative, no good answer in the situation.

Thus, when I said good-bye to my boy friend, we knew that between then and Christmas vacation lay a great unknown, possibly a great impending tragedy. The world around us felt like a globe rolling downhill and no way to stop it.

In the middle of the day, about noon, the radio announced Poland's proclamation denying Germany's ultimatum. Hitler had prepared some provocation on the German-Polish border, wherein they faked an attack by Poles against Germans. Hitler wanted to make sure that the war broke out on that day, September 1.

When I think of it now, 50 years later, it reminds me of the fact that our younger generation often ask: "Where were you when you heard that President Kennedy was shot?" People of my generation think of September 1, 1939 and ask one another this same question. Of course, my generation also asks: "Where were you during the war?" and "Where were you at the end of the war?"

That day changed the history of the 20th century, that day changed everybody's life in Europe, it changed all of Europe, it also brought about Pearl Harbor and the involvement of the United States in the World War. It was a watershed in history, a point where we think of "before" and "after." The 50 million people, who lost their lives and had their fate sealed on that day. Our Jewish people were almost wiped out in Europe and the ones, like my parents and myself, who survived, fought desperately to keep alive. This World War invented the obscenity of genocide on a grand scale and the horror that was Auschwitz.

How fortunate that people don't exactly know what they are about to confront, for they would not dare go through it. My own life could never have turned out the way it did, if not for the war. After all, who could image one's life in a ghetto, living under the Romanians, the Soviets, German-Romanian occupation, the return of the Soviets, during the worst days of Stalin' terror, and towards the end of the war as a refugee in Romania, later in Israel and in the United States. How unstable a time, how bereft of home and friends, how tossed by historic circumstances, how deprived of any security, how defenseless against the turmoil of history.

In a world not of one's own making or of one's own choosing, here I am 50 years later, looking back with very tempered gladness. Some underlying sadness never left me, the times of despair and deprivation branded me with an indelible stamp of tragic experience.

Some survivors rarely think of those years, rarely talk of the daily life of long ago, yet the immediacy of those historic events never left me. Hitlerism and Stalinism, Nazism and Communism played an enormous part in my life. They decided its course, they robbed me of everything, except my parents. They took my belief in the decency of people. What Nazi Germany was capable of I knew, yet I never thought that the Soviet Union would turn out to be one enormous prison. Thus, I became a refugee like most other survivors and the turning point was September 1, 1939. For me, that day will live in infamy, to paraphrase a famous American president.